The Presidential Contest

The Presidential Contest

With a Guide to the 1996 Presidential Race

Fifth Edition

Joseph A. Pika
University of Delaware

Richard A. Watson
Emeritus, University of Missouri—Columbia

A Division of Congressional Quarterly Inc.
Washington, D.C.

Printed in the United States of America

Cover design: Paula Anderson

Photo credits: cover—The White House/Bill Fitz-Patrick; R. Michael Jenkins; Reuters/Bettmann.

Library of Congress Cataloging-in-Publication Data

Pika, Joseph August
    The presidential contest : with a guide to the 1996 presidential race.
— 5th ed. / Joseph A. Pika, Richard A. Watson.
      p. cm.
    Includes bibliographical references and index.
    ISBN 0-87187-837-2 (alk. paper)
    1. Presidents — United States — Election.   I. Watson, Richard
Abernathy   II. Title.
JK524.W38 1995
324.973'092–dc20   95-25241
                                                  CIP

In memory of my parents:
Eleanore T. Pika and Joseph A. Pika Jr.

Contents

c h a p t e r   t h r e e

Election Rules and the Election Campaign   69

c h a p t e r   f o u r

Voting in Presidential Elections   116

c h a p t e r   f i v e

Summary and Assessment of Presidential Contests

a p p e n d i x e s

Tables and Figures

Tables

Figures

Preface

PRESIDENTIAL ELECTIONS are multifaceted events—part spectacle, part governance, part fun, and part tedium. Particularly since 1968, there has been an explosion of detail that one might cover in a book like this. Instead of trying to cover it all, however, the book offers a concise, coherent framework for organizing the major features of the presidential selection process. This approach provides instructors with ample opportunity to expand and elaborate on those features of the process they find most intriguing.

The book contains two frameworks. An explicit chronological framework centers on the stages in a typical presidential election cycle. This four-part time line is briefly set forth in Chapter 1 and then developed throughout the book. Readers should find it a useful device in orienting discussions of previous contests and of contemporary developments in the election cycle. There is also a parallel, analytic framework, and thus common topics (such as campaign finance) can be compared and contrasted for the nomination and general election phases of the contest.

The Presidential Contest is designed to be a supplementary text in regular college courses—particularly those focusing on American government, political parties, and the American presidency—as well as in special election-year courses dealing with the president's selection. It should also prove helpful to journalists, politicians, and citizens in this country and abroad seeking a concise treatment of this elaborate process.

All topics in this revision of the book have been thoroughly updated through the 1992 election with an eye to the upcoming 1996 contest. Several new features from the last edition have been retained: an expanded discussion of race and gender issues; reflections on the question of realignment; and a concluding chapter that examines dissatisfaction with both the nomination and election stages of the presidential contest, as well as proposals to reform them.

Acknowledgments

I WISH TO THANK a number of persons whose assistance has been important for this edition. Richard A. Watson, sole author of the first three editions of this work, was not involved in preparing either the fourth or fifth editions, but readers of the earlier editions will note that his basic approach and treatment remain central throughout. I am also indebted to my colleague Zelma Mosley, who assisted in revising the book's fourth edition but was unable to participate in this revision. Brenda Carter, David Tarr, and their coworkers at CQ Press have once again been particularly helpful, as was my graduate research assistant, Joseph Liberti. Reviews completed by Dr. Janet Blasecki and an unidentified reviewer also proved quite useful.

—Joseph A. Pika

Introduction

THIS BOOK PROVIDES a brief overview of the presidential selection process, the central ritual in American political life. Although most citizens become accustomed to elections as a pervasive decision-making technique in American society, presidential elections are made distinctive by their relative infrequency, greater cost, and expanded media coverage. Most important, they offer the citizen a unique opportunity to engage in a nationwide civic experience. Although their perspectives on candidates and problems may be shaped by very different concerns, there is a shared opportunity to help shape the nation's future. Knowledge of this process should be a critical element of civic education, and this brief but comprehensive discussion is designed with the student in mind.

Elections remain the principal means by which those "outside" the government can judge the performance of those "inside," and thereby redirect the efforts of government officials. Major office holders must periodically come before the populace to renew their right to exercise political power. Voters may also select an alternative group of leaders if they are dissatisfied with the performance of those currently in office. As Joseph Schumpeter observed, in a democracy individuals acquire the right to make political decisions by means of a "competitive struggle for the people's vote."[1]

This "competitive struggle" is a continuous process in which leaders in and out of power attempt to convince the voters that they will fare better under their particular administration. The major effort to win over the electorate, however, is concentrated in the period immediately before the election. During this time, candidates mount campaigns using a variety of political appeals designed to motivate the general public to take the time and effort to vote—and to vote for them.

According to democratic theory, political campaigns and elections perform several important functions in society. As Stephen Hess pointed out, they are primarily a process of "personnel selection," with the electorate operating as a "gigantic search committee" for the nation's political leaders.[2] However, campaigns and elections also serve other purposes. They offer a "corrective" for past electoral mistakes—the chance to "throw the rascals out" and give a new team the opportunity to govern the nation. Campaigns also provide a means to identify the principal problems in a society and to consider policies and programs for dealing with such problems; viewed in this way, campaigns are "educational," a civics lesson for the electorate. The electoral process can also be a catharsis, enabling societal conflicts to be made public and thereby faced squarely. Such a process may lead to another function of democratic elections: the development of attitudes of political compromise and the promotion of social consensus.[3]

Although elections of major public officials are important in any democratic society, they are doubly so in the United States because of its presidential form of government. Under the parliamentary system used in most other democracies in the world, the voters do not directly choose the nation's executive officials. Instead they choose the members of the legislative body, who bargain with one another over the composition of the cabinet, including its leader, who is usually called the prime minister. But in the United States, the presidential election is separate from legislative contests and voters are able to pass judgment on the candidates for the nation's highest office (although their influence on the selection remains indirect, mediated through the electoral college).[4] Because the United States has a two-party instead of a multiparty system, most votes go to the two major candidates, with the winner generally receiving a majority of the total popular vote.

Another distinguishing feature of U.S. presidential contests is the significant role the voters play in *nominating* candidates for the nation's highest office. In most other democratic societies, political party leaders, acting through committees or conferences, choose persons to represent them in the general election. This was also the case throughout most of U.S. history as delegates from the states gathered at the national conventions of the two principal parties to select their candidates. However, the choice of delegates in recent years has been vested more and more in rank-and-file voters instead of traditional party activists. As a result, the nomination as well as the election of the president has become a contest in which candidates must establish their popularity with voters.

This book is organized around four stages in the presidential selection process: 1) defining the pool of candidates; 2) securing the nomination of one of the major political parties—a stage in which citizens and party professionals select delegates to the national party conventions, after which those delegates select a nominee; 3) waging the general election campaign; and 4) validating election results in the electoral college. These stages, introduced in Chapter 1, structure the argument pursued throughout the book. Although the book draws examples from all presidential elections since 1952, increasing reliance has been placed on examples from the four most recent elections.

After outlining the overall process, Chapter 1 provides background information on the rules of the nomination process, the ways they have evolved over the years, and their current nature and impact. It also discusses the pool of candidates from which the voters draw their presidential aspirants. Chapter 2 analyzes the nomination campaign itself: the early maneuvering for position, the targeting of the primary and caucus-convention states, the manipulation of political appeals, the communication of those appeals through the media and campaign workers, the handling of campaign finances, and the ultimate decision—the selection of the presidential and vice-presidential candidates at the parties' national conventions.

Chapter 3 shifts to the general election, analyzing it in the same framework that was used for the nomination process. This enables the reader to see similarities and differences in the two phases of the presidential contest. Chapter 4, which deals with voting in presidential elections, first traces the progressive extension of the franchise to more and more Americans and then analyzes the extent to which citizens have actually exercised their right to vote in recent elections. The chapter then examines the effect of political party affiliation, social group and class identification, candidate appeal, issues, events, and presidential performance on the voting decisions of the American people. The concluding section of the chapter analyzes the consequences of presidential elections for the political party system and for policy making in the United States.

These four chapters thus chronicle the entire presidential contest, reporting and integrating a wide variety of studies of the subject. By contrast, Chapter 5 takes the form of an extended essay or editorial; it presents an assessment of what is right and wrong about the way the nation's highest political official is chosen and of proposals to improve the process. Because this chapter is divided into separate discussions of the nomination and general election processes, some instructors may wish to use appropriate portions of this chapter at the conclusion of Chapter 2 rather than delay evaluation of the process until the end of the book.

The appendixes contain supplemental information on the presidential contest. Appendix A is a schedule of the 1996 primaries and caucuses; Appendix B contains profiles of major candidates likely to contest the 1996 election; Appendix C presents the results of the 1992 presidential primaries; and Appendix D tabulates the results of presidential contests from 1932 through 1992.

Notes

1. Joseph Schumpeter, *Capitalism, Socialism, and Democracy,* 3d ed. (New York: Harper and Row, 1950), 269. As discussed in Chapter 4, the concept of the "people's vote" has changed over the years in the United States as the franchise has been extended to more and more groups; this trend toward broader public participation is also a feature of democratic elections.
2. Stephen Hess, *The Presidential Campaign* (Washington, D.C.: Brookings Institution, 1974), chap. 4.
3. Morris Janowitz and Dwaine Marvick, *Competitive Pressure and Democratic Consent* (Ann Arbor, Mich.: Bureau of Government, Institute of Public Administration, 1956), 2.
4. The winning presidential candidate must receive a majority of the votes in the electoral college. (See Chapter 3.) Since the Civil War, the winner in the electoral college has always received at least 40 percent and usually more than 50 percent of the popular vote.

c h a p t e r   o n e

Nomination Rules
and Candidates

I̶T OPERATED SO SIMPLY in 1789 and 1792. In both instances, George
Washington was selected president by unanimous votes in the electoral
college.[1] John Adams, the second-place finisher both times, became vice
president. In 1789, electors were chosen on the first Wednesday of January and met in their respective states to vote on the first Wednesday in
February. The votes were counted on April 6, a month later than intended
because of delays in convening Congress. The election calendar for 1792
was made more flexible by allowing electors to be chosen within thirty-
four days of the first Wednesday in December, when ballots would be cast.[2]

Today's presidential aspirants and their supporters confront a far
more complicated task. Winning the party nomination is the first hurdle,
an obstacle that may test the candidates' endurance as much as their ability. Then they must mount a nationwide campaign to gain victory over the
candidates in the general election. Today it is customary for candidates to
begin their nomination campaigns two years or more before the election
and to spend millions of dollars in the effort. For example, in the 1996
Republican nomination contest, many experts estimated that candidates
would need to raise at least $20 million by the end of 1995 in order to
mount a viable campaign, which in the end was likely to cost $45 million
for the victorious nominee. Sen. Phil Gramm (R-Tex.) raised a reported
$4.1 million at a single fund-raising event on the eve of his February 24,
1995, announcement as the first official candidate for the 1996 Republican nomination.

As the stark contrast with George Washington's selection illustrates,
the process has evolved substantially over time. Dividing the presidential

FIGURE 1-1   The 1996 Presidential Contest Time Line

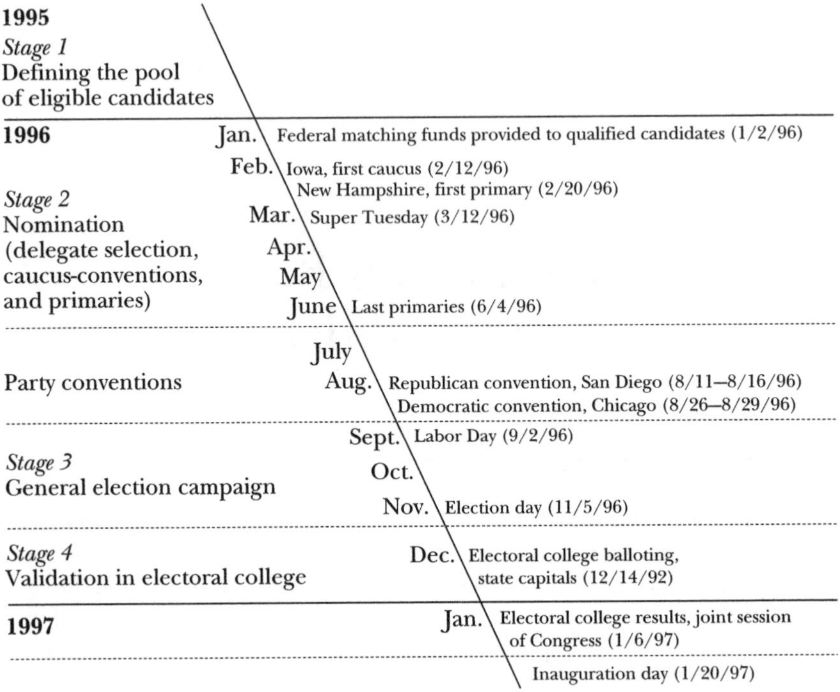

1995

Stage 1
Defining the pool
of eligible candidates

1996	Jan.	Federal matching funds provided to qualified candidates (1/2/96)
	Feb.	Iowa, first caucus (2/12/96)
		New Hampshire, first primary (2/20/96)
Stage 2	Mar.	Super Tuesday (3/12/96)
Nomination	Apr.	
(delegate selection,	May	
caucus-conventions,	June	Last primaries (6/4/96)
and primaries)		

	July	
Party conventions	Aug.	Republican convention, San Diego (8/11–8/16/96)
		Democratic convention, Chicago (8/26–8/29/96)

	Sept.	Labor Day (9/2/96)
Stage 3	Oct.	
General election campaign	Nov.	Election day (11/5/96)

| *Stage 4* | Dec. | Electoral college balloting, |
| Validation in electoral college | | state capitals (12/14/92) |

1997	Jan.	Electoral college results, joint session
		of Congress (1/6/97)
		Inauguration day (1/20/97)

contest into two phases lengthens the electoral process and requires candidates to wage two separate campaigns under quite different sets of rules. Moreover, campaign strategies and techniques must be tailored for the two distinct stages of the presidential battle. Not even the participants in the two contests are the same: Hugh Heclo has labeled the much smaller group of persons who help choose presidential nominees the "selectorate," in contrast to the "electorate," who vote in the general election.[3]

The Founders never contemplated this separation of the campaign into two phases in the procedure they devised for choosing the chief executive. Major developments in the young nation, however, soon divided the selection process into two parts, and after the process was divided, changes continued to occur in both nomination and election procedures. Today we can identify four major stages in the modern process as illustrated in Figure 1-1: 1) defining the pool of eligible candidates; 2) selecting party nominees at national conventions comprised of delegates from throughout the nation; 3) holding the general election at the conclusion of national campaigns; and 4) validating the popular vote in electoral college balloting. Figure 1-1 also shows the time line for the selection process of 1996.

No two presidential election cycles are identical, but the time line is relatively predictable. Potential candidates maneuver for position during the one or two years preceding the election year. Selection of convention delegates begins in January or February of the election year, with conventions typically scheduled in mid-July for the out-party and mid-August for the party that controls the presidency. In 1996, the Republicans chose San Diego and the Democrats chose Chicago as convention sites. Traditionally, the general election campaign begins on Labor Day and runs to the first Tuesday following the second Monday of November, but recent campaigns have begun as soon as the identities of major party nominees have become clear, sometimes even before the conventions have been held. Finally, electors cast ballots in their state capitals in mid-December; those ballots are officially tabulated in the first week of January during a joint session of the U.S. Congress, over which the incumbent vice president and Speaker of the House of Representatives preside.

This chapter first describes the historical evolution of the nomination process, from the establishment of the congressional caucus in 1796 through the national convention system instituted in the 1830s and modified over subsequent years. It then analyzes the nature and impact of current nomination rules. The final section examines "the pool of eligibles" from which nominees are chosen.

Evolution of the Nomination Process

As noted in the previous section, the presidential elections of 1789 and 1792 were conducted without a separate nominating procedure. The system operated as the Founders intended: members of the political elite from the various states, acting through the mechanism of the electoral college, chose George Washington to lead the country. Persons of diverse political views agreed that the nation's wartime hero was a "patriot king" who would rule in the interest of all the people.

In Congress, however, no such political consensus prevailed. In 1790, Alexander Hamilton, the first secretary of the treasury in the Washington administration, presented an economic program that sought to establish a national bank and a tariff to protect U.S. manufacturers and merchants from foreign competition. Thomas Jefferson, then secretary of state, and James Madison, a member of Congress, opposed the program on the grounds that it benefited only mercantile interests and not the nation's farmers, for whom they had great admiration. Subsequently, Jefferson and Madison also differed with Hamilton over the Jay Treaty. Negotiated with England in 1794, the treaty obliged the British to withdraw their troops from forts in the Northwest. However, it failed to satisfy two grievances of Jefferson and Madison: the lack of compensation for slaves carried away by British soldiers during the Revolution and the impressment into the British Navy of sailors from U.S. ships seized by Britain for trading with the French (then at war with Britain).

Out of these controversies over domestic and foreign policy emerged an important institution not provided for by the U.S. Constitution—political parties. The Federalist party had formed by the early 1790s, with Hamilton acting as the principal initiator of policies in Congress and Washington as the popular leader who could rally support for such policies. Federalists soon were running for Congress and, once in office, voting for Hamilton's programs.[4] Jefferson's resignation from the Washington administration in 1793 and Madison's congressional disputes with Hamilton paved the way for a rival political party: the Republicans.[5] By the mid-1790s, cohesive pro- and antiadministration blocs were voting against each other in Congress, and congressional candidates were being identified as Republicans as well as Federalists.[6] Washington's retirement at the end of his second term in 1797 enabled party politics to spread from Congress to the presidency.

The creation of political parties in the United States thus ended the brief period in which the political elite of the day, working through the electoral college, selected the president. From then on, party politics would determine the nation's chief executive, a development that required the parties to devise a means of choosing, or nominating, candidates to run under the party name. Over time, influence over presidential nominations has shifted and broadened within the parties, moving first from members of Congress to local party leaders and later to a broad base of party activists and candidate supporters.

Congressional Caucuses

In 1796, the Federalists chose their candidate, John Adams, by consulting with the prominent leaders of the party. The Republicans turned to their party members in Congress, who nominated Jefferson as their standard-bearer. Four years later, the Federalists followed suit, and the congressional caucus—a meeting of a party's congressional membership—became the nominating mechanism for both parties.

The congressional caucus offered several practical advantages in this early stage of party development. Members of Congress, already assembled in the nation's capital, faced minimal transportation problems in meeting to select a nominee. With so few members participating, the nominating task was kept manageable. Legislators were familiar with potential presidential candidates from all parts of the new country, making them logical agents for choosing candidates for an office with a nationwide constituency, and the caucus provided an organizational base for launching coordinated campaigns. Finally, caucuses provided a means to exercise peer review of candidates' credentials as one group of politicians assessed another's skills and abilities.

But the congressional caucus had serious flaws that eventually proved fatal. First, it violated the separation-of-powers principle of the Constitution in giving members of the legislative body a dominant role in choosing the president, a role much wider than the narrow one provided in the Constitution in the event of an electoral college deadlock. Second, the caucus could not represent areas in which the party had lost the previous congressional election. Third, interested and informed citizens who participated in grassroots party activities (especially campaigns) had no means to participate in congressional caucus deliberations.

The Federalists were the first to be affected by the system's limitations. With the decline of their political fortunes, the size of the party's congressional delegation shrank so much that it ceased to provide geographic representation. The party turned to alternative nominating devices in 1808 and 1812, employing what one political scientist called "primitive national conventions," and holding no organized caucus or convention in 1816, the last presidential contest the Federalists contested.[7] The Republicans used the congressional caucus effectively, though not without criticism, between 1800 and 1820 to nominate three Virginians who had previously served as secretary of state: Jefferson in 1800 and 1804; Madison in 1808 and 1812; and James Monroe in 1816 and 1820. In 1824, however, three-fourths of the Republican members of Congress boycotted the caucus to protest an attempt to nominate Secretary of the Treasury William Crawford, who was seriously ill.

The 1824 election brought an end to the congressional caucus nomination system. That year, five presidential candidates were nominated, principally by state legislatures. One candidate was Andrew Jackson, who was proposed by the Tennessee legislature. Jackson won more popular votes and more electoral votes than any other candidate, but failed to achieve a majority of the electoral votes; as a result, the election was thrown into the House of Representatives, where former secretary of state John Quincy Adams achieved victory through a political deal with House Speaker Henry Clay, another of the candidates. Clay threw his considerable House support to Adams in return for being named secretary of state. "King Caucus," as it had come to be called by critics, was permanently discredited by these shenanigans as an undemocratic selection process thwarting the people's choice.

In 1828, responsibility for presidential nominations was vested entirely in the states; legislatures and conventions put forward citizens of their own states—"favorite sons" such as Jackson and Adams—as candidates. Such a system proved too decentralized to build a nationwide coalition of support behind a candidate who could overcome sectional loyalties. Some device was needed that would represent party elements throughout the country and at the same time facilitate the nomination of a common candidate.

National Party Conventions

The nomination method that emerged to satisfy these needs was the party convention, a truly national meeting that included delegates from all the states. Rail transportation made such assemblies feasible; expanding citizen participation in presidential elections made them necessary. With the advent of the convention, influence over selection of the party nominee shifted to state and local party leaders, particularly those able to commit large blocs of delegate support to a given candidate.

Two minor parties with no appreciable representation in Congress paved the way. The Anti-Masons and National Republicans convened national assemblies in 1831.[8] The Democratic-Republicans, as Jefferson's Republicans had come to be known, held a national convention in 1832 under President Jackson. Jackson, first elected in 1828, viewed the convention as an ideal way of rallying support and securing the vice-presidential nomination for his handpicked candidate, Martin Van Buren.

Since these initial efforts in the early 1830s, major political parties have nominated their presidential and vice-presidential candidates by holding national conventions. National committees call the presidential nominating conventions into session and conventions adopt a platform of common policy positions. Some basic features of the early conventions persist to the present day, though in modified form. Delegates, for example, are allocated to states based roughly on their representation in Congress (senators plus House members). In other respects, however, conventions have undergone substantial change. Until early in the twentieth century, national conventions were periods of intense bargaining among local party leaders from throughout the nation who were willing to trade the voting support of their state delegations in exchange for jobs and other benefits controlled by the federal government. In this era of "brokered conventions," nominees were chosen through negotiations among a relatively small number of party chiefs. This system began to change with the adoption in many states of reforms championed by the Progressive movement. Presidential primaries became an important means to

select convention delegates, although most states continued to rely on traditional party procedures. The result was a *mixed-system,* with delegates
chosen through party-run caucuses outnumbering those chosen through
primaries. Party leaders continued to dominate convention business—
including the presidential nomination—through 1968.

Although today's nominating conventions resemble those that developed more than 150 years ago, the entire nomination process has undergone drastic change since 1968. Influence over the nomination decision
has shifted decisively from party leaders to the voters who participate in
presidential primaries or open party meetings known as *presidential caucuses.* Although convention delegates chosen through these methods do
not formally select the nominee until the party convention, for all intents
and purposes the decision has been made before the convention begins as
delegates are chosen around the country. Because the presidential nomination process is both fluid and complex, party leaders, especially among
the Democrats, have engaged in extensive "institutional tinkering" by
changing the rules. But as observers have noted, the same complexity and
fluidity produce "great latitude for unintended consequences."[9] After
reviewing the current rules governing the nomination of presidential candidates, the final section of this chapter focuses on the kinds of people
who pursue the office.

Current Nomination Rules

The rules that govern any political contest are important. Rules both pre-
scribe behavior in political contests and influence election outcomes. By
determining the strategies and tactics that participants adopt to improve
their chances of winning, rules shape the nominating process. Yet they are
shaped by the process as well. In seeking advantage for their particular
interests, people produce change as they reshape the rules. The prevailing rules are not neutral: inevitably, they favor some individuals and interests over others—sometimes by design, sometimes not.

Since the late 1960s, the rules of the presidential nomination contest
have become especially important. They are highly complicated because
they come from a variety of sources—one-hundred state political parties
and fifty legislatures, the national political parties, and the Congress.
(Individuals also turn to the courts to interpret provisions of these regulations and to reconcile conflicts among them.) In addition, the rules have
been altered so drastically and so often, particularly in the Democratic
party, that it is difficult for candidates and their supporters to keep up
with the changes. These changes have created confusion and uncertainty

for many participants and have favored those who somehow manage to puzzle their way through the welter of rules. Indeed, some contend that Sen. George McGovern won the 1972 Democratic nomination partly because he thoroughly understood the changes in the nomination rules formulated by a commission that he had chaired.

The following three sections examine the rules for apportioning convention delegates among the states, selecting delegates within the states, and financing nomination campaigns.

Allocating National Convention Delegates

A presidential candidate starts out with a well-defined goal: to win a majority of the votes at the party's national convention and so be nominated for the presidency. To win the nomination at the 1992 conventions, the Republican nominee needed 1,106 votes out of 2,210, and the Democratic nominee needed 2,145 out of 4,288. Preliminary figures for 1996 indicate the Republicans will have a total of 1,984 delegate votes and the Democrats 4,295 at their respective conventions.

Although the numbers of convention votes differ, the parties use similar formulas to decide how many votes each state is entitled to cast at the convention. The parties take into account the size of a state's congressional delegation or its population in determining its basic vote allocation, and its record in supporting the party's candidates in recent years in allocating extra, or "bonus," votes to each state. The methods that parties use to determine these bonus votes benefit some states at the expense of others. For the 1996 convention, Utah and Arizona are likely to have the most "bonus" delegates as a result of their strong Republican voting record, in each case five additional delegates. Louisiana is the only state that is likely to have no "bonus" delegates for the 1996 Republican convention; New York will receive three.

The Republican party is interested in a state's recent record in voting not only for the presidential nominee but also for governors, senators, representatives, and state legislators; however, the party does not take into account the *size* of the popular vote for these officials, but simply whether or not they win. The smaller states, especially those in which the Republican party dominates the nonpresidential elections, therefore wield disproportionate influence at the GOP convention. For example, Utah, a state with a small population that has elected a large number of Republican officials, is benefited, even though its small size means that it can cast relatively few popular votes for Republican candidates for president. A large, two-party state such as New York, however, is at a disadvantage. Democratic candidates may win elections for governor, U.S. senator, or U.S. representative, costing the state Republican party bonus votes at the convention. The large number of popular votes the state has cast over the years for Republican presidential candidates is not taken into account, only whether the Republican candidate carried the state.

In contrast, the Democratic party focuses on a state's voting record in recent presidential elections to the exclusion of gubernatorial and congressional contests; moreover, the party is concerned with the average popular vote cast for its presidential candidates in the three previous elections. A populous two-party state such as New York is favored by the system. Its size means that it will cast a large number of popular votes for the Democratic presidential candidate (whether the candidate carries the state or not); the fact that Democratic candidates lose nonpresidential elections will not work to the state's disadvantage at the convention. However, a small state in which the Democrats are traditionally dominant, such as Rhode Island, is disadvantaged. Democratic presidential candidates, while carrying the state, do not win a large number of popular votes, and Democratic victories in nonpresidential elections earn the state no bonus votes.

Selecting Delegates

State delegates to the national conventions of both parties are chosen by one of three methods. In some states party leaders, such as members of the state central committee, the party chair, or the governor (if the party controls that office), select the delegates. In others, a *state convention,* composed of persons themselves elected at caucuses and conventions held in smaller geographical areas, such as precincts, wards, counties, and congressional districts, makes the selection. Finally, in many states the voters select delegates directly in presidential primaries. States sometimes combine methods, using a primary to elect district delegates but allowing their state committees or state conventions to choose "at-large" delegates representing the whole state and they can allow parties to use different methods. State legislatures decide how delegates are to be selected, although they are influenced heavily by national guidelines established by the political parties.

Traditionally, persons active in party affairs—public and party officials referred to as "professionals"—dominated the selection of delegates. This was only natural when party officials formally appointed the delegates. When they manipulated the caucuses and conventions into choosing themselves and their loyal supporters as delegates, professionals also dominated. Moreover, professionals remained influential even after the introduction of presidential primaries by running for delegate positions.

Because many states did not require delegates to vote for the candidate favored by rank-and-file voters in the primary, delegates were free to vote their own presidential preferences instead of the public's.

Between 1968 and 1980, however, there was a pronounced trend away from control by party professionals and toward increased participation by rank-and-file voters. In 1968, only seventeen states chose delegates by a presidential primary; in 1980, thirty-one did so. Meanwhile, the proportion of total national convention delegates chosen by both parties in primaries climbed from 48 percent to nearly 80 percent. In the process, the primary replaced the state convention system as the dominant method for choosing delegates to the national convention. Unlike the past, today's candidates for the presidential nomination of either party must court the support of voters more than that of party chieftains.

Many of the new primary laws passed between 1968 and 1980 increased the influence of rank-and-file voters in selecting their party's ultimate nominee for president. States encouraged delegates chosen in primaries to indicate which candidate they supported for president so that voters could predict how their delegates would vote at the national convention. Some states also permitted voters to indicate their personal preference for president and legally bound the delegates to support the preferred candidates for one or more ballots at the convention. Moreover, under many of the new state laws, a presidential candidate's name was placed on the ballot if his or her candidacy was recognized by the national news media. A candidate who wanted to be removed from the race in such states had to file an affidavit swearing that he or she was not a candidate in any state. This system prevented candidates from choosing the state primaries they would enter, thus allowing voters to pass judgment on a broader range of potential nominees than would otherwise have been available to them.

The trend toward greater influence for rank-and-file voters retreated briefly between 1980 and 1984 as six jurisdictions abandoned the primary in favor of the caucus-convention for selecting delegates to the national convention. As a result, the proportion of delegates for the two major parties' conventions chosen through state presidential primaries declined to about 66 percent in both parties. But these changes proved short-lived; the 1988 and 1992 elections saw a substantial return to the primary method.

During the period 1968–1992, the system of choosing delegates to the national convention underwent massive change. The use of primaries spread, and many were scheduled earlier in the election year. Still, the system is far from uniform. During 1992, thirty-four states, the District of Columbia, and Puerto Rico used some version of a primary, and sixteen

FIGURE 1-2   Presidential Primaries: More and Earlier, plus
State Methods for Choosing National Convention Delegates

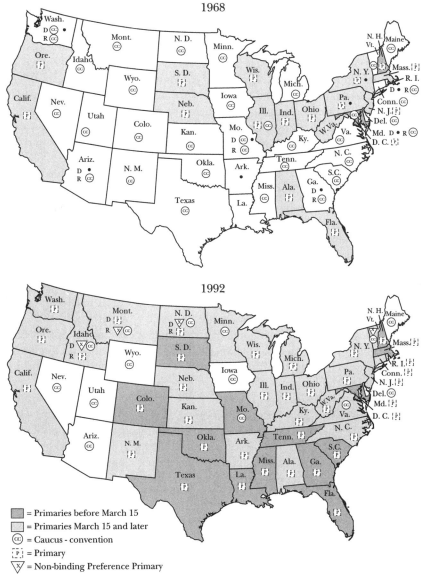

SOURCE: *The Elections of 1988*, ed. Michael Nelson (Washington, D.C.: CQ Press, 1989), Figure 2-1, 30.
Data for 1992 based on Harold W. Stanley and Richard G. Niemi, *Vital Statistics on American Politics*, 4th
ed. (Washington, D.C.: CQ Press, 1994), Table 3-6, 98–99.

states used the caucus-convention method to select delegates. In four states (Idaho, Montana, North Dakota, and Vermont), at least one of the parties held a *nonbinding primary* to gauge voter preferences among candidates, but actually selected delegates through caucus-convention. In six states (Idaho, Montana, North Dakota, South Carolina, West Virginia, and Wisconsin) Republicans and Democrats used different methods or followed different primary rules in selecting delegates. As illustrated in Figure 1-2, there were some regional variations in the use of the two methods: the West remained the only region to rely more heavily on caucus-conventions, whereas primaries outnumbered caucus-conventions in both Midwestern and Northeastern states. Primaries were used to select convention delegates from every state in the southern region except Delaware and Virginia. And selection has been moved earlier in the calendar: in 1968, New Hampshire was the only state to hold its primaries before March 15; in 1992, fourteen states did so. Overall, 83.9 percent of Republican delegates to the 1992 convention were chosen through primaries and 16.1 percent through caucuses. Democratic figures are significantly different because of the presence of a distinctive category, superdelegates (discussed in a later section), who constituted 18 percent of the convention total, but 66.9 percent of Democratic delegates were chosen through primaries and 15.1 percent through caucuses. State legislatures have chosen selection methods in response to reforms introduced by the national political parties for selecting delegates to the national conventions.

Democrats. The vast changes in the Democratic party's procedures after 1968 can be traced to that year's convention in Chicago. The assembly was marked by acrimonious debates over the Vietnam War within the convention hall and by bloody battles outside the convention arena between war protesters and the police. Vice President Hubert Humphrey, who entered the race after President Lyndon Johnson announced in March 1968 that he would not seek reelection, won the nomination without entering a single statewide presidential primary. This would be impossible today, but party leaders still dominated the delegations of the caucus-convention states and were strongly aligned behind Humphrey. Symbolizing this support was Mayor Richard J. ("Boss") Daley of Chicago, who controlled much of what happened both in- and outside the convention hall. Democrats who had supported antiwar candidates in the primaries felt their views had been rejected through the naked exercise of power by old-line party leaders.

Although Daley's candidate emerged triumphant, many delegates to the 1968 convention were concerned that the regular party organization had become unresponsive to the will of rank-and-file Democrats. As a result, the delegates adopted a resolution requiring state parties to give "all Democrats a full, meaningful, and timely opportunity to participate" in the selection of future delegates. The Democratic National Committee (DNC) established a commission chaired by Senator McGovern of South Dakota to assist state parties in meeting the requirement for broader participation. Electoral defeat, of course, spurred reform efforts, and that pattern was repeated following the 1972 election when Baltimore councilwoman, and later senator, Barbara Mikulski chaired a commission again designed to address the delegate selection process. Each commission recommended changes in rules affecting the selection of convention delegates for the next convention; they also struggled with how to expand the number of delegates from groups that had previously been underrepresented at the conventions and how to translate the support candidates received into delegate totals.

For the most part, the battle lines in this series of rules changes were drawn between party professionals and political "amateurs"—the regulars who often held posts in the party organization versus those who became involved because of an interest in a particular candidate or issue. The amateurs won the struggle to open up the selection process when the McGovern Commission recommended that states remove restrictive voter registration laws so that non-Democrats and unaffiliated voters could become party members. At the same time, new regulations forbade traditional party leaders from serving automatically as *ex officio* convention delegates and required written party rules, adequate public notice of meetings, and the elimination of proxy voting, changes that reduced the control that leaders could exercise.

A second issue that plagued party commissions was the representation of particular groups within state delegations to the national convention. The McGovern Commission recommended that minority groups, women, and young people (those age eighteen to thirty) be represented in state delegations "in reasonable relationship to the groups' presence in the state," a victory for amateurs. Many states accomplished this goal through a quota system when they chose their delegates to the 1972 convention. Other minority groups who traditionally had supported the party, such as Italian Americans and Polish Americans, questioned why they had not been included in the quotas. Other Democrats opposed the idea of quotas altogether because using quotas violated their understanding of political equality—ensuring the opportunity to participate rather than determining the results of the political process. The Mikulski Commission replaced quotas with more inclusive "affirmative action plans" designed to encourage "minorities, Native Americans, women, and other traditionally underrepresented groups to participate and to be represented in the delegate selection process and all party affairs." At the 1980 convention, professionals won a 10-percent increase in the size of state delegations to permit inclusion of state party and elected officials; amateurs won the adoption of a rule requiring that state delegations comprise equal numbers of men and women.

A third major problem for the party was how to award state delegation votes to contending candidates. The McGovern Commission recommended that states abolish "winner-take-all" primaries—whereby the candidate who received a plurality of the popular vote is awarded all the delegates—in favor of "fair representation of minority views on presidential candidates," a form of proportional representation. California refused to follow this recommendation, and at the 1972 convention, McGovern ironically received all 271 votes of the California delegates, although he had beaten Humphrey in the primary by only 45 to 39 percent of the popular vote. Democrats abolished statewide winner-take-all contests in 1976, so that candidates winning at least 15 percent of the votes in presidential primaries and caucus-convention meetings would receive their proportional share of a state's delegate votes. Fifteen percent emerged as the Democratic standard for 1980, 1988, and 1992, but was abandoned for a 20-percent threshold in 1984. Moreover, some primary contests awarded "bonus" delegates to statewide winners, preventing the system from being truly proportional and generally throwing the advantage to front-running candidates.

Another commission (the Hunt Commission) developed rules for the 1984 nomination contest. Party professionals were determined to reclaim a greater role in the nomination process and facilitate the selection of "their" kind of candidate rather than an "outsider" such as McGovern or Jimmy Carter. They succeeded in creating a bloc of superdelegates composed of party and elected officials (constituting some 14 percent of the convention votes in 1984, 16 percent in 1988, and 18 percent in 1992); state officials and Democratic members of the House and Senate were responsible for choosing these superdelegates (typically themselves), who attended the conventions uncommitted. Populous states were favored by a rule allowing them to use once again the winner-take-all principle in district-level contests and thereby reward a front-runner with a large bloc of delegate votes.[10] Finally, the new rules no longer bound delegates to vote on the first ballot for the candidate to whom they were linked in the state's delegate selection process. (This provision played a vital part in the 1980 convention, discussed in Chapter 2.) Since 1984, delegates have been legally free to vote as they choose.

Because unsuccessful Democratic candidates Gary Hart and Jesse Jackson were dissatisfied with the 1984 rules (which, they said, favored Walter Mondale), the national convention created the Fairness Commission to study their complaints.[11] As a result, minor changes were made in the 1984 rules. The commission actually increased the number of superdelegates from about 550 to some 650, which meant that all the Democratic governors, all the members of the DNC, and 80 percent of the Democratic members of Congress occupied delegate seats at the 1988 convention. The Fairness Commission also relaxed the 1984 rule that restricted participation in the nomination process to Democrats, so that a number of states such as Wisconsin and Montana were able to conduct "open" primaries in 1988 with the approval of the national party. In 1992, there were five Democratic open primaries that allowed voters to participate in selecting delegates, whether they were Democrats or Republicans, and in another eleven states and Puerto Rico, Democrats allowed independents to participate in the primaries but prohibited registered members of the other party from "crossing over."

Compared to previous rules changes, those for 1992 were relatively minor. In 1984, 1988, and 1992, the Democrats, for the first time in a generation, operated under essentially the same rules in back-to-back contests. For the first time since 1968, no postelection commission was empaneled to review the rules of the nomination struggle after the 1988 and 1992 contests.

Republicans. The Republican party also has made changes in its delegate selection process, even though its leaders have not faced the pressures for reform that confronted Democratic leaders. A committee chaired by Rosemary Ginn, a Missouri member of the Republican National Committee (RNC), recommended proposals for the 1976 convention similar to those of the McGovern Commission: traditional party leaders were prohibited from serving as *ex officio* delegates; party officials were to inform citizens how to participate in the nomination process; and participation was to be increased by opening the primaries and the state conventions to all qualified citizens.

At the same time, the Republican party has not attempted to regulate selection of national convention delegates nearly as extensively as has the Democratic party. The Republican convention rejected recommendations of the Ginn Committee to include persons under twenty-five years of age in "numerical equity to their voting strength in a state" and to have one man, one woman, one person under twenty-five, and one member of a minority group on each of the convention's principal committees. The RNC rejected a later recommendation that it review affirmative action plans, and the party has refused to abolish winner-take-all primaries such as the one in California. The winner-take-all principle proved especially important to the 1988 campaign of George Bush, who finished first in each of the sixteen Republican primaries conducted on March 8, the day known as Super Tuesday, and thereby overwhelmed his competition, who were unable to gain a share of available delegates. Such a practice favors front-runners, enabling them to amass insurmountable leads in convention delegates. In 1992, only fourteen states and the District of Columbia used proportional rules in selecting Republican delegates. Thus the national Republican party has been much less willing than Democrats to intervene in state decisions on the selection of delegates to the national convention, although Republican procedures were affected by state laws that required the same delegate selection procedures for both parties.

Effect of Changes in Delegate Selection Rules

The rules changes adopted from 1968 to 1980 had a profound effect on choosing presidential nominees, particularly for the Democratic party. The proliferation of primaries and the deliberate lessening of the influence of party leaders in caucus-convention states made these leaders far less influential in the nomination process. Such professionals, who traditionally used their skills to select persons considered electable and loyal to the party (such as Humphrey), were largely replaced by political amateurs who supported "issue-oriented" and "antiestablishment" candidates for the presidency (such as McGovern and Carter). Despite these changes, the backgrounds of the new breed of candidates were consistent with those of earlier presidents in that they were still drawn from the same kinds of positions—vice presidents, senators, governors.

Democratic rules designed to increase the representation of traditionally disadvantaged groups in the nomination process also brought the intended results. Women in particular benefited. In 1968, before the Democratic reforms, only 13 percent of the delegates at the Democratic convention were women. In 1972, that figure nearly tripled to 38 percent and, after a slight decline to 33 percent in 1976, rose to almost 50 percent in 1980. It remained at that level in 1984, 1988, and 1992 as a consequence of the party's decision to require that both genders be represented equally at the Democratic national convention. More women delegates have also attended the Republican convention: 16 percent of the delegates were women in 1968, but 33 percent of delegates at the 1988 Republican convention were women and 43 percent at the 1992 convention were women. African American delegates at Democratic conventions increased from 5 percent of delegates in 1968 to 23 percent in 1988, but declined to 18 percent in 1992; the Republican percentage rose from 2 to 5 percent over the same period. Youth was most heavily represented at the Democratic convention of 1972, when 22 percent of the delegates were under thirty, but that figure declined drastically to only 5 percent in 1992. (Similar figures are unavailable for the Republicans.)

Finally, Democratic rules changes ending the winner-take-all primary in favor of a proportional division of states' convention votes made victories in "mega-states" such as California less important than they used to be. Carter, for example, won his party's nomination in 1976 and in 1980 without winning California. The proportional rule encourages candidates to participate in state primaries they do not expect to win, because they have a chance to receive some convention votes rather than being shut out completely, as had occurred in winner-take-all contests.

The rules favored by Democratic party professionals in 1984 helped Mondale go on to win the nomination as he led among superdelegates and in states that used caucuses to select their delegates. (Recall that more states adopted this method in 1984.) Mondale prevailed at the convention, even though his two rivals received a combined share of 55 percent of all votes cast in the primaries. During the 1988 contest, Michael Dukakis had substantial advantages over his principal opponent, Jackson, among delegates chosen through both primaries and caucuses. Jackson's supporters had sought more lenient primary rules, but he actually did better among delegates selected through caucuses (36 percent) than among those chosen through primaries (28 percent).[12] Finally, in 1992, Bill Clinton's 52 percent of ballots cast in Democratic primaries translated into 78 percent of delegates chosen through primaries. He also won 84 percent of delegates chosen in caucus states, giving him an easy victory in the convention over Jerry Brown and Paul Tsongas.[13]

Financing Presidential Nomination Campaigns

Historically, restrictions on contributions to presidential campaigns have not worked. The federal government passed legislation in 1907 forbidding corporations to contribute money to presidential candidates, but corporations easily circumvented the law by paying executives extra compensation, which they and their families subsequently contributed in their own names. The 1947 Taft-Hartley Act prohibited contributions by labor unions, but unions, too, evaded the restrictions by forming political action committees (PACs) to solicit voluntary donations from members and to spend the funds in the committees' names. Finally, the Hatch Act of 1940 (which limited individual contributions to a candidate for federal office to $5,000) and a federal tax law that imposed progressive tax rates on contributions of more than $3,000 to a single committee both proved ineffective because numerous committees were formed for a single candidate, and each committee was entitled to accept a $5,000 contribution.

The move for campaign reform began with President John F. Kennedy, who knew the advantages wealth gave a candidate.[14] He appointed the Commission on Campaign Costs, which in 1962 issued a report proposing public mandatory filing of reports of campaign expenditures, tax incentives for contributors, and matching funds for presidential candidates. Nothing came of the proposals during the 1960s, but they laid the groundwork for the wave of reform that swept the country in the 1970s. In 1971 and again in 1974, Congress passed legislation affecting campaign financing. In January 1976, however, in *Buckley v. Valeo*, the Supreme Court ruled certain provisions of the legislation unconstitutional;[15] later that year Congress responded by enacting still further regulations governing the use of money in federal elections. Finally, in 1979 Congress added more amendments to the campaign finance legislation that reduced reporting requirements, but also included provisions to strengthen state and local party organizations by encouraging voter registration and get-out-the-vote drives. The latter changes, termed "soft-money," have become controversial and are discussed in Chapter 3.

A variety of financial regulations govern the conduct of presidential campaigns. The following sections discuss the major ones affecting the nomination process. (Some of the provisions also apply to the general election campaign, which is treated in Chapter 3.)

Disclosure of Information. Presidential candidates and committees are required to provide full information on the financing of their campaigns. They must report the names of all contributors who give $200 or more and must itemize expenses of $200 or more. This information is filed with the Federal Election Commission (FEC), the agency responsible for administering the campaign legislation. The FEC is a bipartisan body of six members nominated by the president and confirmed by the Senate.

Limits on Contributions. Individuals may contribute no more than $1,000 to a presidential candidate for each election (the nomination and general election are considered separate contests), $5,000 to a PAC (one that contributes to more than one candidate), and $20,000 to the national committee of a political party. The total contribution may not exceed $25,000 a year. Presidential candidates are free to spend an unlimited amount of their own money and their immediate family's money on their campaigns, but if they accept public financing, their contributions to their own campaign are limited to $50,000 per election.

Limits on Spending. Candidates may spend as much as they wish on presidential campaigns unless they accept public financing, in which case limitations apply. For the 1992 presidential campaign, limits for the prenomination process included a national ceiling of $28.2 million plus $5.6 million for fund-raising costs—a total of $33.8 million. In addition, there are state spending limitations based on population. For example, in 1988, California had the highest spending limit ($7.1 million); the lowest figure, which applied to a number of small states, was $444,600. These figures will be adjusted in 1996 to reflect population and inflation data.

Independent Campaign Expenditures. There is no limitation on independent campaign expenditures, that is, those made by individuals or political committees advocating the defeat or election of a candidate but not made in conjunction with the candidate's campaign. However, individuals or committees making such expenditures in amounts of more than $250 must file a report with the FEC and must state, under penalty of perjury, that the expenditure was not made in collusion with the candidate. Such expenditures have been more significant during the general election than during the nomination process.

Public Financing. Candidates for the presidential nomination who are able to raise $100,000 in individual contributions, with at least $5,000 collected in twenty different states, receive federal matching funds equal to the total amount of contributions of $250 or less. By checking a box on their federal income tax forms, taxpayers authorize the federal government to set aside $3 of their tax payments for public financing of campaigns. By August 1995, $43.4 million had been certified to twelve qualifying primary candidates from the 1992 contest. Clinton led the pack with $12,536,135 in matching funds, nearly three times the total of his closest Democratic competitor, Brown; Bush received $10,658,521, double the total of Patrick Buchanan, his principal challenger for the Republican nomination. The matching fund total was down from 1988 when sixteen candidates qualified for a total of $67.5 million in matching funds. The federal government also provided grants of more than $11 million each to the Democratic and Republican parties to finance their nominating conventions, expected to rise to $12 million in 1996.

As with delegate selection rules, campaign finance laws have had a significant effect on presidential nominations. The sources and techniques for raising funds have changed radically. Rather than depending on a few "fat cats" to finance their campaigns (in 1968, insurance executive W. Clement Stone gave $2.8 million to Richard Nixon's campaign), candidates now raise funds from a large number of small individual contributors, primarily through direct mail solicitation.[16] Public funds also make it possible for persons who formerly could not afford to mount a nomination campaign to do so. Sen. Fred Harris (D-Okla.) had to abandon a presidential bid in 1972 because he could not raise money from large contributors; but with federal matching funds available, he was able to run in 1976. Right-to-Life candidate Ellen McCormack was also able to qualify for federal funds that year, as was Leonora Fulani of the New

Alliance Party in 1988 and 1992. At the same time, the new method of rais-ing money from a large number of individuals and thereby qualifying for federal matching funds means that candidates tend to start their cam-paigns earlier than they formerly did. As election specialist Herbert Alexander suggests, public funding helps "free each candidate's personal organization from the party hierarchy," [17] but it may make fund-raising an even greater concern of candidates. Relying on a few fat cats required less time than raising large sums in smaller contributions. In addition to the matching funds they received, Bush raised $27.7 million in 1992 and Clin-ton $25.4 million. In order to raise $20 million by the end of 1995, the consensus goal of political consultants, candidates for the 1996 nomina-tion would have to raise nearly $358,000 a week, a considerable invest-ment of time and effort.[18]

Thus a variety of rules help shape the nomination contest. The remainder of this chapter focuses on the people directly affected by such rules—the presidential candidates themselves.

Defining the Pool of Eligible Candidates

As the unanimous selection of Washington demonstrates, there was little doubt about who would become America's first president. However, the constitutional qualifications for president are so general that nearly 100 million Americans meet them. To be eligible for the presidency, individu-als need to meet only three requirements, set forth in Article II, Section 1, of the U.S. Constitution. One must be a "natural born" citizen,[19] at least thirty-five years of age, and a resident of the United States for fourteen years or longer. But the pool of "plausible" candidates is far smaller than that of "possible" candidates.[20]

Far more important than the *formal* requirements for the presidency are the *informal* ones. Persons who entertain presidential ambitions (the bug is considered to be virtually incurable once it strikes) must possess what is generally called "political availability"; that is, they must offer the political experience and personal characteristics that presumably make them attractive to political activists and to the general voting public. Although there is no simple checklist of job qualifications for the presi-dency, one can look at past candidates to gain an understanding of the political and personal backgrounds that put an individual in line for a presidential nomination. Even this approach poses some difficulties, since the attitudes of political leaders and the American public change over time. The following discussion, which focuses on the period since the election of Franklin D. Roosevelt in 1932, analyzes the informal standards of presidential "availability" that operated during that era, including how some of those standards have changed.

Political Experience of Presidential Candidates

In terms of the electoral time line set forth in Figure 1-1, we can think of candidates' strategic career decisions as occurring over an extended period, long before the election year begins. As with their predecessors, most nominees and other major presidential candidates since 1932 had previous service in a civilian, elective, political office. (See Appendix B for a list of the 1996 aspirants.) The two exceptions among nominees were Wendell Willkie, who was president of a public utility company when he was nominated by the Republicans in 1940, and Dwight D. Eisenhower, a career military officer and World War II hero who became the successful GOP candidate in 1952. Recent elections have found an unusually large number of aspirants who lacked experience in elected office. In 1988, campaigns were mounted by Jackson, a civil rights organizer; Pat Robertson, a television evangelist and business person; and Alexander Haig, a retired military officer. Buchanan, a former White House aide in three Republican administrations and a television commentator, challenged Bush in 1992 and entered the 1996 contest as well. Finally, H. Ross Perot, a billionaire business person, sought the presidency as an independent candidate in 1992.

Ordinarily, party nominees and most major candidates can claim to have occupied a variety of political posts during the course of their political careers, but the particular offices they held immediately before becoming presidential candidates are relatively limited. Candidates of the party out of power follow paths somewhat different from those of the party holding the presidency, but it is striking how little the background characteristics of nominees have changed even when one compares today's candidates with those from the last half of the nineteenth century.[21]

Since 1932, a principal recruiting ground for the party out of power—one that has long been popular in U.S. politics—has been a state governorship. Throughout this era, both major parties have looked to governors as promising candidates. From 1932 through 1956, governors tended to become the nominees: Democrat Roosevelt of New York in 1932, Republican Alfred Landon of Kansas in 1936, and Republican Thomas Dewey of New York in 1944. After a hiatus from 1960 through 1972, the state governorship once again emerged as the dominant background for successful presidential nominees of the party out of power: former Georgia governor Carter led the Democrats in 1976; former California governor Ronald Reagan became the Republicans' 1980 standard-bearer; the sitting governor of Massachusetts, Dukakis, was the Democratic nominee in 1988, and Clinton was the sitting governor of Arkansas when nominated by the party in 1992. Only in 1984, when Democrats nominated former vice president Mondale, did the party out of power not turn to a governor during this twenty-year period, although Mondale, Carter, and Reagan had one important trait in common—none of the three held an elected office at the time he sought the nomination. Each had the freedom to run a full-time campaign. Paul Abramson, John Aldrich, and David Rohde note that throughout the period of 1972–1992, typically one-quarter to one-half of the presidential candidates were not in office at the time of the campaign. This was true for six of the fourteen major party candidates in 1988 and three of the eight in 1992. The reformed selection process has become much more demanding, making it critical that candidates minimize competing responsibilities if they hope to be successful.[22]

The other major source of presidential candidates for the party out of power since 1932 is the U.S. Senate. Many senators have been presidential candidates throughout the period, particularly between 1960 and 1972. During these years, the Democrats nominated senators Kennedy of Massachusetts in 1960 and McGovern of South Dakota in 1972, and the Republicans chose Barry Goldwater of Arizona in 1964.[23] Johnson, the Democratic nominee in 1964, and Nixon, the Republican nominee in 1968, had served in the Senate before moving on to the vice presidency.

For a while, the Senate seemed to be the most fertile recruiting ground for presidential candidates. Nationalization of American politics shifted political attention away from the state capitals to Washington, D.C., and senators took advantage of the opportunity to project themselves over the national news media concentrated there.[24] Senators associated themselves with major public policies and took advantage of the new prominence accorded foreign affairs since World War II, a traditional area of Senate responsibility. The six-year term of senators enables them to try for the presidency without giving up their legislative seat. Of the senators who have run for the presidency since 1932, only Goldwater lost his place in the upper chamber as a result of his candidacy.[25] But despite these factors, only twice have senators been elected directly to the White House (Warren Harding in 1920 and Kennedy in 1960).

The competitive advantages of governors is somewhat surprising. State chief executives were more powerful players in the presidential selection process when they headed state delegations and negotiated with their peers at brokered conventions to choose the party's nominee. Governors from states with large cities that serve as communications centers for the nation, such as New York, Los Angeles, and Chicago, would seem to have advantages in pursuing the nomination, but Carter, Dukakis, and Clinton were not severely disadvantaged by being from smaller states. Governors have no significant responsibilities in foreign affairs and are more closely tied to their home states (particularly if they are serving and the state legislature is in session) than are senators. Finally, many governors serve short stints in office—in some cases because of legal limitations on their tenure, in others because they fail to meet public expectations that they will solve major domestic problems without increasing taxes. They therefore find it difficult to become sufficiently well known to be viable presidential candidates.

Carter's election in 1976 and Reagan's bid for the Republican nomination that year and election in 1980 indicate that governors possess some advantages as candidates, particularly if they are *not* occupying the governor's mansion at the time they seek the presidency (a point driven home by Dukakis's defeat). Unlike Dukakis, Carter and Reagan were free to devote their energies full time to the demanding task of winning the nomination, an opportunity not available to senators with heavy legislative duties who sought the presidency in both of those years (Democrats Frank Church and Henry Jackson in 1976, Republicans Howard Baker and Bob Dole in 1980, and Dole again in 1988). Perhaps most importantly, both Carter and Reagan also benefited from the anti-Washington mood of the populace, which made voters receptive to candidates who had not served in a national office. Citizen concern with the burgeoning costs of government and the problems of controlling the federal bureaucracy could continue to make governors attractive presidential candidates: governors can claim valuable executive experience in managing large-scale public enterprises and thousands of state government employees, in contrast to a senator's legislative duties and small personal staff. Finally, the decline in the public's concern over foreign affairs compared with domestic problems during the 1976–1988 period may counteract the foreign policy advantages senators held over governors as presidential candidates. It is probable that the offices of both U.S. senator and state governor will continue to be major recruitment grounds for presidential candidates of the party out of power. As of June 1995, prominently mentioned Republican hopefuls include one sitting governor (Pete Wilson, California), a former governor (Lamar Alexander, Tennessee), and four senators (Dole, Kansas; Gramm, Texas; Richard Lugar, Indiana; and Arlen Specter, Pennsylvania). Buchanan had also declared his candidacy. Several prominent potential candidates took themselves out of the race early in 1995, including former vice president Dan Quayle and former presidential candidate Jack Kemp, as well as several sitting governors. (See Appendix B for the backgrounds of major candidates in 1996.)

For the party that occupies the presidency, *that office itself* is the major source of candidates. In only four instances since 1932 has the incumbent chief executive not been his party's subsequent nominee. In 1960 and 1988, Republican incumbents Eisenhower and Reagan were precluded from running again by the Twenty-second Amendment, and in 1952 and 1968 Democratic presidents Harry S. Truman and Johnson chose not to seek another term. The exact reasons for Truman's and Johnson's decisions are unknown, but both held office at the time of highly unpopular wars in Korea and in Vietnam. In addition, both had been challenged and embarrassed politically in the New Hampshire primary—Truman by Sen. Estes Kefauver of Tennessee and Johnson by Sen. Eugene McCarthy of Minnesota.

When the incumbent president decides not to run or is constitutionally barred from doing so, recent experiences indicate that the office of vice president becomes the major source of presidential candidates for the party in power. In 1960, the Republicans chose Nixon, who won the nomination virtually without opposition. (Governor Nelson Rockefeller of New York had considered making a bid that year, but decided not to run when he determined early on that the vice president had the nomination locked up.) In 1968, the Democrats chose Vice President Humphrey as their nominee, but only after he had overcome the challenge of Senator McCarthy and after the assassination of Sen. Robert Kennedy of New York in early June. Bush overcame five major challengers to win the nomination in 1988 and the opportunity to succeed Reagan. Only in 1952 was the incumbent vice president, Alben Barkley, denied the presidential nomination. At the time he was seventy-five years old and not considered to be a major figure in the party.[26] In that instance, the principal candidates came from the traditional training grounds already discussed: the party's nominee, Adlai Stevenson, was the governor of Illinois; contenders Kefauver of Tennessee and Richard Russell of Georgia represented their states in the U.S. Senate.

Incumbent presidents have important advantages when it comes to winning their party's nomination. It is difficult for a party to admit to the voters that it made a mistake four years before when it nominated the candidate who won the presidency. As discussed in the next chapter, incumbents also have several political weapons they can use against candidates who seek to deny them their party's nomination. As a result, even unpopular presidents tend to be renominated. The Republicans chose Herbert Hoover again in 1932 in the midst of the Great Depression; and the Democrats renominated Carter in 1980 when both inflation and unemployment were high, Americans were being held hostage in Iran, and Soviet troops occupied Afghanistan. Bush regained the nomination in

1992 despite a steep decline in public approval during the preceding year. Since 1932, three vice presidents who succeeded to the presidency on the death or resignation of their predecessors were subsequently nominated by their party—Democrats Truman and Johnson and Republican Gerald R. Ford.

Incumbent vice presidents are now more likely to win their party's nomination in their own right than they were in the past.[27] Presidential candidates of late tend to choose more capable running mates, individuals who are viable prospects for the presidency itself. In addition, recent presidents are assigning their vice presidents more meaningful responsibilities than did their predecessors. These duties include participating in political party activities (especially campaigning in off-year elections), which helps them forge ties with party chieftains; serving as liaisons with social groups, which draws vice presidents to the attention of group leaders; and acting as emissaries to foreign countries, which makes them visible to the general public. In the postwar era, however, vice presidents were successful in winning nominations but not the general election. Nixon and Humphrey lost in 1960 and 1968, as did Mondale in 1984. In 1988, Bush broke a long string of failed campaign efforts when he became the first incumbent vice president to win the presidency since Van Buren in 1836.

Independent Candidates: The Ultimate Outsiders

The 1992 candidacy of Perot demonstrated that candidates who lack any sort of previous electoral experience and the backing of a national political party can generate considerable public support, although he was not even the typical independent. Unlike the independent candidacies of George Wallace in 1968 and John Anderson in 1980, Perot's run for the presidency did not arise from an unsuccessful effort to gain a party nomination; Wallace had sought to be the Democratic nominee in 1968 and Anderson ran for the Republican nomination in 1980. Nor had Perot ever held public office; Wallace had served as governor of Alabama and Anderson as a member of the House of Representatives from Illinois. Also setting him apart was Perot's personal wealth, estimated to be about $3 billion, which provided him with resources that no other candidate could hope to match. He took full advantage of that wealth, spending an estimated $64 million of his own money in 1992.

While Clinton and Bush were pursuing convention delegates in a seemingly interminable schedule of primaries and caucuses (described more fully in Chapter 2), Perot confronted a different challenge: getting his name on the November ballot in each of the fifty states and the Dis-

trict of Columbia via nominating petitions. Getting on the ballot is virtually automatic for major-party nominees. Independent candidates for the
presidency must, in most states, meet the same requirements established
by each law for independent (that is, non-party) candidates seeking state-
wide office. These standards vary widely, which presents a daunting task
that requires money, organization, coordinated efforts, and broad support.

As of March 27, 1992, a point at which Bush had virtually secured the
Republican nomination and Clinton had very nearly done the same for
the Democratic nomination, Perot was guaranteed access to the ballot
only in Tennessee, although petition efforts had begun in fourteen other
states.[28] To have his name listed in November, Perot's organization and
the petition committees that had sprung up around the country needed
to secure a specified number of signatures on petitions by an official deadline. In some states, the task must have seemed impossible. California, for
example, required that 134,781 signatures be collected with petitions sub-
mitted by August 7. New York had three major requirements: 20,000 signatures had to come from registered voters who had not voted in the
state's presidential primary; at least 100 signatures had to come from citizens in each of one-half of the state's congressional districts; and the signatures had to be compiled between July 1 and August 18. When multi-
plied by fifty-one separate sets of guidelines, the complexity of the task was
substantial. Nine states and the District of Columbia specified that signatures be collected within a stated time period, and twenty-seven states and
D.C. required that a presidential candidate also file with a vice-presidential running mate. Most of the deadlines were in July and August, but
Texas required action by May 11, and Arizona set the latest date, September 18.[29]

Thus, the Perot organization and his supporters had to perform different activities and meet deadlines that were quite different from the
major parties' candidates. When Perot gained access to Arizona's ballot
in mid-September, he had completed the task that was rather off-hand-
edly launched when he announced his availability on television in mid-
February.

Personal Characteristics of Presidential Candidates

Despite the large pool of people who meet the formal requirements for
president, far fewer meet the informal criteria that have been commonly
employed. Most constraining have been the limitations of gender and
race. No woman, African American, Hispanic, or Asian American has ever
been nominated for president by a national convention, although in the

past twenty years several have waged national campaigns. Geraldine Ferraro was part of the Democrats' national ticket in 1984 as a vice-presidential nominee. Jackson sought the Democratic nomination in 1984 and 1988.

Other "tests" based on personal characteristics have also been applied to presidential aspirants. Journalist Sidney Hyman listed several of these informal qualifications in 1959, and we discuss later the changes that have occurred over the past eight presidential elections.[30] Hyman concluded:

- Preferred candidates come from states that have a large electoral vote and a two-party voting record.
- Candidates from big northern states are favored over those from southern states.
- Conventions nominate only persons who are, or who can be made to appear, hospitable to the many economic interests in the nation.
- Presidential candidates are expected to represent an idealized version of home and family life.
- Although the majority of Americans live in large urban centers, preferred candidates come from small towns.
- Preferred candidates come from English ethnic stock.
- Nominating conventions have created an extraconstitutional religious test by their decisive preference for Protestant hopefuls.

Although many of the candidates in presidential contests since 1960 satisfied these tests, some clearly did not. Past geographical preferences for nominees from northern, two-party states with a large electoral vote failed to prevent the nomination of Goldwater from Arizona; Johnson and Bush from Texas; Humphrey and Mondale from Minnesota; McGovern from South Dakota; Carter from Georgia; Dukakis from Massachusetts; or Clinton from Arkansas. Nor were all the candidates from small towns. Nixon grew up on the outskirts of Los Angeles; John and Robert Kennedy, as well as Dukakis, were raised in the Boston area. Goldwater spent his young adult years in Phoenix; Humphrey in Minneapolis; and Jerry Brown in Sacramento. Reagan was raised in the small town of Dixon, Illinois, but his political career had its roots in the Los Angeles area.

Other of Hyman's tests pertaining to social background also fail to apply to several candidates since 1960. John Kennedy's candidacy in 1960 violated the traditional preference for Protestants. Once he won, little was made of the fact that his brothers Robert and Edward were also Roman Catholic, as were other subsequent Democratic hopefuls—McCarthy and Brown. Nor did Republicans seem concerned that Senator Goldwater, though an Episcopalian, had a Jewish background on one side of his family. The related, traditional preference for English stock did little to deter the candidacies of the Kennedys, McCarthy, and Reagan of Irish background; Goldwater of Russian background; Mondale of Norwegian background; or Dukakis of Greek background.

In addition, several presidential candidates since 1960 could not be said to represent an idealized version of home and family life. In 1963, Rockefeller divorced his wife of more than thirty years and married a much younger, divorced woman whose previous husband won custody of the children of that marriage. In 1976, Democratic candidate Morris Udall was divorced, and in 1980 it was widely known that Edward Kennedy's marriage was in serious trouble (he and his wife subsequently divorced and he has remarried). Brown was unmarried and at one time reputed to have had an affair with rock singer Linda Ronstadt. Although none of these candidates won their party's nomination, Reagan, also divorced, was both nominated and elected in the 1980 contest and thereby became the country's first president to have divorced and remarried. But the electorate has been less comfortable with some candidates' extra-marital experiences. Hart's widely reported relationship with a much younger woman who was not his wife ended his 1988 presidential hopes, even though he had entered the campaign as the front-runner. Clinton's successful campaign in 1992 was nearly derailed during the New Hampshire primary when a former nightclub singer, Gennifer Flowers, claimed to have had a twelve-year affair with the governor, charges that appeared in many tabloid newspapers and that were repeated in the mainstream media. To reestablish the image of marital unity, Clinton and his wife, Hillary, appeared on CBS's program *60 Minutes* to discuss their marriage.

Finally, several recent presidential candidates failed to meet Hyman's 1959 test of being or appearing to be hospitable to the full range of the nation's economic interests. Goldwater had private business interests (his family owned a department store), and Nixon had close political ties to conservative California business people, as did Reagan. Reagan and Goldwater firmly espoused the tenets of private enterprise. Bush made a fortune as an oil drilling contractor in Texas before turning to politics. Humphrey, Edward Kennedy, and Mondale were allied closely with organized labor; McGovern was identified with economic underdogs, as indicated in the 1972 campaign by his espousal of a $1,000 grant for all Americans.

Thus, none of Hyman's informal qualifications have endured unchanged. Changes in the nomination process itself, as well as broader currents in U.S. society, have altered many of the major considerations underlying the choice of presidential candidates. Divorce is far more prevalent and acceptable today than in the past. The proliferation of presidential primaries "provides a forum in which prejudices can be addressed openly,"[31] and the vice-presidential nomination offers a way to address such social views indirectly, as was the case with Ferraro's nomination in 1984. The development of a more common culture and the nationalization of American life in general, brought about by improved means of communication and transportation, have reduced the importance of parochial concerns—the religious, ethnic, or geographical background of a candidate—and increased the emphasis on the experience presidential candidates have had in the national political arena and their association with national issues.

Hyman's 1959 list excluded some important informal requirements. Although personal wealth is not essential, access to large amounts of financial support is critical. Persons of modest means need not apply for the presidency. Nor is this purely an individual issue. Some analysts have suggested that as members of socially or politically disadvantaged groups—African Americans; women; immigrants from Mexico, eastern and southern Europe, and the Far East—ascend the socioeconomic ladder and begin to occupy governorships and seats in the U.S. Senate, from which U.S. chief executives traditionally have been recruited, they will enhance their chances of becoming serious candidates for the presidency.[32] This view, however, may offer misleading reassurances of an open political system. For example, until a female candidate is nominated by a major political party, gender will remain the most exclusionary informal requirement for the office. Gender was not even included on Hyman's list in 1959.

Notes

1. James Monroe is the only other candidate to have approached this distinction. He won all but one electoral vote in 1820.
2. Michael Nelson, *Guide to the American Presidency* (Washington, D.C.: CQ Press, 1990), 266–267, 1403.
3. Hugh Heclo, "Presidential and Prime Ministerial Selection," in *Perspectives on Presidential Selection*, ed. Donald R. Matthews (Washington, D.C.: Brookings Institution, 1973), 25.
4. William Chambers, *Political Parties in a New Nation: The American Experience, 1776–1809* (New York: Oxford University Press, 1963), chap. 2.
5. In the early 1820s, the Republican party became known as the Democratic-Republicans, and in 1840 was officially designated as the Democratic party. Paul David, Ralph Goldman, and Richard Bain, *The Politics of National Party Conventions* (New York: Vintage, 1964), chap. 3.
6. Joseph Charles, *The Origins of the American Party System* (New York: Harper Torch, 1956), 83–94.
7. Gerald Pomper, *Nominating the President: The Politics of Convention Choice* (New York: Norton, 1966), 17.

8. David, Goldman, and Bain, *The Politics of National Party Conventions*, 50. The National Republican party was soon to give way to the Whigs, with many Whig supporters joining the modern Republican party when it was formed in the 1850s.

9. David, Goldman, and Bain, *The Politics of National Party Conventions*, 61.

10. Some states used another variant in 1984 and 1988, the "winner-take-more" principle, whereby the leading candidate in a district received a "bonus" delegate, and the remainder of the delegates were divided among the candidates in proportion to the votes they received.

11. There is evidence that Hart and Jackson's complaints were warranted. One study found that Mondale particularly benefited from the support of super-delegates and his ability to outlast a number of his opponents. Priscilla L. Southwell, "Rules as 'Unseen Participants': The Democratic Presidential Nomination Process," *American Politics Quarterly* 20, no. 1 (January 1992): 54–68.

12. Rhodes Cook, "The Nominating Process," in *The Elections of 1988*, ed. Michael Nelson (Washington, D.C.: CQ Press, 1989), 53.

13. Harold G. Stanley and Richard G. Niemi, *Vital Statistics on American Politics*, 4th ed. (Washington, D.C.: CQ Press, 1994), Tables 3-3 and 3-8, 92 and 103.

14. Herbert E. Alexander, *Financing Politics: Money, Elections, and Political Reform*, 2d ed. (Washington, D.C.: CQ Press, 1980), 27.

15. 424 U.S. 1 (1976).

16. Although political action committees can help finance nomination campaigns, their contributions, unlike those of individuals, are not matched by federal funds.

17. Alexander, *Financing Politics*, 98.

18. Richard Berke, "In GOP Field, A Race to Raise Money Is On," *New York Times*, February 2, 1995, A1.

19. Naturalized citizens (such as former secretary of state Henry Kissinger, who was born in Germany) do not meet this requirement. There is some question whether persons with American parents who are born abroad (such as George Romney, former governor of Michigan and 1968 presidential aspirant, who was born of American parents in France) are also legally barred from the presidency by this stipulation.

20. Michael Nelson, "Who Vies for President?" in *Presidential Selection*, ed. Alexander Heard and Michael Nelson (Durham, N.C.: Duke University Press, 1987), 129.

21. John Aldrich, "Methods and Actors: The Relationship of Processes to Candidates," in *Presidential Selection*, ed. Heard and Nelson.

22. Paul R. Abramson, John H. Aldrich, and David W. Rohde, *Change and Continuity in the 1992 Elections* (Washington, D.C.: CQ Press, 1994), 18–20.

23. It should be noted that on occasion the party out of power draws on a third source for candidates—defeated presidential candidates. Since 1932, the Republicans have chosen Dewey and Nixon, and the Democrats, Stevenson, to run for the presidency a second time. Only Nixon was successful.

24. Nelson Polsby, *Congress and the Presidency*, 3d ed. (Englewood Cliffs, N.J.: Prentice-Hall, 1976), 99–102.

25. William Keech and Donald Matthews, *The Party's Choice* (Washington, D.C.: Brookings Institution, 1976), 23. During the early 1980s, aspiring nominees believed that unemployment was an advantage to seeking the nomination, causing several potential candidates to avoid seeking election or reelection to

the Senate. This was true for Senators Baker and Hart, who declined to seek reelection in 1984 and 1986, as well as for former senator and vice president Mondale, who declined to pursue a vacant Senate seat from Minnesota in 1982.

26. It should also be noted that a former vice president may ultimately become a presidential candidate: Nixon ran successfully in 1968 after losing in 1960, and Mondale served in that office from 1977 to 1981 and became the Democratic presidential candidate in 1984.

27. Before Nixon's selection in 1960, the last incumbent vice president to be nominated was Van Buren in 1836.

28. *Congressional Quarterly Weekly Report,* April 4, 1992, 900.

29. See also National Clearinghouse on Election Administration, *Ballot Access, Volume I: Administrative Issues, Problems, and Recommendations* (Washington, D.C.: Federal Election Commission, 1978), for a state-by-state listing of access requirements.

30. Sidney Hyman, "Nine Tests for the Presidential Hopeful," *New York Times,* January 4, 1959, sec. 5, 1–11.

31. Michael Nelson, "Who Vies for President?" in *Presidential Selection,* 144.

32. Jackson finished third behind Mondale and Hart for the 1984 Democratic nomination and second for the 1988 nomination. In the 1988 contest, Rep. Patricia Schroeder of Colorado was widely mentioned as a possible Democratic candidate. No women were major-party candidates in 1992; African American Douglas Wilder withdrew from the contest after only a brief candidacy.

Selected Readings

Alexander, Herbert E., and Anthony Corrado. *Financing the 1992 Election.* Armonk, N.Y.: M.E. Sharpe, 1995.

Crotty, William, and John S. Jackson III. *Presidential Primaries and Nominations.* Washington, D.C.: CQ Press, 1985.

Grassmuck, George, ed. *Before Nomination: Our Primary Problems.* Washington, D.C.: AEI Press, 1985.

Heard, Alexander, and Michael Nelson, eds. *Presidential Selection.* Durham, N.C.: Duke University Press, 1987.

Loevy, Robert D. *The Flawed Path to the Presidency, 1992: Unfairness and Inequality in the Presidential Selection Process.* Albany, N.Y.: State University of New York Press, 1995.

Shafer, Byron E. *Quiet Revolution: The Struggle for the Democratic Party and the Shaping of Post-Reform Politics.* New York: Russell Sage Foundation, 1983.

c h a p t e r   t w o

The Nomination Campaign

FIVE PRINCIPAL DEMOCRATIC CANDIDATES emerged early in 1992 to compete for the right to face the Republican nominee, presumed to be George Bush, in November. None of the five—former California governor Jerry Brown, Gov. Bill Clinton of Arkansas, Sen. Tom Harkin of Iowa, Sen. Bob Kerrey of Nebraska, and former senator Paul Tsongas of Massachusetts—could be considered a major national figure in his party, although Clinton arguably had the strongest claim. In fact, commentators referred to the group as the "B-team" since more notable potential candidates, the "A-team," chose not to run—a group that included Gov. Mario Cuomo of New York, Sen. Al Gore of Tennessee, and Rep. Richard Gephardt of Missouri. Their hesitation could hardly be faulted. Early in 1991, President Bush looked unbeatable, registering an all-time high approval rating of 89 percent shortly after the victory over Iraq in the Persian Gulf War. As the year progressed, however, and the economy eased into a modest recession without a response from the administration, Bush's ratings steadily declined, and a Democratic victory in the fall appeared more likely. In addition, a challenger emerged within the Republican party—Patrick Buchanan—to contest the president's renomination.

The situation in early 1995 was quite different. A long list of Republican aspirants explored the possibility of launching a presidential campaign after their party reclaimed majorities in both the House and Senate for the first time in forty years during the 1994 mid-term elections. President Clinton's public approval ratings wallowed below 50 percent, Democrats were in disarray, and there was speculation about whether someone might challenge the president for the nomination. Republican senators, governors, former cabinet members, and military heroes were mentioned as presidential possibilities. Even some top-tier candidates, including former vice president Dan Quayle, decided not to run in such a crowded and unpredictable field of challengers. President Clinton confronted the very real prospect of joining three of his predecessors—Gerald Ford, Jimmy Carter, and Bush—as an incumbent rejected at the polls. If so, he would become the fourth incumbent of the past five who sought reelection only to suffer this fate.

As these histories reveal, the nomination campaign is a winnowing process in which each of the two major parties chooses from a large pool of potential candidates the one person who will represent it in the general election. As political scientist Austin Ranney points out, the nomination phase is more important than the election stage of the campaign, because "the parties' nominating processes eliminate far more presidential possibilities than do the voters' electing processes."[1]

There are several important differences between the campaign for the nomination and the campaign preceding the general election. A nomination campaign is much less structured. Rather than contending with one known opponent representing the other major political party and a possible independent candidate, aspirants for their party's nomination typically do not know how many opponents they will face or who they will be. In contrast to the general election's relatively short campaign period (extending roughly from Labor Day in early September to election day in early November), the nomination campaign is long and indefinite. Candidates may start their quest for the presidency up to two years before election year. The general election campaign occurs in all fifty states simultaneously, but the nomination campaign takes place in uneven stages, and candidates must hopscotch the nation in pursuit of votes. Finally, presidential nominees can use their party label to attract votes and can count on party leaders to work in their campaign, but candidates for the party's nomination must develop other types of political appeals to attract the support of the "selectorate" and a personal organization to work on their behalf.

The highly unstructured nature of the presidential nominating process causes great uncertainties for candidates in planning and conducting the campaign. A further complication is that most first-time candidates must organize a nationwide political campaign, a task that, by comparison, dwarfs the effort of winning a Senate seat or governorship in even the largest states. As the following discussion indicates, important decisions have to be made all along the road to the party's nomination.

Early Maneuvering

Although the formal nomination process does not start until the beginning of the election year (the Iowa caucuses are likely to be the kickoff event in 1996), political maneuvering takes place long before that time. A few days after the 1972 presidential election, for example, Carter's staff laid out a plan for winning the 1976 Democratic nomination. Shortly after vice-presidential candidate Walter Mondale lost the 1980 election, he began his quest for the 1984 Democratic presidential nomination.

Journalist Arthur Hadley calls this political interval between the election of one president and the first contest before the next presidential election "the invisible primary." [2] By this he means that the competition during this time has many of the characteristics of the actual state primaries. The invisible primary, however, takes place behind the scenes as far as the general public is concerned, whereas American voters are very conscious of the regular primaries.

The invisible primary is a testing ground for the would-be presidents to determine whether their candidacies are viable. One factor is psychological: is the candidate willing to undergo the grueling process needed to win, a process characterized by extended absences from home, long hours on the campaign trail, endless fund-raising, and short, sometimes sleepless nights? Mondale, an early casualty of the period preceding the 1976 election, withdrew from the race in November 1974 with the following statement: "I found I did not have the overwhelming desire to be President which is essential for the kind of campaign that is required. I don't think anyone should be President who is not willing to go through fire." [3] Jack Kemp offered a similar explanation when he decided not to run in 1996: "My passion for ideas is not matched by my passion for partisan or electoral politics," and Kemp made it clear that fund-raising would be a particularly onerous task. [4] Quayle noted that his decision not to run was intended to "put our family first," but many speculated that fund-raising was also Quayle's major concern, just as it had been for Gov. Carroll Campbell of South Carolina, former secretary of education William Bennett, and former defense secretary Dick Cheney, all of whom also bowed out of the 1996 race. [5]

At this stage of the contest, candidates are concerned with MOMM—money, organization, message, and media coverage. Each must recruit a staff of key aides who will help plan the campaign strategy, begin fund-raising efforts, and assemble a larger group of workers who will organize states for the upcoming primary and caucus-convention contests. Assembling a group of dedicated, experienced, and skilled aides is critical to success. Perhaps the most important factor in this early phase is how would-be candidates fare with the media. As columnist Russell Baker notes, the members of the media are the "great mentioner," the source of name recognition and favorable publicity. Candidates who are ignored because reporters and commentators do not regard them as serious contenders find it almost impossible to emerge as viable presidential possibilities. Before any votes are cast, the media evaluates candidates' success in raising money, recruiting well-known political operatives to their banner, and weathering pre-election year straw polls conducted among party activists in various states.[6]

The media also begin the process of looking into the candidates' personal lives and records—"vetting," as it is sometimes called. Adverse comments can seriously damage a candidacy: in his quest for the 1980 Democratic nomination, Brown was portrayed by the media as a "spacey," "far-out" politician whose ideas, rhetoric, and lifestyle disqualified him for the presidency. Those images resurfaced in 1996, as well, to dog his campaign. Edward Kennedy's 1979 interview with CBS commentator Roger Mudd turned into a disaster as the senator seemed unable to give an adequate explanation of his actions in the 1969 drowning of Mary Jo Kopechne in Chappaquiddick; of his strained relationship with his wife, Joan, and his alleged affairs with other women; and of why he wanted to be president and how his policies and political views differed from those of President Carter. Many observers concluded that the Massachusetts senator never recovered from that interview, which occurred before his official presidential campaign even began.

Personal character became the focus of media inquiries that resulted in two candidates withdrawing from the race in 1987. Gary Hart, the early Democratic front-runner, was unable to defuse womanizing charges stemming from a story that alleged he was having an affair with a younger woman. The campaign of Sen. Joseph Biden was also plagued by a negative media image and questions of personal character. Biden admitted plagiarizing a law review article while attending the Syracuse Law School in 1965. He also admitted quoting Robert F. Kennedy, Hubert H. Humphrey, and British Labour party leader Neil Kinnock without attribution. Although the latter practice is not unusual among politicians, media attention to his misstatements overshadowed his candidacy. Biden, too, withdrew from the 1988 race before it even began.

In contrast, candidates who tend to do well in the invisible primary exploit the advantages provided by the media. Early in Carter's 1976 campaign, his staff recommended that he cultivate important political columnists and editors—such as *New York Times* columnist Tom Wicker and *Washington Post* chair Katharine Graham—by making favorable comments on their articles and columns and, if possible, by scheduling visits with them. Some candidates enhance their presence in the print media through magazine articles or books published either earlier in their careers or during the nomination campaign itself; examples include Kennedy's *Profiles in Courage,* Richard Nixon's *Six Crises,* and Carter's *Why Not the Best?* They also use television and radio, appearing regularly on news programs such as *Meet the Press.* They may even use a syndicated radio program or news column of their own, as Ronald Reagan did to advance his political views and, indirectly, his candidacy. In 1992, Clinton delivered a series of issue speeches at Georgetown University, his alma mater, presumably in hopes that the media would cover these Washington events.

People with presidential ambitions typically take additional steps to enhance their prospects with leaders of their party as well as with the public. In anticipation of the 1972 election, Edmund Muskie, Humphrey's running mate in 1968, began accepting speaking engagements outside his home state of Maine soon after he and Humphrey were defeated. Looking toward the 1976 election, Carter assumed the position of coordinator of the 1974 Democratic congressional campaign, a job that took him to thirty states, where he had the opportunity to get acquainted with Democratic leaders. Clinton had served as chair of the National Governors Association and then later became chair of the Democratic Leadership Council in 1990. Both positions provided him with advantages—the chance for endorsements from prominent state party leaders and a prominent position within the principal group that was pushing the national party toward greater moderation. Both Bob Dole and Phil Gramm, potential candidates in 1996, campaigned extensively for Republican candidates in 1994, and some critics accused Gramm of using his position as chair of the Republicans' Senate campaign committee to expand his fund-raising base. For some candidates, a trip abroad may also keep them in the news and, if they have not had much experience in foreign affairs, help to counteract the charge that they are not knowledgeable in this vital area that consumes so much of the U.S. president's time.

Another key aspect of the invisible primary is the raising of funds necessary for the nomination campaign. The new finance legislation, reviewed in Chapter 1, favors raising money in small amounts from many individuals and encourages candidates to get an early start in soliciting funds. Once certified as eligible and agreeing to the conditions that establish expenditure limits, candidates begin receiving federal matching funds in January of the election year. This does not preclude other financial maneuvering, however. One area in which this is possible is the organization of *leadership PACs,* committees organized by prospective presidential candidates in the years before the campaign. In January 1977, with $1 million left over from his 1976 campaign, Reagan established a political action committee (PAC) called Citizens for the Republic. Ultimately, Reagan's PAC spent close to $6.3 million, most of which went to pay operating expenses and traveling costs for Reagan, who served as the principal speaker at political gatherings for GOP candidates. Mondale's 1984 PAC, Committee for the Future of America, contributed to more than 200 House, Senate, and gubernatorial candidates in 1982. Bush raised more than $11 million for a similar effort, Fund for America's Future, leading up to 1988, and a number of other candidates did likewise with nearly $25 million raised by all candidates that year. Neither Bush nor Clinton made use of the device in 1992, although Jesse Jackson, Cuomo, and Gephardt organized such efforts in anticipation of 1992 candidacies that never were.[7]

As the presidential election year approaches, campaign fund-raising moves into high gear. By the end of 1987, Bush (with $18.1 million), Pat Robertson (with $14.2 million), and Michael Dukakis (with $10.2 million) led the field of candidates in collecting individual campaign contributions, thus freeing them to compete in more of the early nomination contests. In late 1991, Clinton released his fund-raising reports as a way to force his opponents to do likewise and thereby demonstrate that he had raised the most.[8] Clinton had raised a relatively modest total of $3.3 million by December 31, 1991, with Harkin second at $2.2 million; Bush had raised $10.0 million to Buchanan's $0.7 million. Clinton continued to raise money throughout the prenomination period and eventually totaled $12,536,135, even more than Bush's final total of $10,658,521.[9] As noted in Chapter 1, Republican candidates expect to need at least $20 million by the end of 1995 in order to mount an effective campaign, giving rise to herculean efforts. Phil Gramm set the all-time fund-raising record with more than $4 million in a single event, and he transferred a $5-million surplus from his Senate campaign committee into his presidential account. Those trailing the 1996 pack needed to try harder; Lamar Alexander scheduled twenty-three fund-raising events from March 6 to April 15, 1995.[10] These figures are substantially higher than those for Democrats during 1992 because the field is more congested at an earlier stage of the contest and because several "major" candidates have chosen to pursue the nomination.

In recent years presidential candidates have also found it wise to enter prenomination "popularity" contests held in some states, even though such contests have no legal effect on the composition of the state delegation to the national convention. Robertson scored a surprise victory in the Iowa straw poll sponsored by the state GOP in September 1987. He formally entered the race the following month and went on to register another surprise victory in the Iowa caucuses. Clinton won a straw poll at the Florida Democratic state convention on December 15, 1991, in time to help shape his media image as the front-runner, particularly after Cuomo announced on December 20 that he was not a candidate. Gramm registered early victories in straw polls held in Louisiana and Arizona in 1995, further cementing his credentials as a major force early in the nomination race.

Candidates may also seek early endorsements from groups closely associated with their parties. In the 1984 contest, both the AFL-CIO, with its 14 million members and 98 affiliated unions, and the National Education Association (NEA), the nation's largest individual labor union with 1.7 million members, endorsed Mondale as the Democratic candidate before the official state contests. Shortly thereafter, the National Organization of Women endorsed Mondale as well. These early endorsements later became a target of Republican criticism, and the Democratic national chair asked organized interests to refrain during the 1988 contest from endorsing any candidate prior to the state contests. Long-shot candidates may also begin campaigning in novel ways. In 1987, Bruce Babbitt, the former Arizona governor, began television advertising in Iowa far earlier than usual, hoping to create curiosity about his candidacy among party activists who would dominate the precinct caucuses there. He also engaged in an interparty debate with Republican candidate Pete du Pont, who, like Babbitt, was given little chance of winning his party's nomination. (Two more prominent candidates, Gephardt [D-Mo.] and Kemp [R-N.Y.], also participated in an interparty debate.) All seven Democratic candidates appeared in a televised debate on William F. Buckley's program, *Firing Line.*

The early phase of the nomination campaign, which we have termed "defining the pool of eligibles," serves as a testing period for would-be candidates, especially those in the party out of office. An eligible incumbent president is typically the front-running candidate for the nomination of the party in power. Some candidates drop out before the official campaign begins, as did Democratic senator Mondale in 1975, Republican senator Lowell Weicker in 1979, and Democrats Hart and Biden in 1987. Others establish themselves as leaders in the public opinion polls taken at the beginning of the year and go on to win their party's nomination. As Table 2-1 illustrates, this was the prevailing pattern from 1936 through 1968. In three recent instances, however, the front-runner was ultimately replaced by a dark horse—George McGovern, who was preferred by only 3 percent of the Democrats in January 1972, and Carter, the choice of only 4 percent in January 1976. Dukakis was preferred by only 3 percent of Democrats in a January 1987 Gallup poll that showed Hart to be the

TABLE 2-1 Leading Presidential Candidates and Nominees, 1936–1992

	Party in power			Party out of power		
Year	Party	Leading candidate at beginning of election year	Nominee	Party	Leading candidate at beginning of election year[a]	Nominee
1936	D	Roosevelt	Roosevelt	R	Landon	Landon
1940	D	Roosevelt	Roosevelt	R	—	Willkie
1944	D	Roosevelt	Roosevelt	R	Dewey	Dewey
1948	D	Truman	Truman	R	Dewey-Taft	Dewey
1952	D	Truman	Stevenson	R	Eisenhower-Taft	Eisenhower
1956	R	Eisenhower	Eisenhower	D	Stevenson	Stevenson
1960	R	Nixon	Nixon	D	Kennedy	Kennedy
1964	D	Johnson	Johnson	R	—	Goldwater
1968	D	Johnson	Humphrey	R	Nixon	Nixon
1972	R	Nixon	Nixon	D	Muskie	McGovern
1976	R	Ford[b]	Ford	D	Humphrey[b]	Carter
1980	D	Carter[c]	Carter	R	—[c]	Reagan
1984	R	Reagan[d]	Reagan	D	Mondale[d]	Mondale
1988	R	Bush	Bush	D	—[e]	Dukakis
1992	R	Bush[f]	Bush	D	Brown[f]	Clinton

SOURCE: Donald Matthews, "Presidential Nominations: Process and Outcomes," in *Choosing the President*, ed. James David Barber (Englewood Cliffs, N.J.: Prentice-Hall, 1974), 54. Subsequent elections updated using Gallup poll data.

[a] Dash (–) indicates that no single candidate led in the polls.

[b] The 1976 information was taken from the January Gallup poll.

[c] Carter led Kennedy in all Gallup polls conducted after the seizure of the hostages by Iran in November 1979. In a February 1980 Gallup poll listing eight candidates, 34 percent of Republican voters named Reagan as their first choice and 32 percent chose Ford; however, when the choice was narrowed to those two candidates, 56 percent preferred Ford and 40 percent, Reagan.

[d] Since President Reagan was unopposed for the Republican nomination, no preference poll was taken. A Gallup poll in mid-February 1984 showed, however, that 86 percent of Republicans approved the president's performance in office. The Gallup poll indicating Mondale to be the leading candidate among Democrats was taken in mid-November 1983.

[e] In an October 1987 Gallup poll, Jackson led Dukakis 22–14 percent but after Hart reentered the contest, he vaulted to the lead in a January 1988 poll with 23 percent to 16 for Dukakis and 15 for Jackson. By mid-March, after Hart's second withdrawal, Dukakis lead 32–23 percent over Jackson. Among Democrats, Brown led Clinton by 21.

[f] In a Gallup poll conducted January 3–6, 1992, Bush led Buchananan by 85 percent to 10 percent. Among Democrats, Brown led Clinton by 21 percent to 17 percent.

choice of a full 53 percent. By January 1988, Hart led by a narrow margin of 23 percent to 16 percent. Dukakis increased his support to 32 percent when Hart dropped out of the race for the second time. In 1992, Clinton was a close second to Brown, who led in a Gallup poll conducted during the first week of 1992. Brown was preferred by 21 percent and Clinton by 17 percent of registered Democrats. Leaders in the polls therefore cannot afford to relax after achieving early popularity: the final choice of the nominee depends on presidential primaries as well as on caucus-convention contests.

Targeting the Nomination Campaign

The number of state contests in which candidates participate has risen drastically since 1969. Primary laws in some states automatically place nationally recognized candidates on the ballot, thus forcing them to participate in contests they may prefer to bypass. The proportional representation feature of most Democratic and some Republican contests encourages candidates to enter even those races they are likely to lose because they can still receive some delegate votes. Moreover, the selectorate expects candidates to show that they have political support in all parts of the country. As a result, serious candidates plan to enter all contests, but once a candidate withdraws from the race, plans are changed accordingly. For example, three of the leading Democratic contenders withdrew early in 1992—Senator Kerrey on March 6, Senator Harkin on March 9, and former senator Tsongas on March 19. There were twenty-four primaries contested between the date Tsongas withdrew and the last event on June 9. Thus, although candidates may plan to compete everywhere, the reality may be quite different. Only Clinton and the persistent Brown remained active to the end of the process. The outcome of early contests is extremely important, but today's candidates can no longer base their campaigns on a limited number of contests, as was the case prior to 1972.

Limitations of time and energy prevent active campaigning in every state. The allocation of money also becomes a major problem. Not only is there an overall restriction on spending ($27.6 million, with $5.5 million allowed for fund-raising, was the limit for those accepting public financing in 1992; the combined total is likely to be a little more than $36 million in 1996), but spending limits also apply in each state.[11] Such considerations require presidential candidates to establish priorities among the large number of primaries and caucus-convention contests. The primaries, in particular, are important because they determine two-thirds to four-fifths of the delegates to the national conventions. Moreover, candidates are much more likely to campaign personally and spend more money in states that hold primaries than in those that have caucus-conventions.[12]

Candidates take several factors into account when deciding which primaries they should emphasize in their nomination campaigns. One is the date of the primary. The earliest contest, traditionally New Hampshire, attracts most of the major contenders because it is the first popular test of voter sentiment. Although the number of New Hampshire delegates is small (in 1992, only 18 of 4,288 Democratic delegates and 23 of 2,210 Republicans), it focuses immediate attention on the winner, as it did on Kennedy in 1960 and Carter in 1976. Even an unexpectedly good showing in a losing cause can benefit a candidate by producing sudden notoriety, as it did Eugene McCarthy in 1968, McGovern in 1972, and Clinton in 1992. New Hampshire appeals to presidential candidates for another reason: its small area and population make campaigning there manageable. Most of the population is concentrated in a thirty-mile strip in the southern part of the state. Slightly more than 120,000 Democrats were registered in 1976, and the Carter organization claimed that it contacted about 95 percent of them, an ideal situation for the former governor who had not yet acquired substantial financial resources for media expenditures and whose contingent of Georgia volunteers could conduct an effective door-to-door campaign. Tsongas tried to achieve much the same goal in 1992 when he reportedly spent seventy campaign days in New Hampshire to compensate for his inability to buy extensive television time, an easy task to accomplish since his home in Lowell, Massachusetts, is just seventeen miles from the New Hampshire border.[13]

In the 1988 campaign, the primaries held on Tuesday, March 8—Super Tuesday as it came to be called—presented a formidable strategic hurdle for the candidates. Delegates were selected from twenty states, most of them in the South. Southern politicos hoped that Super Tuesday would provide momentum early in the nomination process for a candidate more to the liking of southern voters. Al Gore (D-Tenn.), the only southerner in the race, mounted minimal efforts in the New Hampshire and Iowa events and focused on Super Tuesday. But he won only five states (the same success enjoyed by Jackson, who received most of the southern Black vote); Gore suspended his campaign six weeks later.[14] For the Republican party, Super Tuesday was a crucial contest between Bush and Dole. Dole had won in Iowa, but Bush later swamped Dole in the New Hampshire contest. Bush hoped to build on the momentum gained in New Hampshire and did so by winning each of the day's sixteen Republican primaries.

In 1992, only eleven states selected delegates on Super Tuesday (March 10), though most were again concentrated in the South; fourteen states had selected delegates in the preceding two weeks, seven on "Junior Tuesday," one week earlier. Clinton had finished a strong second to Tsongas in New Hampshire (33.2 percent to 24.7) and stole much of the media hype that followed the contest by claiming to be the "Comeback Kid." Prior to the showdown on Super Tuesday, Clinton won the Georgia primary, Tsongas won in Maryland and Utah, while Brown eked out a narrow victory in Colorado and won the caucuses in Maine. Kerrey and Harkin left the race after poor showings in these contests, but there seemed to be no front-runner. Clinton assumed this position when he defeated Tsongas in seven of Super Tuesday's contests, including Florida and Texas, while losing only in Massachusetts, Rhode Island, and Delaware. Florida was the most important of these contests because Tsongas had hoped to score a breakthrough in the South as Dukakis had done in 1988. Clinton and Tsongas appeared to enjoy support that was largely regional; but that issue was resolved the following week in Illinois and Michigan when Clinton scored solid victories. Tsongas suspended his campaign shortly thereafter, leaving Brown to register a surprising victory in Connecticut on March 24 but lose the crucial New York primary on April 7.

Not all contests produce such an early victor. If the earlier primaries have not produced a clear favorite, California voters have often been in a position to determine who the party's nominee will be. Both Barry Goldwater in 1964 and McGovern in 1972 owed their selection to their primary victories in California, which showed them as "winners" shortly before the national convention began. But in recent years the California primary has been less important in determining the nominee, even though it selects the largest number of delegates. Recognizing that contests during the first five weeks of the process have become more numerous (thirty-one states and the District of Columbia selected delegates during February and March while twenty states waited until April to June 1992) and most important in determining the eventual winner, California has joined the many other states that have moved up their delegate selection date. In 1996, the California primary will be held on March 26 (the date was June 2 in 1992). New York has also moved its primary to March 7, a month earlier than in 1992. This pattern of concentrating delegate selection early in the process is termed "front-loading" and has a significant impact on candidate strategies. It places a premium on maximizing campaign contributions before the election year begins (hence the $20 million target for 1996). Campaign organization must be established earlier and messages clearly formulated. Moreover, early missteps are likely to be devastating since the time available for making corrections is so short.

In addition to large states moving up in the schedule, smaller states have challenged New Hampshire's primacy as the nation's first primary.

This traditional position in the calendar is acknowledged by the Democratic party, which has specified a "window" for delegate selection that runs from the first Tuesday in March to the first Tuesday in June (March 5 through June 4, 1996). States selecting delegates outside these limits must receive party permission. The New Hampshire legislature is determined to defend the state's position by scheduling its primary one week earlier than any one else's, as formalized in a 1975 statute. An interstate feud broke out when Arizona and then Delaware threatened New Hampshire's traditional role for 1996. Unless other plans emerge for 1996, Delaware Republicans will hold their primary on February 24, the Saturday following New Hampshire's (therefore allowing less than the one-week interval), and Arizona will join South Dakota with primaries on February 27. Delaware Democrats were having difficulty obtaining permission for the earlier date, forcing them to form alternative plans or conduct an "unsanctioned" primary. This scramble for national attention and political impact is likely to continue in the future.[15]

Considerations other than timing and delegate strength affect candidates' decisions about where to concentrate campaign efforts. Naturally, candidates try to choose states in which they think they have the best chance of winning. In 1984, Mondale selected Pennsylvania and Illinois because of the concentrations of organized labor, Jewish voters, and African American voters from whom he expected to garner support. Both Gore and Jackson targeted southern states in the 1988 Super Tuesday contests. Gore hoped to transform favorite-son status into nationwide support, and Jackson to mobilize his support by African Americans throughout the region. Buchanan hoped to build on his 1992 New Hampshire success by scoring another surprise in Georgia, a state viewed as receptive to his conservative themes. At times, however, candidates have chosen to contest primaries that were not considered advantageous to them to demonstrate that they had a broader appeal than was generally recognized. John Kennedy went into the West Virginia primary in 1960 to prove that a Catholic could win in a state in which the population was 95 percent Protestant. In 1976, Carter chose to emphasize the Pennsylvania primary to show that a southern Baptist could do well in a northern industrial state with a large Catholic population. Both risks proved to be good ones that greatly advanced the Kennedy and Carter candidacies. Tsongas was not as lucky in 1992 when he sought to win Florida and prevent Clinton from sweeping the South.

A major problem for candidates is managing properly a primary they clearly expect to lose. Many contenders have found that the most successful approach is to convince the public and particularly the media that they are not making a major effort so that a loss is not considered a genuine defeat. Most important, candidates must avoid raising false expectations during the nomination campaign. In 1976, shortly before the New Hampshire primary, the Reagan staff released the results of a public opinion poll showing him to be ahead of Ford. When the California governor lost that primary by a single percentage point, the media interpreted the results as a serious defeat for him and a major victory for Ford. In 1980, John Connally decided to focus on the South Carolina primary as the one that would establish his candidacy; when he lost to Reagan there, the Texas governor felt obliged to withdraw from the race altogether. In most cases, candidates downplay their chances so that expectations will be exceeded.

In some instances, caucus-conventions can be crucial even though they have become generally less important than primaries. The Iowa caucuses, held even before the New Hampshire primary, have taken on major importance because they are the first tests of the candidates' political strength, and the media therefore attach great significance to an Iowa victory.[16] In 1976, Carter's successful campaign in Iowa established him as the Democrats' leading candidate; in 1980, his victory over Senator Kennedy in that state gave him a psychological edge in the New Hampshire primary a month later. But the importance of the Iowa caucuses as a launching pad for presidential contenders diminished in 1988 and 1992. Democrat Gephardt and Republican Dole, Iowa's winners, dropped out of the nomination contest by the end of March in 1988. Iowa senator Harkin, a favorite son, dominated the contest in 1992, as expected, so that other candidates did not devote resources to the state and the media directed even greater attention to New Hampshire.

Caucus-convention states also become important if no clear victor emerges during early contests. In 1976, both Ford and Reagan diligently pursued delegates chosen in Republican party caucuses and conventions, especially in the period immediately preceding the Republican convention. In the end, Ford owed his nomination to previously uncommitted delegations, such as that of Mississippi, that cast their ballots for him at the national convention.

Manipulating Political Appeals

With the exception of 1988 when Reagan was constitutionally prohibited from seeking a third term, every election since the post-1968 reforms went into effect has included an incumbent president seeking reelection. Although no candidates in the nomination campaign have the option of using the party label against opponents in the same way they can in the general election, presidents seeking renomination can emphasize that they are leaders of their party. Bush, for example, had been an extremely active party leader and campaigner while he was president. He reportedly provided support at 115 fund-raising events in the 1988–1990 period and made sixty-five personal appearances leading up to the 1990 mid-term.[17] Thus, presidents can suggest that persons who challenge them for the nomination are casting doubts on the good judgment of the party, which nominated them previously, and that a challenge would divide the party in the upcoming general election. Presidents can even imply that attacks on them constitute attacks on the country.

In contrast, the challenger of an incumbent president must find ways to make the challenge appear legitimate. One is to suggest that the incumbent president is not providing the leadership the nation requires. Another is to intimate that the president is such a weak candidate that the party and its congressional, state, and local candidates will be brought down in defeat in November. Yet another is to avow that the president has not kept promises made in the previous campaign and that the president has strayed from the traditional policies of the party. These strategies were perfectly illustrated in 1980 when Senator Kennedy sought to wrest the 1980 Democratic nomination from President Carter. In a similar way, Buchanan made the same charges in his challenge to President Bush in 1992.

Incumbent presidents also can use the powers of the office to great advantage. In a speech early in the 1980 campaign, Senator Kennedy charged that the Carter administration's offer of $7 million to relieve starvation in Cambodia was woefully inadequate; two hours later the president called in television camera crews to announce that $69 million would be given to combat famine and to resettle Cambodian refugees in Thailand. Presidents can use their leverage over federal grants and support for legislation as a way to exact endorsements from party leaders. They also enjoy other prerogatives of office. For example, the Sunday before the Iowa caucuses, President Carter appeared on *Meet the Press* and announced that he would insist that U.S. athletes boycott the summer Olympics in Moscow unless the Soviet Union withdrew its troops from Afghanistan. On the eve of the New Hampshire primary the president invited the U.S. Olympic hockey team to the White House for a televised congratulatory ceremony for its victory over the Soviet team. On the morning of the Wisconsin and Kansas primaries, Carter made a public announcement of a "positive step" toward the release of the hostages in Iran.

Incumbent presidents therefore assume a clear role in a nomination campaign. Not only do they invoke the symbol of party unity, they also

TABLE 2-2 Major Candidates for 1992 Democratic Nomination

Candidate	Background	Political views	Assets	Liabilities
Jerry Brown	lawyer, former governor of California, born April 17, 1938	offered a distinctive—some say "flaky"—lifestyle and "antipolitics" approach to office; expressed doubts about big government and the need for policies to adjust to environment and economic limits	former governor of large, economically viable state; "antipolitics" approach aligned with the public mood, one of anti-big government and anti-incumbency	sometimes seen as too radical and unpredictable
Bill Clinton	lawyer, governor of Arkansas, born August 19, 1946	championed himself as a "new Democrat"; favored the death penalty, supported abortion with restrictions, advocated reform in welfare and health care, and emphasized economic revitalization via public-private initiatives	governor of southern state, able to garner support in recent Republican-dominated South; centrist stance offered broad appeal; highly competent and well organized campaign, able to amass $3.3 million by the end of 1991	experience limited to smaller, lower-ranking state; character called into question over non-military service (Vietnam-era draft) and an alleged extra-marital affair while in office
Tom Harkin	lawyer, U.S. senator from Iowa, born November 19, 1939	labeled himself a traditional New Deal Democrat; openly endorsed a traditional progressive agenda for the party and the nation; during ten years in the House and seven in the Senate had been rated as a liberal, especially on foreign affairs	seventeen years of experience in the House and Senate; was odds-on favorite to win in Iowa's February 1992 caucuses; strongly supported by organized labor in reelection bid; appealed most strongly to traditional elements of the Democratic coalition	limited appeal, representing Iowa, a homogenous, agricultural state, for seventeen years

Bob Kerrey	U.S. senator, former governor of Nebraska, born August 27, 1943	antiwar position, vocally opposed the use of military force to oust Iraq from Kuwait; could attract Democratic party activists with liberal voting record and antiwar position, and had shown the ability to win votes from a Republican-leaning electorate; first to call for national health insurance	decorated war veteran with an antiwar stance; ability to appeal to right-of-center constituency	vocally opposed the Gulf War, which later received high public approval; untested on the national scene
Paul Tsongas	lawyer, former U.S. senator from Massachusetts, born February 14, 1941	a liberal campaigning on the need for a new national industrial policy to revitalize America's economic base and restore America's competitiveness in the international marketplace; proposed cut in capital-gains tax, tax credits to stimulate research and development, and relaxed antitrust laws	combined experience in local government and service in the Peace Corps with ten years in the U.S. Congress, six as senator; became the first candidate to raise more than $500,000 by the end of June	health called into question as result of former bout with cancer; reminded many of Michael Dukakis
Douglas Wilder	lawyer, governor of Virginia, born January 17, 1931	as governor, urged fiscal responsibility; endorsed austere budget of program cuts and public employee layoffs to deal with $2 billion state deficit and refusal to raise taxes; highly visible stand in favor of abortion rights gained broader appeal among White voters	first African American governor elected in the nation's history; military service	political feud with Senator Robb, Virginia's other presidential hopeful, damaged both men's careers; charges, counter-charges, and revelations covered heavily by national media

TABLE 2-3 Major Candidates for 1992 Republican Nomination

Candidate	Background	Political Views	Assets	Liabilities
George Bush	president of the United States, former vice president of the United States, businessperson, born June 12, 1924	perceived by many as a "moderate" Republican, advocated fewer taxes, less spending, and less big government, and persistent opposition to abortion; victory in the Gulf War and abortion stance helped ease tension with the far right	served in the White House for twelve years; very strong diplomatic skills; commander in chief of the successful Gulf War, which gained him one of the highest recorded approval ratings; was able to take credit for the fall of the Berlin Wall	often perceived as a "wimp," out of touch with mainstream America, and born with a silver spoon in his mouth
Pat Buchanan	conservative television commentator, journalist, presidential speechwriter, director of communications in Reagan administration, born November 2, 1938	ultra-conservative, reverted to old-fashioned form of political isolationism in foreign policy views, focused on domestic affairs believed to have been shirked by Bush	highly recognized name, received abundance of television air time, strong support with the far right	perceived as anti-Semitic and too far right to have broad-based appeal

manipulate events to benefit their candidacies. Incumbency is particularly advantageous if foreign crises occur during the campaign period, for Americans tend to "rally 'round the flag," and hence their president, as they initially did in 1980 for Carter when Americans were taken hostage in Iran. Events can conspire to highlight a president's weakness, however. Bush was fortunate in 1992 that the Republican nomination campaign was largely decided before the outbreak of riots in Los Angeles that followed announcement of the Rodney King verdict.

In the long view, U.S. history shows the superior campaign position of the incumbent. Franklin Pierce was the last president who actively sought his party's renomination and failed to obtain it; James Buchanan won the Democratic nomination from him in 1856. President Chester Arthur lost the GOP nomination in 1884, but there is some question about how actively he sought it. Nonetheless, recent defeats suffered by incumbent presidents show us that an internal party challenge for the nomination can later have devastating effects in the general election: Ford, Carter, and Bush, the three incumbents recently denied reelection, confronted nomination challenges that bruised their images and left unhealed wounds within their parties.

Presidential candidates in the party out of power face an entirely different campaign situation. Although they do not have the problem of how legitimately to challenge an incumbent president, they do experience other difficulties. Typically, many candidates vie for their party's nomination, and all aspirants must find a way to distinguish themselves from their opponents. Tables 2-2 and 2-3 present information on the range of persons who sought the 1992 Democratic and Republican nominations. A further complication is that the range of political views of the selectorate in the nomination campaign is narrower than that of the electorate in the general election: most Republicans participating in the nomination process are more conservative than the average Republican voter; most Democratic participants are more liberal than the average Democratic voter.

The limited range of the selectorate's views creates problems and opportunities for those who try to advance their candidacy by taking stands on the issues. A candidate who departs from the standard positions runs the risk of alienating a large number of party members; yet one who does not do so remains indistinguishable from the other candidates. In the crowded field of 1988, du Pont offered a number of radically different policy proposals as a way to distinguish himself from the field, but he failed to win substantial support. Clinton had expected to run as the moderate in 1992, but the Tsongas economic plan, which urged government assistance to business, led Clinton to develop a more liberal message. Candidates may also be forced to match their opponents' appeals. Clinton, for example, had to issue an economic plan in order to match the Tsongas blueprint for economic reform, "A Call to Economic Arms." Health care, originally Kerrey's major issue, quickly became a topic that all candidates had to address.

Facing the problems associated with taking stands on issues, candidates develop other types of political appeals in nomination campaigns. Most important is the projection of a personal image that reflects their most attractive attributes. Carter recognized the nation's distrust of public officials after the Vietnam War and Watergate and emphasized his commitment to make the government as "truthful, capable, and filled with love as the American people." Clinton sought to overcome campaign and media criticism of his personal life in 1992 by emphasizing another trait—action—illustrated by his accomplishments as governor of Arkansas in the areas of education reform, job creation, and welfare reform. Tsongas had a very different problem to combat: his health. Having recovered from lymphatic cancer, a notable Tsongas campaign ad showed him swimming vigorously to demonstrate his full recovery.

Candidates also project themselves as "winners." This appeal usually is adopted by candidates who do well in the early nomination contests. Confident after his victory over Reagan in the 1980 Iowa caucuses, Bush suddenly announced that his campaign had momentum, or what he referred to as "Big Mo." Unfortunately for Bush, Big Mo lasted only until the New Hampshire primary, which Reagan clearly won. Mondale asserted his invincibility after his decisive victory in Iowa, only one week before being upset by Hart in New Hampshire. Clinton found a way to project upbeat interpretations of the New Hampshire, South Dakota, Maine, Colorado, and Maryland contests in 1992 when he finished second or third but ahead of expectations.

Presidential nomination campaigns, therefore, are characterized more by the manipulation of personal images and claims of winner status than by a discussion of the issues. Contributing greatly to this situation is the influence of the media in the nomination process.

Communicating Political Appeals

In 1988 and again in 1992, more than 20 million voters participated in the Democratic primaries and another 12 to 13 million in the Republican primaries. Thousands more attended party caucuses. To communicate with this vast number of people, candidates turn to the mass media and novel ways of commanding public attention. These are often referred to as "wholesale" campaign tactics that reach large numbers of voters rather than "retail" techniques that are more personal. Candidates in the 1988 campaign prepared videotapes for distribution at gatherings they were unable to attend. Televised call-in shows beamed up to a satellite allowed candidates to link up with voters and reporters around the country.[18] In 1992, the Clinton campaign distributed videos of the candidate door-to-door the same way candidates traditionally have dropped literature, and Buchanan wired himself for sound so that reporters could monitor all his interactions with voters. These innovations complemented the usual techniques of modern campaigning.

Major candidates depend heavily on short television commercials to carry their messages. In 1980, Carter's advertisements stressed his character: one showed the president with his family and concluded with the statement, "Husband, Father, President. He's done these three jobs with distinction." Edward Kennedy's commercials carried a leadership theme: they focused on the senator looking forceful in Senate hearings and walking through enthusiastic crowds. In 1992, Kerrey reminded voters of his decorated service in Vietnam, while Harkin sought to strike a populist pose by addressing groups of workers and farmers in rousing tones of outrage. Buchanan's ads heavily criticized Bush's record as president with particular emphasis on his reversal of the "No New Taxes" pledge made in 1988 and the jobs that would be lost through the proposed North American Free Trade Agreement.

Candidate debates have become increasingly important beginning with the 1980 GOP nomination contest. Reagan refused to participate in the initial nationally televised debate held in Iowa on the grounds that such verbal encounters would destroy party unity; Bush did well in the debate (paraphrasing Yogi Berra in asserting that Carter had made the "wrong mistake" by imposing an embargo on grain shipments to the Soviet Union) and went on to win the caucuses there. Reagan then switched tactics and engaged in two debates in New Hampshire. In the second one, originally scheduled to include only Reagan and Bush, the California governor outmaneuvered his opponent by suggesting that the debate be opened to other candidates; when Bush insisted on sticking to the terms of the original two-person encounter, he came across as selfish to the other Republican contenders and to many voters as well. Reagan won the New Hampshire primary and also prevailed in Illinois, where he did well in a multicandidate debate that included John Anderson of Illinois.

The Democratic candidates held about a dozen debates in 1984, but none proved as crucial as the Reagan-Bush New Hampshire debate of 1980, partly because the field was so large. With eight in the debate that preceded the Iowa caucus, it was difficult for viewers to keep straight which candidate said what. There were still important confrontations: in Iowa, Hart asked Mondale to indicate a single, major domestic issue on which he disagreed with the AFL-CIO; in Atlanta, Mondale challenged Hart to spell out the substance of his "new ideas," making his point by using the famous line from a fast-food chain's commercial, "Where's the beef?" During the 1988 nominating season, approximately 100 candidate debates were held; toward the end of the campaign, several weary candidates began declining invitations to participate. The 1992 events held some local importance: Brown benefited from a preelection debate in Colorado where the Tsongas position on nuclear power was a major issue; agriculture issues were appropriately highlighted in the South Dakota debate.

Even more important than candidate commercials or debates in campaign communications is the coverage of the nomination process by the news media. Particularly influential are nationally syndicated newspaper columnists, such as David Broder, Jack Germond, and Jules Witcover; writers for local newspapers, among others, take their cues about the candidates and the nomination contest itself from these media "heavies," a phenomenon known as "pack journalism." [19] Principal network newscasters such as Dan Rather, Peter Jennings, and Tom Brokaw, as well as Sunday morning news commentators such as George Will and Sam Donaldson, have played an important role in recent nomination campaigns since television is the main source of political information for most voters. The coverage is sometimes dramatic, as in early 1988 when Bush and Rather confronted each other in a live interview on the *CBS Evening News.* Rather persistently pressed Bush on his role in the Iran-Contra scandal, particularly his knowledge about the details of the arms-for-hostages trade. Bush refused to answer directly and took the offensive by reminding Rather of an evening when he had walked off the set to protest a late beginning of the newscast. Bush's point was that people should be judged by their entire records, not by a single event in their careers. Bush had successfully avoided embarrassment and used the encounter to his political advantage.

Such dramatic encounters are rare. Instead, the mass media focus primarily on the presidential "game"—who is winning and losing, campaign strategy and logistics, and appearances and "hoopla." [20] The contestants' competitive chances are calculated and their candidacies assessed by the extent to which they surpass or fall short of the media's predictions. The media also offer analyses of the strategies of the candidates and how successful they are likely to be. Television in particular concentrates its attention on candidate appearances and crowd reactions to such appearances, as it tries to convey the visually exciting aspects of the campaign. In 1992, Buchanan enhanced the visual effects with a novel "porta-crowd" strategy. Traveling around New Hampshire in a bus with twenty die-hard supporters, Buchanan and his group would disembark in a small town and the candidate would engage in conversation with local citizens while the porta-crowd provided television crews with the desired atmosphere, but the media did not comment on the event's contrived nature.[21]

Most studies contend that the media devote far less coverage to the "substance" of the campaign—discussion of issues and policies, the traits and records of the candidates, and endorsements by political leaders—for several reasons. It is difficult to focus effectively on issues when a number of candidates in a nomination contest hold very similar views. With today's nomination campaigns so long, candidates' speeches become, from the media's point of view, "unnewsworthy," as the contenders repeat their stands on the issues again and again. Finally, many media representatives assume that most voters are not interested in the issues; in any event, it is difficult to present issues in depth—especially on television, where the average evening news story lasts only a little longer than one minute.

Patterson points out that there are two kinds of issues in which the media are interested.[22] One is when candidates take diametrically opposed stands on a matter of public policy—the "clear-cut" issue. There are also "campaign" issues, where candidates commit an error of judgment, such as Carter's remark in 1976 about the desirability of preserving the "ethnic purity" of city neighborhoods. Mudd's previously mentioned interview with Kennedy is a graphic illustration: it concentrated primarily on Mary Jo Kopechne's death at Chappaquiddick and barely touched on Kennedy's voting record in his seventeen years in the Senate. More recently, Clinton's alleged affair with Gennifer Flowers, the details of his draft deferment at the time of the Vietnam War, and his possible use of marijuana as a college student drew far more media attention than his issue positions.

Media coverage can shape public perceptions about a candidate's viability. One analysis of coverage given to Jackson's campaigns in 1984 and 1988 found that reporters gave Jackson less presidential "game" coverage than the other candidates in the Democratic field. Stories focused on his personality and on his role as an outsider with little chance for the nomination. Though the media presented Jackson as a legitimate candidate, they also implied that he was different from the other candidates, reinforcing the idea that he had a slim chance of nomination.

The media also devote little attention to how candidates have fared in prior public offices. Before the state caucuses and primaries begin, commentators give some coverage to the candidates' records, but that interest declines when the presidential "game" begins. Only when a hiatus occurs in the primary campaign do the media generally return to an examination of the record. In April 1980, for example, during the three weeks between the Wisconsin and Pennsylvania primaries, the media suddenly began producing detailed comparisons of Reagan's campaign statements and his actual performance as the governor of California.

Thus the media shape the nature of the nomination campaign. They tend to focus attention on the game aspects of the early contests, particularly those in Iowa and New Hampshire. They typically employ a winner-take-all principle that gives virtually all the publicity, regardless of how narrow the victory or the number of popular votes involved, to the victorious candidate in a state contest. In the 1976 Iowa caucuses, Carter's capture of about 14,000 voters (just 28 percent of the 50,000 cast) was interpreted by Mudd as making the Georgia governor a "clear winner" and as opening the "ground between himself and the rest of the so-called pack." [23] At times, however, the media may provide greater coverage to the runner-up: after winning a mere 16 percent of the votes in the Iowa caucuses in 1984, Hart received as much publicity as Mondale, who captured three times as many votes.[24] In a similar way, in 1992, Buchanan's success in winning almost 40 percent of the New Hampshire vote (his actual total was 37 percent to Bush's 53 percent) overshadowed the president's victory. On the Democratic side, Clinton's 24.7 percent showing exceeded the predictions based on preelection polls, thereby overshadowing Tsongas's first-place showing of 33.2 percent.

Campaign Organization and Workers

Although the mass media play a major role in communicating political appeals to the selectorate, interpersonal contacts remain an important element in nomination campaigns. This is particularly true in small state primaries and in states that use caucus-conventions to choose their delegates to the national convention. In the latter states, voters do not simply arrive at the local polling place and cast ballots; rather, they typically participate in a lengthy meeting in which candidates' supporters gather into groups, engage in discussion of the contestants' relative merits, and possibly shift their preferences if their own candidate has too little support to win representation at the next step, a county or district convention. Thus, the caucus is the first, local stage of this process with conventions held to reflect views at successively larger geographic areas. Delegates to the national convention are ultimately chosen at a state convention. Most people are unwilling to commit as much time and effort as even the first stage requires unless campaign workers have contacted them personally, and it is critical that someone monitor progress at each successive stage of this process.

As the campaign progresses, a candidate must expand the core of support that developed in the early, prenomination stage of the process. Before 1972, candidates relied heavily on political professionals to sponsor and organize their campaign, as Humphrey did in 1968. But today, the endorsement and campaign efforts of party professionals do not ensure the nomination. Party and public officials heavily endorsed Sen. Edmund Muskie in 1976, but McGovern was the nominee, a candidate with whom many professionals were uncomfortable. In the same way, Carter won the Democratic nomination in 1972, even though he had virtually no initial support from his fellow governors or other members of the Democratic political establishment, leading him to be regarded as an "outsider." However, Mondale was the choice of "insiders" in 1984 and party officials rallied behind Dukakis and Clinton in 1988 and 1992, despite some discomfort with each. Because intraparty disputes have been less prominent in their party, Republicans have had less difficulty with such disputes, although the number of outsider Republican candidates has increased in recent years, including Robertson in 1988 and Buchanan in 1992 and 1996. Probably the only candidate today who can line up the support of party professionals is an incumbent president who can use the influence of the office over the dispensation of federal grants as political leverage against opponents.

Today's candidates build personal organizations based on loyal supporters who have helped them in previous campaigns, political consultants providing campaign services and advice, and political amateurs who offer support because they agree with a candidate's stands on the issues or are attracted to his or her personality or political style. Amateurs constituted the base for the Goldwater movement in 1964, for McCarthy's "Children's Crusade" in 1968, for McGovern's "guerrilla army" in 1972, and for Reagan's conservative constituency in 1976 and again in 1980. Political scientist Jeane Kirkpatrick identified a new class of political activists that had emerged during the 1960s and 1970s that she called the "new presidential elite." [25] Usually members of the upper–middle class, such people had neither experience in nor loyalty to traditional party organizations. They took a keen interest in the intellectual and moral aspects of politics and used their verbal skills to great advantage in nomination politics. Some of these participants remained active in presidential politics (Hart had been McGovern's campaign manager in 1972), and some candidates relied on grassroots enthusiasts as the base of their support (Brown and Buchanan in 1992). But the amateur campaigns seldom produced winners in November, and candidates had to rely on political pros to perform the most critical tasks. Nonetheless, tapping a source of enthusiastic support could be a distinct campaign asset. Thus, there were warning signs for Dole at the outset of the 1996 race when Gramm appeared to be the favorite among many Republican activists. For example, Gramm led Dole by 40 percent to 12 percent in a survey taken of attendees at the annual Conservative Political Action Conference held in Washington early in 1995.[26] Dole also could not afford to cede the support of the Christian Coalition to his principal opponent and may have adjusted both his policy views and his legislative strategy in an effort to maintain credibility with this important source of Republican activists.

At times, members of interest groups explicitly endorse candidates for the nomination and furnish campaign workers for them. Edward Kennedy drew support from the International Association of Machinists and Aerospace Workers, and the NEA worked hard on President Carter's behalf in 1980. Both the AFL-CIO and the NEA endorsed Mondale before the formal 1984 nomination process began and then played an important part in helping him secure the Democratic nomination. But after Mondale was labeled the "candidate of the special interests" because of these group endorsements, candidates in subsequent races were reluctant to risk a similar sobriquet. Nonetheless, Harkin worked hard to enlist the support of organized labor behind his campaign in 1992 and Clinton sought the support of women's groups.

Campaign Finance

Presidential candidates since the 1970s raise funds for their campaigns before the state contests begin, and the effort continues throughout the official campaign period. As in 1992, candidates who do not do well in the first few primaries tend to drop out of the race early on. One reason is that, under the campaign finance law, federal matching funds must be cut off within thirty days if a candidate obtains less than 10 percent of the votes in two consecutive primaries. Even candidates who score some successes in primaries may nonetheless develop financial problems if their opponents are doing even better. In 1980, Senator Kennedy found that President Carter was outspending him in virtually every state, including his home state of Massachusetts (New Hampshire was one exception). That same year, Bush was forced to take out a bank loan of $2.8 million after losing to Reagan in several primaries.

Candidates must decide not only how to raise funds but also how to spend them. The overall spending limits for the entire campaign ($17.6

million in 1980, $24.4 million in 1984, $27.7 million in 1988, and $33.1 million in 1992), as well as expenditure limits in each state, require that money be carefully allocated. Because they want to win in initial primaries and caucuses, candidates are inclined to spend heavily in the very early stages of the campaign. By February 26, 1980, the date of the New Hampshire primary, Reagan had spent two-thirds of his allowable limit for a campaign consisting of thirty-four primaries.[27] Clinton reportedly had only $102,068 in cash at the end of February while facing $711,406 in debts. He was able, however, to borrow heavily against a line-of-credit arranged with an Arkansas bank. Thus, even though he led the Democratic field in fund-raising, debts accumulated rapidly in the contest; as he pulled away from the field, however, campaign contributions rose significantly.[28] Front-loading the schedule makes it even more important that a substantial campaign war chest has been accumulated.

Summary of Developments in Recent Nomination Campaigns

As suggested in the preceding sections, presidential nomination campaigns are highly complex operations that call for a variety of specialists. Pollsters help candidates assess their nomination prospects and provide vital feedback on the reactions of voters to the candidates and their campaigns, on the issues that people are thinking about, and on the attitudes of social and economic groups about such issues. Media consultants help candidates develop a favorable image, write their speeches, and plan their television appearances. Direct-mail specialists help raise money and get out the vote. Since the 1952 presidential election, candidates have turned more and more to political consultants to organize these diverse operations, to develop strategy, and to manage the overall campaign.

Since the late 1960s, control over the fate of presidential candidates has passed from a relatively few party professionals to rank-and-file voters. The attitudes of these voters evolve during the course of the nomination contest, in large part under the influence of the media. In the early stages of the contest, the media help determine who the viable candidates are; then, once the state primaries and caucuses begin, they label the "winners" and "losers," often influencing the results of future state contests, for voters gravitate toward the winners and desert the losers. Periodic public opinion polls reflect the presidential preferences of U.S. voters, as do the results of state primaries and caucuses.

Moreover, the attitudes of voters, the media, the polls, and the state contest results influence one another. Candidates who receive favorable treatment from the media tend to do well in the primaries, and their showing there, in turn, raises their standings in the polls. Favorable polls impress representatives of the media as well as political activists and many rank-and-file voters, leading to more victories for the poll leaders in both nonprimary and primary contests. The result of this reinforcement process is that one candidate typically has emerged by the time the delegates gather for their party's national convention. This candidate has received the most extensive and the most favorable media coverage, has led in the polls, and has won more primary and caucus-convention contests than any other candidate.[29] However, one more hurdle remains for the front-runner to cross—the party's national convention.

The National Convention

The national convention is important to presidential candidates for two reasons. First, whatever may have happened before, the actual nomination occurs at the convention. Second, the convention provides opportunities for candidates to strengthen their chances to win the general election the following November.

Rules and Politics of the Proceedings

Several decisions that precede the balloting for the nomination can affect significantly both the choice of nominee and the outcome of the general election. Sometimes the location of the convention is important. (The party's national committee officially makes this decision: for the party out of power, the national committee chair has the greatest say in the matter; for the party in power, the U.S. president does.) The welcoming speech of Illinois governor Adlai Stevenson to the Democratic delegates assembled in Chicago in 1952 is credited with influencing their decision to nominate him that year. In 1968, the confrontation in Chicago between protestors and Mayor Richard Daley's police contributed to Humphrey's defeat in the general election. Some Democrats fear that returning to the scene of that debacle in 1996 will only serve to remind voters of the Democrats' past difficulties. On the other hand, Republicans hope that by meeting in San Diego, their candidate will gain a head start toward winning the most important electoral prize for November: California.

Also important are the struggles that occasionally emerge between rival slates of delegates from states in which the selection process was disputed. At the 1952 Republican convention, the party's credentials committee awarded Robert Taft a majority of the delegates in several southern states, but this decision was overturned on the floor of the convention in favor of the ultimate nominee, Dwight Eisenhower. At the 1972 Democratic convention, there were eighty-two separate challenges involving thirty states and more than 40 percent of the delegates; most of the disputes stemmed from alleged violations of the McGovern Commission guidelines. Eventually, all but two were settled by the credentials committee; these went to the convention floor and were resolved in Senator McGovern's favor. He was awarded all of California's delegate votes, even though, as previously noted, he won only 45 percent of that state's primary vote. Fights over rules of convention proceedings sometimes take on great significance. One such battle occurred at the 1976 Republican convention when the Reagan forces moved to amend the rules to require candidates to name their vice-presidential choice before the balloting on presidential candidates; they hoped thereby to force Ford to name a running mate and thus risk the loss of supporters who would be disappointed with his decision. (Before the convention, Reagan had chosen liberal-to-moderate Pennsylvania senator Richard Schweiker as his vice president, a move calculated to bring him needed support from uncommitted delegates in large eastern states such as New York and Pennsylvania.) The defeat of that amendment helped pave the way for President Ford's victory on the first ballot that year. In 1980, Edward Kennedy's forces attempted to persuade the Democratic convention delegates to throw out a rule that required delegates to vote on the first ballot for a presidential candidate to whom they were pledged in their home state's primary or caucus-convention. When the convention upheld the rule, the Massachusetts senator knew he had no chance of winning the Democratic nomination, for a majority of the delegates were pledged to Carter. Kennedy immediately withdrew his candidacy. At the 1988 Democratic convention, Jackson realized he had lost the nomination but sought to win concessions on the rules governing the 1992 contest. Rather than risk a publicly embarrassing and potentially unity-shattering battle over the rules, the Dukakis forces gave Jackson what he wanted. Delegate selection was tied more closely to the share of the vote earned in the primary and caucus contests, and the number of superdelegates was reduced, though the latter agreement was later broken.

Writing and adopting the party platform entails other important convention decisions. Although critics have ridiculed the platforms for containing promises the party does not intend to keep, presidents of both parties have used their influence to enact the promises into law.[30] Moreover, many delegates and party leaders take them seriously.[31] In 1948, some of the delegates to the Democratic convention felt that the platform was too liberal on civil rights; twenty years later the Democrats bitterly debated the Vietnam plank in the platform. Republicans also have experienced major conflicts over their party platform: in 1964, the conservative Goldwater forces, who controlled that convention, refused to make any concessions to party moderates, such as governors Nelson Rockefeller of New York and George Romney of Michigan, on civil rights and political extremism.

One of the problems of platform fights is that the intraparty conflict may influence the general election campaign. In 1948, a group of southerners headed by South Carolina governor Strom Thurmond (then a Democrat) formed the States' Rights party, which actually carried four southern states—Alabama, Louisiana, Mississippi, and South Carolina. Republican governors Rockefeller and Romney did little to help Goldwater in 1964, and many Democrats opposed to the pro-administration Vietnam plank in the party's 1968 platform did not rouse themselves in the general election campaign that year. Bush, reportedly fearing that conservatives would stay at home in 1992, allowed several spokespersons for the party's conservative wing to deliver prime-time speeches that projected an especially unattractive image to moderates and independents.

Because of the possibility of splitting the party in the fall campaign, presidential candidates and their supporters sometimes decide not to fight their major rivals over the platform. After defeating Reagan for the 1976 Republican nomination, President Ford allowed the views of the California governor to prevail in several major provisions of the platform, including advocating a "moral" foreign policy in contrast to the Ford administration's policy of détente with the Soviet Union. In 1980, President Carter followed a similar procedure in permitting the Kennedy forces to add to the Democratic platform a provision for a $12 billion, antirecession job program. In 1984, Mondale allowed Hart to add a plank spelling out the conditions under which a Democratic president would use U.S. forces abroad and permitted Jackson to add a provision for "affirmative action goals and timetables and other verifiable measurements." In 1988, three of Jackson's proposed platform amendments were not included, but the Dukakis forces accepted modified versions of nine other Jackson planks in exchange for Jackson's acceptance of a short platform.

Credentials contests, the adoption of rules of procedure, and the writing of the party platform are tests of strength for the candidates and often determine who will prevail in the most important decision of the convention—the balloting for president, which typically takes place on the third day of the proceedings. In the interim, preparations are made for the roll-call vote. Presidential hopefuls frequently call caucuses of state delegations and sometimes contact individual delegates for their support. Polls are taken of delegates so that candidates know how many votes they can count on and from whom they may pick up additional support. In 1960, Edward Kennedy retained contacts with the Wyoming delegates he had worked with the previous spring and was in their midst when that delegation cast its decisive vote for his brother on the first ballot.[32] Also in 1960, Nixon arranged to have his picture taken with each delegate at the Republican convention.[33]

The strategy candidates employ in the balloting depends on the amount of delegate support they have. A front-runner, as President Ford asserted he was in 1976, can concentrate on holding the votes he or she has been promised and on picking up any additional votes needed to win a majority on the initial ballot. The candidates and their workers use the bandwagon technique to achieve this goal—that is, they argue that because the candidate will win the nomination anyway, smart delegation chairs or individual members should support the candidacy early on, rather than wait until the matter has already been settled. The candidate, the workers imply, will remember early support in the future and will grant political favors accordingly. Franklin Roosevelt did so quite specifically after he was elected in 1932, determining whether a person seeking a political position had backed him "before Chicago" (where the convention had been held).

Candidates with less delegate support attempt to counter the bandwagon technique with their own strategies. They try to create the impression that the nomination is still uncertain, as the Reagan forces did at the 1976 Republican convention. At times, they may encourage delegates who do not support them to cast their ballots for favorite sons or other minor candidates; their objective is to hold down the vote for the front-runner on the first roll call. Candidates also attempt to forge alliances to stop the leader. They may agree, for example, that at some time during the balloting, those who fall behind in the voting will throw their support to others. The difficulty with making such an arrangement is that minor candidates frequently have greater differences among themselves than they have with the leader. The only alliance that conceivably might have stopped Nixon at the 1968 Republican convention would have been one between Rockefeller and Reagan. However, given their divergent views on vital issues of the day, and Rockefeller's failure to support Goldwater in 1964 (in contrast to Reagan's famous convention speech on Goldwater's behalf), the two governors were hardly a compatible political combination.

The leader, along with other candidates, offers various enticements in bargaining with possible political supporters. Some delegates may be interested in persuading the party to take a particular stand on the platform. Others may have more tangible concerns: senators or governors may seek the candidate's support in their own campaigns; other political leaders may be looking toward a cabinet post. Although a presidential candidate may refuse to make such commitments in order to remain free and beholden to no one, the candidate's supporters do not hesitate to make promises. One delegate to the 1960 convention claimed to be the nineteenth person to whom the Kennedy forces had offered the vice presidency.[34]

A definite trend in recent conventions is early victory for the candidate who arrives at the convention with the greatest number of pledged delegates. In the twenty-four conventions the two major parties have held since World War II, only two nominees—Thomas Dewey in 1948 and Stevenson in 1952—failed to win a majority of the convention votes on the first ballot. Thus, the convention has become a body that typically legitimizes a decision made some time before the delegates gather to confer the nomination on their candidate.

The selection of the vice-presidential nominee is the final decision of the convention. Although in theory the delegates make the choice, it has been political custom since 1940 to allow presidential nominees to pick their own running mates. On rare occasions nominees may decide not to express their preference and to permit the convention to make an open choice, as Stevenson did in 1956. The typical presidential nominee, however, confers with leaders whose judgment he trusts, and, when he makes the decision, the word is passed on to the delegates. Even though some delegates may resist a particular vice-presidential candidate, nominees generally get their way. In 1940, Roosevelt threatened to refuse the presidential nomination unless Henry Wallace were chosen as his vice president. In 1960, Kennedy insisted on Lyndon Johnson as his running mate over the objections of some liberal members of the party, including his brother Robert. In effect, the vice president is the first political appointment of the winning presidential nominee.

Various considerations underlie the choice of a vice-presidential candidate. Parties traditionally attempt to balance the ticket—that is, to select a person who differs in certain ways from the presidential nominee. For example, the two candidates may come from separate parts of the country. Over the years, the Democratic party often has chosen southerners to run with presidential nominees who were typically from other, two-party regions; the Kennedy-Johnson ticket in 1960 and the Dukakis-Bentsen ticket in 1988 were two such combinations. In 1976, when a southerner, Carter, won the Democratic presidential contest for the first time since before the Civil War, the process worked in reverse; he chose as his running mate Mondale from the northern state of Minnesota. In 1972, McGovern originally chose Sen. Thomas Eagleton as his running mate, because the Missourian possessed certain characteristics the South

Dakotan lacked: affiliation with the Roman Catholic church, ties to organized labor, and previous residence in a large city (St. Louis). In 1980, Reagan chose Bush (whom he reportedly did not much admire) in order to win the support of moderates in the Republican party. In 1984, Mondale selected as his running mate Rep. Geraldine Ferraro of New York, who not only complemented the ticket geographically but also was the first woman and first Italian American to serve as a major party candidate in a presidential contest. The ticket is balanced in these ways to broaden its appeal and thereby strengthen the party's chances in the general election. In a striking break with this tradition, Clinton selected another southern moderate, Gore, as his running mate in 1992, a move that highlighted the generational shift represented by two baby boomers and contrasted Gore's strong credentials for the presidency—he had campaigned for the office in 1988—with the suspect preparation of Quayle.

At least some presidential nominees consider how the vice-presidential candidate will perform in office. The trend toward assigning important responsibilities to the second in command has led some candidates to choose running mates with whom they feel they can work effectively. This was the main reason Carter chose Mondale over other northern liberal senators he had interviewed for the position, including Muskie of Maine, Frank Church of Idaho, John Glenn of Ohio, and Adlai Stevenson III of Illinois. The possibility of succession also has led presidents to choose the running mate who seems most able to assume the duties of the nation's highest office. Kennedy reportedly chose Johnson not only because he balanced the Democratic ticket in 1960 but also because Kennedy considered the Texan to be the most capable leader among his rivals for the presidential nomination.

Whatever the considerations that prompt the choice of a running mate, there is no doubt that presidential nominees often make the decision too quickly, and frequently without complete knowledge of the candidate's background. A notable example is McGovern's choice of Eagleton in 1972. McGovern and his staff met the morning after his nomination (many of them having had only two or three hours of sleep), and by five o'clock that afternoon they settled on Eagleton. The Missourian accepted the nomination after several other persons had either turned it down, could not be contacted, or were vetoed by key McGovern supporters. During that time no one on the candidate's staff discovered Eagleton's history of mental illness, which ultimately led McGovern to force him off the ticket after a storm of public controversy. Media reaction to the choice made by a presidential nominee can become a complication for the ticket. In 1988, the reaction to Bush's selection of Dan Quayle nearly overshadowed the Republican convention. Questions were raised about Quayle's ability to perform as president should the need arise, his service in the National Guard during the Vietnam War, and the circumstances of his admission to law school. Following the controversy, Quayle may have benefited temporarily from a sympathetic backlash to the media's feeding frenzy, but his problems at the outset of the campaign probably explain why he virtually disappeared during the general election.

The Democrats' choice also produced problems in 1988, though of a different sort. Dukakis and Lloyd Bentsen had substantial policy differences that attracted immediate Republican comment. More significantly, however, Jackson was rebuffed in his pointed pursuit of the vice-presidential nomination, a position to which he felt entitled given his second-place finish in the competition for the presidential nomination. Dukakis not only denied Jackson this chance but managed to alienate Jackson and many of his supporters in the process. Jackson had expected Dukakis to give him the courtesy of a telephone call before announcing his choice, but the decision was announced publicly before Jackson could be reached. The bad feelings carried over into the fall campaign.

After the vice-presidential candidate is chosen, the final night of the convention proceedings is given over to acceptance speeches. On this occasion the presidential nominee tries to reunite the candidates and various party elements that have confronted one another during the long pre-convention campaign and the hectic days of the convention. Major party figures usually come to the convention stage and pledge their support for the winner in the upcoming campaign. At times, however, personal feelings run too high and wounds fail to heal sufficiently for a show of party unity. In 1964, for example, important members of the liberal wing of the Republican party did not support the GOP standard-bearer, Goldwater. In 1968, many McCarthyites (including McCarthy himself) refused, at least immediately, to endorse the Democrats' nominee, Humphrey. In 1972, prominent Democratic leaders, including George Meany of the AFL-CIO, did not support McGovern. Senator Kennedy apparently refused to shake President Carter's hand on the final night of the 1980 Democratic convention. Thus, the convention does not always achieve one of its main objectives: to rally the party faithful for the general election.

Recent Changes in Conventions

Conventions today strive to project their party's nominee in the best possible light and boost the chances for victory in the general election. In this regard, the 1992 Democratic and Republican conventions offered a contrast almost as sharp as those in 1968. The Democratic assembly was carefully choreographed to avoid controversy while projecting an image of party reform and moderation befitting the "New Democrats." The process of drafting the party platform was carefully controlled by the Clinton forces and produced a noncontroversial document. Access to the speaker's podium was limited to those who had endorsed Clinton—which meant that opponents of abortion such as Pennsylvania governor Bob Casey were not allowed to address either the delegates or a national audience. Brown, the nominee's most persistent opponent, was allowed to speak only through a contrivance of the rules. On the third night of the convention, Clinton's nomination was finalized and television cameras followed his dramatically slow walk to greet the convention after a celebration with his family and supporters, all of which had been carefully scripted. His formal, convention-ending acceptance speech on the final night was delivered after another dramatic twist: Perot's sudden withdrawal from the race as an independent candidate. The total effect provided Clinton with an enormous post-convention bounce that Bush was never able to overcome.

In contrast, the Republican convention did little to help Bush, who by then trailed badly in the polls. Buchanan's opening night speech proclaimed "a religious war going on in our country for the soul of America," included sharp attacks on Hillary Clinton and Gore, and offered digs at homosexuals. The party platform was equally dominated by themes from the party's right wing, including a strong antiabortion plank. The media commentary stressed the party's "mean-spirited" tone, which was softened only when Barbara Bush's appearance with her children and grandchildren highlighted an emphasis on traditional family values. The president also visited the convention hall on Wednesday night, but delayed his moderately successful acceptance speech until the following night. Overall, the convention may have damaged the Republican candidate's chances almost as much as the Democrats' 1968 convention in Chicago.

The 1992 conventions illustrated several of the changes that have occurred in national conventions. Although their principal activities are much the same as they were more than 150 years ago (devising the rules of procedure, adopting platforms, and, most important, nominating presidential and vice-presidential candidates), the conventions are no longer deliberative assemblies. Rather, they ratify decisions that have been made during the delegate selection process. Because they merely confirm decisions reached before the convention has started, these gatherings have lost virtually all of the drama and excitement that they provided for citizens and the media in the 1950s and 1960s when the major networks provided "gavel-to-gavel" coverage, a thing of the past.

Presidential candidates are no longer forced to negotiate with party leaders, particularly with those who chair state delegations (often governors), to secure the nomination or gain favorable treatment. Today, candidates' personal organizations dominate the convention proceedings and contact individual delegates directly rather than working through the leaders who chair state delegations. Thus the growth in importance of candidate (rather than party) organizations, which has occurred in presidential nomination campaigns, has carried over into the national convention itself. The character of convention delegates has also changed: in the late 1960s and 1970s, amateur delegates replaced professionals as the wielders of power, but in the 1980s and 1990s, the distinction between the two types of delegates has blurred as former amateurs share power with professionals and take on many of the latter's characteristics. In some conventions, delegate caucuses that transcend state boundaries, such as those organized by women, African Americans, and Hispanics, have gained prominence. These groups have taken the leadership in platform fights, as women did at the 1976 Republican convention over the ratification of the Equal Rights Amendment (ERA) and at the 1980 Democratic convention over the use of Medicaid funds for abortions and the denial of financial and technical campaign support to candidates not supporting the ERA.

Technological developments have fundamentally altered recent nominating conventions. Sophisticated electronic equipment enables centralized candidate organizations to communicate directly with their organizers and with individual delegates on the crowded convention floor. The mass media's capacity to provide thorough and immediate coverage of convention proceedings is vitally important—as is their reluctance to provide such coverage. Extensive coverage has forced the parties to stage proceedings in a way that appeals to a nationwide audience; visually important events must be scheduled to take advantage of prime-time viewing, and the parties strive to avoid the tone and divisiveness that projects a negative image. Modern television coverage may have changed the nature of conventions; party members can no longer "take the time for the slow and sometimes secretive bargaining that in the past allowed their national conventions to function successfully as coalition-building institutions." [35] But television increasingly finds the proceedings lacking in newsworthiness. The result is staged extravaganzas that have become the opening gambit for the fall campaign.

Notes

1. Austin Ranney, "Changing the Rules of the Nominating Game," in *Choosing the President,* ed. James David Barber (Englewood Cliffs, N.J.: Prentice-Hall, 1974), 71.
2. Arthur Hadley, *The Invisible Primary* (Englewood Cliffs, N.J.: Prentice-Hall, 1976).

3. Jules Witcover, "Sen. Mondale Won't Seek Presidential Nomination," *Washington Post*, November 22, 1974, A1.

4. Editorial, "Kemp Bows Out," *Wall Street Journal*, February 1, 1995, A12.

5. Richard Berke, "Facing Financial Squeeze, Quayle Pulls Out of '96 Race," *New York Times*, February 10, 1995.

6. For example, see the reports by Richard L. Berke, "In GOP Field, A Race to Raise Money Is On," *New York Times*, February 2, 1995, A1, and Gerald F. Seib, "With Race for the Presidency Still a Year Away, GOP Hopefuls Already Court Campaign Talent," *Wall Street Journal*, January 30, 1995, A22.

7. The Federal Election Commission, *The Presidential Public Funding Program* (Washington, D.C.: Federal Election Commission, April 1993), Chart 1-4, 10, and 4-1, 31. Also see discussion in Herbert E. Alexander and Anthony Corrado, *Financing the 1992 Election* (Armonk, N.Y.: M.E. Sharpe, 1995), chap. 3.

8. Robert D. Loevy, *The Flawed Path to the Presidency 1992* (Albany, N.Y.: SUNY Press, 1995), 11. Also see Alexander and Corrado, *Financing the 1992 Election*, chap. 3.

9. Alexander and Corrado, *Financing the 1992 Election*, chap. 2, especially Table 2.6.

10. Richard L. Berke, "In GOP Field, A Race to Raise Money Is On," *New York Times*, February 2, 1995, A1.

11. If the election had been held in 1995, the spending limit for California would have been $10,943,283, while for the least populated states, including New Hampshire and Delaware, it would have been $601,200. The Federal Election Commission issues such figures one year in advance of the election year to help in campaign planning. Final totals for 1996 are expected to vary only slightly. Press Office Release of the Federal Election Commission, March 3, 1995.

12. John Aldrich, *Before the Convention: A Theory of Presidential Nomination Campaigns* (Chicago: University of Chicago Press, 1980), 70. Also see Robert Loevy's discussion of Junior Tuesday in 1992, *The Flawed Path to the Presidency 1992*, 80–83.

13. Ronald D. Elving and Beth Donovan, "Candidates Spread Their Bets In Presidential Gamble," *Congressional Quarterly Weekly Report*, February 22, 1992, 421. Kerrey had spent 57 days, Harkin 52, Clinton 43, and Brown 40.

14. Thomas B. Edsall and Richard Marin, "Super Tuesday's Showing," *Washington Post National Weekly Edition*, March 14–20, 1988, 37.

15. In the case of Delaware, state Republicans were overjoyed with the prospect of playing a greater role in the 1996 contest, but Democrats were confronted with the possibility that they could only hold a nonbinding "beauty contest" since they had violated the party-specified dates and would have to rely again on the caucus-convention method.

16. Three states have scheduled Republican caucuses prior to Iowa's in 1996: Alaska, Hawaii, and Louisiana. It remains to be seen whether Iowa will move its date up in the calendar in order to remain first.

17. Alexander and Corrado, *Financing the 1992 Election*, chap. 3.

18. Pat Dunham, *Electoral Behavior in the United States* (Englewood Cliffs, N.J.: Prentice-Hall, 1991), 163; "Beaming at the Voters," *Time*, February 15, 1988, 78–79.

19. Timothy Crouse, *The Boys on the Bus* (New York: Ballantine Books, 1972).

20. Thomas Patterson, *The Mass Media Election: How Americans Choose Their President* (New York: Praeger, 1980), chap. 3.

21. Loevy, *The Flawed Path to the Presidency*, 27.
22. Patterson, *The Mass Media Election*, chap. 4.
23. C. Anthony Broh, *A Horse of a Different Color: Television's Treatment of Jesse Jackson's 1984 Presidential Campaign* (Washington, D.C.: Joint Center for Political Studies, 1987), 44.
24. William C. Adams, "Media Coverage of Campaign '84: A Preliminary Report," *Public Opinion*, April–May 1984, 10–11, cited in Gary R. Orren, "The Nomination Process: Vicissitudes of Candidate Selection," in *The Elections of 1984*, ed. Michael Nelson (Washington, D.C.: CQ Press, 1985), 53.
25. Jeane Kirkpatrick, *The New Presidential Elite: Men and Women in National Politics* (New York: Russell Sage Foundation and the Twentieth Century Fund, 1976).
26. Steven Thomma, "For Republicans, Time to Think New Hampshire," *Philadelphia Inquirer*, February 2, 1995, E1.
27. Cannon and Peterson, "GOP," 128.
28. Alexander and Corrado, *Financing the 1992 Election*, chap. 3.
29. Recent exceptions to that trend, when two candidates ended the preconvention period fairly even in all respects, are Ford and Reagan in 1976, McGovern and Humphrey in 1972, and Mondale and Hart in 1984.
30. Gerald Pomper and Susan Lederman, *Elections in America: Control and Influence in Democratic Politics*, 2d ed. (New York: Longman, 1980), chap. 8.
31. Judith Parris, *The Convention Problem: Issues in Reform of Presidential Nominating Procedures* (Washington, D.C.: Brookings Institution, 1972), 110.
32. Theodore H. White, *The Making of the President, 1960* (New York: Pocket Books, 1961), 203.
33. Nelson Polsby and Aaron Wildavsky, *Presidential Elections: Strategies of American Electoral Politics* (New York: Scribners, 1964), 82.
34. Polsby and Wildavsky, *Presidential Elections*, 144.
35. David Broder, "Political Reporters in Presidential Politics," in *Inside the System*, 2d ed., ed. Charles Peters and John Rothchild (New York: Praeger, 1973), 7.

Selected Readings

Bartels, Larry M. *Presidential Primaries and the Dynamics of Public Choice*. Princeton, N.J.: Princeton University Press, 1988.

Geer, John G. *Nominating Presidents: An Evaluation of Voters and Primaries*. New York: Greenwood Press, 1989.

Kessel, John. *Presidential Campaign Politics*. Homewood, Ill.: Dorsey, 1988.

Nelson, Michael, ed. *The Elections of 1992*. Washington, D.C.: CQ Press, 1993.

Pomper, Gerald, ed. *The Election of 1992: Reports and Interpretations*. Chatham, N.J.: Chatham House, 1993.

Wayne, Stephen J. *The Road to the White House 1992: The Politics of Presidential Elections*. 4th ed. New York: St. Martin's, 1992.

Election Rules and the Election Campaign

WILLIAM JEFFERSON CLINTON was officially declared the nation's forty-second president on January 6, 1993, when ballots from members of the electoral college were opened and recorded during a joint session of Congress. Electors had met in their respective state capitals on December 14, 1992, to cast presidential and vice-presidential ballots. Clinton was inaugurated on January 20, 1993, in accordance with the timetable set forth in the Twentieth Amendment to the Constitution, ratified in 1933. These events validated the popular vote outcome reported by the media on election night and brought to a conclusion the election phase of the selection process, a phase in which candidates face very different problems from those confronted in winning the nomination.

New political appeals must be developed for this stage of the campaign, which is typically a one-on-one contest pitting the nominees of the two major parties against each other. On occasion, as in 1992, a strong third-party candidate may run. The audience of the campaign increases greatly during the general election—more than 100 million people voted in the 1992 general election, three times the number that participated in the nomination process.[1]

Candidates and their staff members, therefore, must decide how they can win the support of these additional voters as well as those who backed losing candidates in the nomination process. A further complication is the length of the campaign: this new, expanded phase of the presidential contest is compressed into the roughly twelve-week period that extends from the second convention to election day.

The first section of this chapter traces the evolution of the electoral college system and explains how it and recent campaign finance laws affect the general election campaign. The second section analyzes the campaign in the same framework as was used in Chapter 1 for the nomination contest: its early stages and targeting efforts, the kinds of political appeals directed toward the electorate, the communication of these appeals through the media and campaign workers, and the sources and types of expenditures.

Rules of the Election Contest

Rules covering the general election phase differ in two central respects from those governing the nomination phase: the constitutional requirement that the electoral college choose the president and the distinctive provisions of the campaign finance laws. The constitutional requirements have been remarkably stable over time, particularly when compared to the extensive changes found in the nomination process, but campaign finance laws have undergone significant changes over the past twenty-five years.

The Electoral College

The method of selecting the president was among the most difficult problems the delegates to the Constitutional Convention faced.[2] Numerous plans were proposed, the two most important being selection by the Congress and direct election by the people. The first, derived from the practice in most states of the legislature's choosing the governor, had the backing of a number of delegates, including Roger Sherman of Connecticut. It was eventually discarded as a result of fear of legislative supremacy and also because the delegates could not choose between "state-unit voting," which favored the small states, and joint action of the two chambers, which benefited the large states with their greater voting power in the House of Representatives. Three of the most influential members of the convention—James Madison of Virginia and James Wilson and Gouverneur Morris of Pennsylvania—supported direct popular election, but most delegates considered that method too democratic. As George Mason of Virginia said, "It would be as unnatural to refer the choice of a proper magistrate to the people as it would to refer a trial of colors to a blind man."

Having decided against both popular election and selection by legislative bodies, the delegates proceeded to adopt an entirely new plan put forth by one of their committees. The proposal, which some historians believe was based on a method used in Maryland to elect state senators, specified that each state legislature could choose electors, by whatever means it desired, equal to its total number of senators and representatives in Congress, but that none of the electors could be members of Congress or hold other national office.[3] The individual electors would assemble at a fixed time in their respective state capitals and cast two votes each for president. These votes were then to be transmitted to Washington, D.C., where they would be opened and counted during a joint session of Congress. Whoever received the largest number of electoral votes would be declared president, provided an absolute majority (one more than half) had been obtained; if no candidate received a majority, the House of Representatives, voting by states (with each state delegation having one vote), would choose the president from among the five candidates receiving the highest number of electoral votes. After the president was chosen, the person with the next highest number of electoral votes would be declared vice president. If two or more contenders received an equal number of electoral votes, the Senate would choose the vice president from among them.

This complicated procedure reflected values and assumptions about human nature enunciated in *The Federalist Papers,* Number 68, attributed to Alexander Hamilton, whose views were somewhat more elitist than those of the majority of the delegates to the Constitutional Convention. Most of the Founders believed that the average person lacked the ability to make sound judgments about the qualifications of the presidential candidates and that the decision therefore should be left to a small group of electors—a political elite that would have both the information and the wisdom necessary to choose the best persons for the nation's two highest offices. Because the electors could not be national office holders with connections to the president, they could approach their task without bias; because they assembled separately in their respective state capitals rather than as a single body, there would be less chance of them being corrupted or exposed to popular unrest. Moreover, because they were convened for a single purpose and would be dissolved when their task was completed, the possibility of tampering with them in advance or rewarding them with future favors was eliminated.

Some of the delegates may have expected the electors to respond to popular preferences.[4] They anticipated that each state's electors would cast one vote for a "native son," a locally popular political figure, and the other for a "continental character," an individual with a national reputation known to members of the political elite if not to the average citizen. (Evidence for this assumption is provided by Article II, Section 1, of the

Constitution, which states that at least one of the two persons for whom an elector votes must not be an inhabitant of the elector's state.)

The Founders also expected that after George Washington's presidency, the electoral votes would be so widely distributed that few candidates would receive a majority, and, therefore, most elections (Mason estimated nineteen out of twenty) would ultimately be decided by the House of Representatives. The electors would thus serve to "screen" (or, in today's terms, "nominate") the candidates, and the House would choose ("elect") the president from among them. The conflict between large and small states, which was settled by the Connecticut Compromise on the composition of the Senate and House, also arose in the plan the delegates worked out for the selection of the chief executive. In the initial vote by the electors, the large states had the advantage, because the number of each state's votes reflected the size of its House delegation. If no candidate received a majority, the small states were favored in the second selection because votes would be cast by states, not by individual representatives.

This selection method, then, was a compromise. In addition to resolving the large-state/small-state conflict, the electoral college device took into account advocates of states' rights by allowing the state legislatures to decide how the electors should be chosen. It also held open, for those who favored letting the people choose the president, the possibility of the electors' actually reflecting the popular vote for the president in their state. As political scientist John Roche has pointed out, the intermediate elector scheme gave "everybody a piece of the cake"; he also notes, however, that "the future was left to cope with the problem of what to do with this Rube Goldberg mechanism,"[5] and it was not long before problems developed.

The formation and organization of political parties in the 1790s proceeded so quickly that by the election of 1800, the electors no longer served as independent persons exercising their own judgments on candidates' capabilities; instead, they acted as agents of political parties and the general public. In 1800, the Republican party was so disciplined that all Republican electors cast their two votes for Thomas Jefferson and Aaron Burr. Although it was generally understood that Jefferson was the Republican candidate for president and Burr the candidate for vice president, the Constitution provided no means for the electors to make that distinction on their ballots. The result was a tie in electoral votes; neither won a majority, and the matter was handed to the House of Representatives for a final decision. Ironically, the Federalists, despite their major defeat in the congressional elections of 1800, still controlled the lame-duck Congress (which did not expire until March 1801) and therefore were in a position to help decide which Republican would serve as president and which as vice president. At the urging of Hamilton, who disagreed with Jefferson on policy matters but distrusted Burr personally, some of the Federalist representatives eventually cast blank ballots, which permitted the Republican legislators to choose Jefferson as president on the thirty-sixth ballot.

One result of this bizarre chain of events was the ratification in 1804 of the Twelfth Amendment, stipulating that electors cast separate ballots for president and vice president. The amendment also provides that if no presidential candidate receives a majority of the electoral votes, the House of Representatives, balloting by states, will select the president by majority vote from among the three (instead of five) candidates who receive the highest number of electoral votes. If no vice-presidential candidate receives a majority of electoral votes, similar procedures are to be used by the Senate in choosing between the two persons with the highest number of electoral ballots.

Other changes in the selection of the president followed; however, they emerged as political developments rather than constitutional amendments. Thus, state legislators, who held the power to determine how electors should be chosen, began to cede this right to the general electorate. By 1832, all states except South Carolina had done so.

Another matter left to the discretion of the states—how their electoral votes would be counted—soon underwent change. States initially were inclined to divide the vote by congressional districts; the candidate who won the plurality of the popular votes (that is, more votes than anyone else) in each district received its electoral vote, and the remaining two electoral votes (representing the two Senate seats) were awarded to the state-wide popular winner.

However, legislatures soon began to adopt the "unit" or "general-ticket" rule, whereby all the state's electoral votes went to the candidate who received the plurality of the state-wide popular vote. This change benefited the state's majority party because it did not have to award any electoral votes to a minority party that might be successful in individual congressional districts. Also, this system maximized the influence of the state in the presidential election by permitting it to throw all its electoral votes to one candidate. Once some states adopted this procedure, others, wanting to maintain their influence on the presidential contest, felt they had to follow. As a result, by 1836, the district plan had vanished, and the unit system had taken its place. Since then, a few states have returned to the district plan; Maine has used it for several decades and Nebraska adopted the plan for 1992.

Another political development of the era changed the nature of the presidential election contest: the elimination of property qualifications for voting. By the early 1840s, White manhood suffrage was virtually complete in the United States. The increasing democratization of U.S. political life was expressed in voting for the president, but the formal provisions of the electoral college remain the same today as they were in 1804 when the Twelfth Amendment was adopted.

Today, these formal provisions provide a strange system for choosing the chief executive. Although most Americans view the presidential election as a popular one, it really is not. When voters mark their ballots in November for a presidential candidate, the vote actually determines which pledged slate of electors will have the opportunity to cast electoral votes. In mid-December, the state electors associated with the winning candidate (party faithfuls who may be chosen in primaries, at conventions, or by state committees) meet in their state capitals to cast ballots. About one-third of the states attempt by law to bind the electors to vote for the popular-vote winner, but there is some question whether such laws are constitutional. The results of the electoral balloting are transmitted to Washington, D.C.; they are counted early in January of the following year, and the incumbent vice president, as presiding officer of the Senate, announces the outcome before a joint session of the Congress. If, as usually happens, one candidate receives an absolute majority of the electoral votes, the vice president officially declares that candidate to be president. (Because the popular-vote winner usually wins in the electoral college as well, we call this a "validation" of the popular vote outcome.)

The formal procedure has occasionally created some ironic moments. In January 1961, Richard Nixon declared his opponent, John Kennedy, to be president; eight years later another vice president, Hubert Humphrey, declared his opponent, this time Nixon, to be the chief executive. George Bush had the distinction in 1988 of being the first vice president since Martin Van Buren to declare his own victory.

The electoral college system as it operates today is considered by many students of presidential elections to be not only strange but also grossly unfair; some even consider it dangerous. Chapter 5 assesses the arguments for and against the electoral college; this section examines only the effects the present arrangements have on campaign strategies.

Under the electoral college system, election results are decided state by state. In effect, there are fifty-one separate presidential contests—with a "winner-take-all" principle in forty-nine—which puts a premium on a popular vote victory in each state and the District of Columbia, no matter how small the margin of that victory may be. Even in Maine and Nebraska, the other two contests, state-wide results are likely to be determinative.

A built-in bias in the electoral college works to the advantage of certain states over others. The present system benefits the very small and the very large states. The small states have the advantage of what political scientist Lawrence Longley calls the "constant two" votes, that is, the two electoral votes, representing the two senators, that all states receive, regardless of size.[6] This arrangement—the constant two, plus the additional vote for their House member—means that the smallest states control three electoral votes, even though their population alone might entitle them to just one or two votes. The very large states have an even greater advantage; they benefit from the unit or general-ticket system because all their electoral votes are awarded to their popular-vote winner. Thus in 1992, Clinton, the popular-vote winner in California, received all 54 electoral votes, 20 percent of the total 270 electoral votes required for election, although the combined total of popular votes for Bush and independent candidate H. Ross Perot exceeded Clinton's total by more than 800,000.[7]

Electoral votes were reallocated for the 1992 presidential election reflecting the results of the 1990 census; those figures were finalized in mid-July 1991.[8] Eight states gained seats in the House of Representatives and thirteen lost seats; the states' electoral vote totals were adjusted accordingly. California gained seven seats, Florida four, and Texas three. On the losing end, New York lost three seats, while Illinois, Michigan, Ohio, and Pennsylvania each lost two seats. Eight other states lost one seat. (See Figure 3-1 for an illustration of the size of the states based on their number of electoral votes for the 1992 elections.)

Longley shows that residency in the very small and the very large states of the far West and, to a lesser extent, the East is an advantage for some ethnic groups. Voters concentrated in urban areas, both central cities and the suburbs, also benefit. In general, however, African Americans do not benefit by the rules of the system because the rules put the South, where many African Americans live, at a disadvantage. (The South contains a disproportionate number of medium-sized states—those with from four to fourteen electoral votes. Medium-sized states offer candidates neither a great many electoral votes, as the big states do, nor a disproportionately large number of electoral votes, as the small states do.)

Finally, the electoral college benefits certain kinds of candidates. These include not only those of the two major parties, who are in a position to win enough popular votes in a state to be awarded its electoral votes, but also third-party candidates who have a regional appeal sufficient to win some states. At a disadvantage, however, are third-party candidates without regional appeal. In 1948, Dixiecrat presidential candidate Strom Thurmond carried four states, with a total of thirty-nine electoral votes, even though he won only about 2.4 percent of the national popular vote; that same year the Progressive party candidate, Henry Wallace, with the

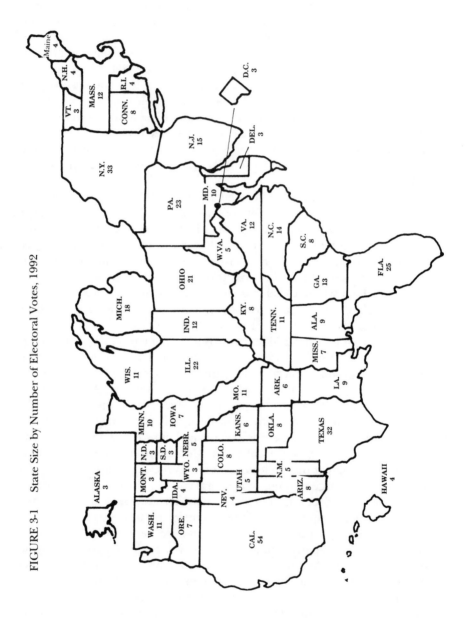

FIGURE 3-1   State Size by Number of Electoral Votes, 1992

same percentage of the nationwide vote, did not carry any states and thus received no electoral votes at all.[9] More recently, John Anderson polled 5,720,060 votes in 1980 (five times the total of Thurmond and Wallace in 1948 and 6.6 percent of the total votes cast), but he received no electoral votes because his support was distributed nationally rather than concentrated regionally. The same fate befell Perot in 1992; although he received 19,741,048 votes, 18.9 percent of the total votes cast nationally, he won no electoral votes because he finished first in no states nor in any of the house districts in Maine and Nebraska.

Because candidates wish to maximize the return on limited resources available during the campaign—particularly time and money—they focus heavily on those states likely to contribute the largest number of electoral votes toward a victory. Thus, the electoral map is a critical consideration in formulating their campaign strategy.

Rules Affecting Campaign Finance

The legal provisions for financing the general election differ considerably from those governing presidential nominations. For the general election, complete public financing is provided to nominees of the major parties (those parties that won 25 percent or more of the popular vote in the past presidential election) provided they observe rules specified by the Federal Election Commission (FEC), including a prohibition on additional contributions. In the 1992 presidential election, the federal government allocated $55.2 million to the Republicans' and Democrats' candidates and $10.2 million to each national committee to fund the conventions. Candidates of minor parties (those parties that won between 5 and 25 percent of the vote in the previous election) may receive partial public financing if they observed the regulations. Candidates of parties ineligible for public financing (those parties that won less than 5 percent of the vote in the previous election) can be partially reimbursed after the current election if they receive at least 5 percent of the vote. Independent candidate Perot spent $69 million in pursuit of the presidency, only $4 million of which came from contributions. The rest was Perot's own money. Because Perot did not observe the expenditure limits, he will not be eligible for matching funds in 1996.

Two provisions of the campaign finance law permit the major-party candidates to benefit from campaign expenditures besides those made from public funds. As is true of the nomination process, there is no limitation on *independent expenditures,* that is, those made by individuals or political committees that advocate the defeat or election of a presidential candidate but that are not made in conjunction with the candidate's own

TABLE 3-1   Cost of Presidential General Elections, 1940–1972
             (in millions of dollars)

Year	Expenditure	Candidate	Expenditure	Candidate
	Republican		Democrat	
1940	3.45	Willkie	2.78	F. Roosevelt*
1944	2.83	Dewey	2.17	F. Roosevelt*
1948	2.13	Dewey	2.74	Truman*
1952	6.61	Eisenhower*	5.03	Stevenson
1956	7.78	Eisenhower*	5.11	Stevenson
1960	10.13	Nixon	9.80	Kennedy*
1964	16.03	Goldwater	8.76	Johnson*
1968	25.40	Nixon*	11.59	Humphrey
1972	61.40	Nixon*	30.00	McGovern

SOURCE: Excerpted from Herbert E. Alexander, *Financing Politics: Money, Elections, and Political Reform* (Washington, D.C.: CQ Press, 1976), Table 2-1, 20.

NOTE: Asterisk (*) indicates winner.

campaign. Such individuals and committees must file reports with the FEC stating, under penalty of perjury, that the expenditure was not made in collusion with the candidate. In addition, an amendment to the campaign finance law enacted in 1979 permits state and local party organizations to spend money for any purpose except campaign advertising and the hiring of outside personnel; this so-called "soft money" can be used for grassroots activities such as distributing campaign buttons, stickers, and yard signs; registering voters; and transporting them to the polls to vote. The guidelines for these funds are set by state laws.

As with the provisions for financing presidential nomination campaigns, those governing the general election have brought significant changes in the funding of fall presidential campaigns. The two major party candidates no longer need to depend on wealthy contributors and other private sources to finance their campaigns. (They may still benefit, however, from the independent expenditures of such sources and from the grassroots activities of state and local parties.) The law also has the effect of limiting and equalizing the expenditures made by the two major party candidates, which is a distinct advantage for the Democrats because, historically, Republican presidential candidates have spent more than their opponents.[10] (Table 3-1 shows that, except for 1948, the Republican presidential candidate outspent his Democratic opponent in every election from 1940 through 1972, the last contest before the enactment of the campaign finance law providing public funding.) Finally, the law typically benefits the candidates of the two major parties over minor-party candidates, who are entitled to only partial public financing, if any at all. This was not the case in 1992, of course, because of Perot's enormous personal wealth, which could be used to support his candidacy. With the exception of "soft money," Perot's campaign resources were remarkably similar to those of the two major-party candidates, although his spending pattern was different.

The General Election Campaign

Traditionally, U.S. presidential campaigns have begun on Labor Day, but individual candidates are free to choose other times, depending on the political circumstances. Gerald R. Ford, seeking to reorganize his forces after a bruising battle with challenger Ronald Reagan at the 1976 Republican national convention, waited until a week after Labor Day to launch his fall campaign. In contrast, Reagan, with the Republican nomination locked up in both 1980 and 1984, hit the campaign trail early to counteract the favorable publicity generated by the Democratic national conventions of those two years. Bush also got started early in 1988, as a way to narrow the gap with Michael Dukakis. Bush began to criticize Dukakis and portray him as a liberal in June, a full month before the nomination was decided.[11] In contrast, Dukakis was slow to focus his general election campaign and fell behind Bush, a pattern that the Democrats were not about to repeat in 1992. Clinton began to campaign aggressively immediately after the Democratic convention rather than waiting for the traditional start. Thus the conditions under which candidates win their party's nomination, plus the circumstances surrounding their opponent's choice, shape decisions on the beginning of the fall campaign.

Targeting the Campaign

As in the nomination process, presidential candidates must decide in which states and toward which population groups they will focus their efforts in the fall campaign.[12] The decision is harder at this stage because the general election takes place simultaneously in all fifty states and the District of Columbia, rather than in stages, and campaign efforts must be concentrated into a much shorter period of time than is available for the nomination campaign. But in the general election, unlike the nomination process, there are no legal limits on the amount of money presidential candidates can spend in individual states; they have a freer hand in their choices, but those choices are more difficult.

By far the most important consideration in targeting the fall campaign is the electoral college. The candidate's task is clear: to win the presidency, he or she must win a majority (270) of the 538 electoral votes. This fact places a premium on carrying those states with the largest number of electoral votes. In 1992 and 1996, by winning the eleven largest states—California, New York, Texas, Florida, Pennsylvania, Illinois, Ohio, Michigan, New Jersey, North Carolina, and either Georgia or Virginia—a candidate could win the presidency while losing the other forty contests. Naturally, candidates from both major political parties concentrate their personal campaign time and money on the largest states.

Another element that affects candidates' decisions on where to campaign is the political situation in a particular state; that is, whether the state generally goes to one party's candidate or whether it swings back and forth from one election to the next. Distinctly one-party states are likely to be slighted by both of the major-party candidates. The party in control does not think it is necessary to waste time there. In 1968, for example, Nixon did not visit or spend money in Kansas; as one campaign aide, Robert Ellsworth, said of his home state, "If you have to worry about Kansas, you don't have a campaign anyway."[13] In contrast, the opposition party is likely to think it futile to exert much effort in what is obviously enemy territory.[14] The "swing" states naturally draw the greatest attention from presidential candidates of both parties.

Since 1968, there has been a major geographic revolution in American politics. Historically, the South has been vital to the electoral fortunes of Democratic candidates, recently playing an essential role in the electoral victories of Kennedy in 1960 and Carter in 1976. In fact, until 1992, no Democrat had ever won the White House without carrying a majority of southern states. But since 1968, with the lone exception of 1976, when Jimmy Carter attracted support as a favorite son from Georgia, the Solid South—long a mainstay of Democratic campaigns—has moved into the Republican camp. One of the keys to Clinton's victory was reducing this Republican advantage when he won four southern states, including Arkansas and Al Gore's home state of Tennessee, as well as Louisiana and Georgia. Humphrey in 1968 and George McGovern in 1972 wrote off the region; in 1980, even with Carter on the ticket, only Georgia went for the Democratic candidate.[15] No southern state supported the Democratic ticket in 1984 or 1988, even though Dukakis had chosen Lloyd Bentsen, senator from Texas, as his running mate, partly in an effort to attract southern votes. Several factors contributed to the South's political reorientation: the Democrats' endorsement of aggressive action on civil rights violated a long-standing regional commitment to local control of race relations; the debate among Democrats over Vietnam policy was perceived by many southern voters as unpatriotic; the emergence on the national agenda of law and order and social issues such as abortion and school prayer renewed the salience of the region's deep-seated traditional values; and the influx of new residents attracted by the region's rapid economic growth created a new group of voters who were less closely tied to the traditional Democratic party identification. Thus, the Republicans have added the South to their already substantial support in the West; prior to 1992, one would say that the Democrats, if they retained an area of regional strength, were strongest in the Northeast.

The regions that have been crucial in recent presidential contests are the Middle Atlantic states of New York, Pennsylvania, and New Jersey, and the Middle West states of Ohio, Michigan, Illinois, and Missouri. Together, this tier of seven highly industrial states controlled 155 electoral votes in the 1984 and 1988 elections. These states also tend to be extremely competitive, which means that campaign efforts there can be very important in deciding which candidate prevails. Even though these states collectively lost twelve electoral votes for the 1992 election following reapportionment, they remained significant; during the last two days of the 1992 campaign, New Jersey, Michigan, and Ohio were visited by both Bush and Clinton, while the latter also stopped in Pennsylvania and Missouri.[16]

Until 1992, the most systematic plan for targeting a presidential campaign was developed for Carter in 1976 by Hamilton Jordan. Jordan assigned points to each state, using three criteria: its number of electoral votes; its Democratic potential, based on the number of Democratic office holders in the state and how well McGovern had done there in 1972; and how concerted a campaign was needed in a particular state, taking into account how well Carter had done in the preconvention period, how much time or resources he had previously expended in the state, and how close to Ford he was in the polls. Each campaigner was allocated points as well: for example, a day's campaigning by Carter was worth seven points; by Walter Mondale, five points; and by a Carter child, one point. Jordan then assigned campaigners to states so that scheduling points were matched with those developed under the political-importance formula.[17]

Clinton's campaign began by dividing the states into four categories: fourteen states with 182 electoral votes were regarded as likely victories based on polling data; ten with 63 votes were conceded to Bush and another nine with 99 votes were regarded as unlikely areas for success; but eighteen states with 194 electoral votes were targeted as the contests on which to concentrate. The Clinton camp found computer-assisted planning essential to coordinate candidate travel schedules, media purchases, and grassroots efforts within this larger framework. Their principal analytical technique was data-mapping. Media markets were "ranked in terms of the number of persuadable voters ... weighted by the Electoral College votes and the perceived strategic importance of the states reached in that market." This produced a color-coded map that shaped planners' resource-allocation decisions. These thirty-two states with 376 electoral votes were the focus of Clinton's efforts, only one of which was lost on election day.[18]

Electoral college considerations remain crucial throughout the entire campaign. Bush's strategy in 1988 sought to solidify expected support in the Southern and Rocky Mountain states and then to confront Dukakis in potential swing states that would be essential for his victory, particularly Ohio and New Jersey. Dukakis, still trailing Bush after the second debate in 1988, focused his efforts on eighteen states with just enough electoral votes to win. The tables were turned in 1992. Entering the campaign's final week, Bush was behind, but the national polls showed a narrowing of Clinton's lead; one had it at 2 percentage points. With California, New York, and Illinois comfortably going for Clinton, Bush's hopes were reduced to holding as many southern states as possible (including Texas and Florida), running strong in the Mountain and upper–Middle West states, and winning virtually all the remaining swing states, including New Jersey, Ohio, Kentucky, Michigan, Missouri, and Wisconsin. This strategy was complicated by Perot's strong appeal to selected voting groups. However, Clinton held on to win in each of these swing states, several by small pluralities. With such a narrow margin for error, it is not surprising to find that both Bush in 1992 and Dukakis in 1988 went down to defeat.

Manipulating Political Appeals

Candidates need to attract voters' attention and support. To do so, they employ a variety of appeals that draw on existing loyalties and attitudes held by the voters.

Party Labels. Political party labels, unimportant in the nomination process, become a focal point in general election campaigns. Given the Democrats' status as the majority party for more than fifty years, starting with Franklin Roosevelt, it is natural that Democratic candidates throughout the years emphasized their party affiliation and linked their opponents with the minority Republican party. In 1960, Kennedy stressed that he "stood" with Woodrow Wilson, Franklin Roosevelt, and Harry S. Truman, whereas his opponent, Nixon, "stood" with William McKinley, William Howard Taft, Warren Harding, Alfred Landon, and Thomas Dewey. (Not surprisingly, Kennedy did not mention popular Republican presidents such as Abraham Lincoln, Theodore Roosevelt, or Dwight D.

Eisenhower.) Twenty years later, Carter pursued a similar strategy, emphasizing that he represented the party of Roosevelt, Truman, Kennedy, and Lyndon B. Johnson (leading Reagan to quip that the only Democratic president Carter was not talking about was himself).

Over the years, Republican presidential candidates have devised tactics to counteract the partisan advantage enjoyed by their Democratic opponents, with whom a far larger portion of the populace had been willing to identify. (See Chapter 4.) One is to advise the voters to ignore party labels and vote for the best person. Nixon used this approach in his 1960 campaign, urging Americans to cast their ballots for the person who had experience in foreign affairs, who had stood up to Soviet leader Nikita Khrushchev and bested him in a "kitchen debate" in Moscow. Another tactic is to suggest that the Democratic presidential candidate does not represent the views of the rank-and-file members of the party. In 1972, Nixon charged that the Democratic convention had rejected the historic principles of that party and implored, "To those millions who have been driven out of their home in the Democratic party, we say come home." Another ploy open to Republican presidential candidates is to associate themselves with past Democratic presidents. In 1976, Ford tied his candidacy to that of Democrat Truman, who, as an underdog incumbent, struggled successfully for the same goal as Ford: election to the office in his own right, not merely by succession. Four years later, Reagan linked his desire for major changes in U.S. society with the New Deal, Fair Deal, and New Frontier administrations of Roosevelt, Truman, and Kennedy. In 1984, he participated in anniversary ceremonies for Roosevelt and Truman and held receptions at the White House in honor of Humphrey and former senator Henry Jackson.[19] In 1992, Bush compared his own campaign to Truman's victory over Dewey in 1948; like Bush, Truman blamed the nation's troubles on Congress, had trailed badly in the polls, and was counted out as a sure loser, but unlike Bush, he prevailed.

Party labels, however, have been losing their power to attract voters as more and more citizens declare themselves to be "Independents." Thus, Perot could express contempt for the two parties, blame both of them for "gridlock," and hope to strike a responsive chord among voters looking for an answer to frustrating national problems. Party candidates, seeking to garner support from the Independents who are nearly as numerous as either party's identifiers, may find that overly partisan appeals can backfire.

Incumbency. Historically, incumbent presidents have found that their office provides more advantages than disadvantages in running for reelection. They are better known to the voters than their opponents, who must work to narrow the recognition gap. The incumbent president frequently assumes the role of statesperson, often too busy with the affairs of the nation to participate in a demeaning, partisan campaign. In 1976, Ford followed his advisers' recommendation by conducting the early stages of the campaign from the White House Rose Garden—gathering presidential publicity by receiving visitors, signing or vetoing bills, and calling press conferences to make announcements. Carter did much the same in 1980 until the race tightened.

While the incumbent is operating above the partisan fray, others are free to make political attacks on the opposition. Vice-presidential candidates frequently assume that role, as Humphrey did for the Democrats in 1964 and Bob Dole did for the Republicans in 1976. Or the president's supporters may develop an entire team of "surrogates" to carry on the effort—White House aides, cabinet members, members of Congress, and party officials—as was the case with Nixon in 1972.

The incumbent president is also in a position to use the prerogatives of the office to good advantage during the election campaign. In 1976, President Ford suddenly recommended legislation to expand the national park system and to reduce the amount of the down payments required for mortgages guaranteed by the Federal Housing Administration. The president also can disburse forms of political "patronage" available to the nation's chief executive. In 1980, President Carter announced his support for water projects in Kentucky and Tennessee that he had previously opposed, offered the steel industry protection against foreign imports, approved financial aid to enable residents of Love Canal (the polluted area near Niagara Falls, New York) to move away from that region, and announced federally subsidized loans for drought-stricken farms. In 1984, President Reagan provided assistance to U.S. farmers by allowing the Soviet Union to purchase an extra 10 million metric tons of grain and by changing credit arrangements to grant greater relief to farmers who were heavily in debt. Bush announced the sale of fighter planes to Taiwan and Saudi Arabia that would save jobs in Texas, California, Connecticut, Missouri, and Oklahoma; he reversed a plan to close Homestead Air Force Base in Florida, the scene of extensive damage from Hurricane Andrew; and he announced crop subsidies for wheat farmers and disaster assistance to farmers.[20]

Incumbent presidents can also use their office to publicize important events in foreign and military policy. In 1972, President Nixon visited both Communist China and the Soviet Union, garnering extensive media coverage in the process. In the spring of 1984, President Reagan went to China; in June of that year he journeyed to the Normandy beaches to lead the fortieth anniversary commemoration of the Allied invasion of France in World War II, an occasion attended by veterans and their families. Bush met with the president of Mexico and prime minister of Canada to initial the North American Free Trade Agreement, even though it had been settled months earlier; the photo opportunity and the chance to appear "presidential" were irresistible.

Of the past four incumbents who ran for reelection, only Reagan was successful. The electoral defeats of Presidents Ford, Carter, and Bush suggest some disadvantages associated with incumbency, particularly if service in the presidency coincides with negative economic developments (such as recession and high inflation) or an unresolved foreign crisis for which the president might be blamed. Thus, if a sitting president's record is considered weak or national conditions seem to have deteriorated, the president is likely to be held accountable by voters who cast their ballots retrospectively rather than prospectively—that is, based on a judgment of past performance rather than an estimate of future performance. This has been suggested as the major reason for Carter's defeat in 1980 and Bush's in 1992.

To illustrate the problem, one can contrast what many perceived to be Carter's failure to resolve the Iranian hostage crisis with the newfound respect many believed the nation enjoyed after Reagan's first term. Bush's foreign policy success in the Persian Gulf, however, made his apparent inaction on the slowing economy all the more vivid.

Even in these instances, incumbency may have been more beneficial than detrimental. It must be remembered that both the 1976 and 1980 elections were extremely close. In the former, an incumbent who had never run for national office came very close to victory in the final weeks of the campaign; in the latter, polls indicated that Carter and Reagan were virtually neck-and-neck going into the final weekend of the campaign. Bush was fighting against two major opponents; Perot's criticism of Bush's record was added to Clinton's, making a powerful appeal, particularly to Independents.

Until 1988, incumbency seemed to benefit presidents but not vice presidents. Nixon in 1960 and Humphrey in 1968 failed in their attempts to succeed an outgoing president. Bush found himself in a far more advantageous position, however. During his final year in office, Reagan's public approval ratings bounced back from the beating they had taken in 1986–1987 following public disclosure of the secret Iran-contra transactions; from a low of 40 percent approval and 53 percent disapproval in February 1987, Reagan's rating rose to 54 percent approval and 37 percent disapproval in September 1988.[21] Unlike Eisenhower in 1960, who seemed to harbor doubts about Nixon, Reagan unequivocally endorsed Bush as his successor, thereby transferring the mantle of his legacy. Reagan was also an active campaigner, visiting sixteen states to demonstrate his support.[22] Finally, Bush drew on a number of Reagan's most experienced campaign aides for his own effort in 1988, including campaign chair James A. Baker and campaign director Lee Atwater. Atwater, later named chair of the Republican National Committee, had twenty-eight people working for him in 1988 who had experience in two or more successful presidential campaigns.[23] Thus, by drawing closer to his popular predecessor than could Nixon or Humphrey, Bush turned vice-presidential incumbency into a campaign asset. He was less successful with presidential incumbency, however.

Candidate Image. Because the public focuses so much attention in a presidential campaign on the candidates themselves, the personality and character that the aspirants project are particularly important. Each campaign organization strives to create a composite image of the most attractive attributes of its candidate. Although the image necessarily deviates from reality, it must still reflect enough of the essential characteristics of the candidate to be believable. One effective tactic is to take a potential flaw and convert it into an asset. Thus, the somewhat elderly Eisenhower (he was sixty-six at the time of his second campaign in 1956) was pictured as a benevolent father (or even grandfather) whose mature judgment was needed to lead the nation in times of stress.[24] In contrast, the youthful Kennedy, who was forty-three when he ran for the presidency in 1960, was characterized as a man of "vigor" who would make the United States "feel young again" after the Eisenhower years.

Presidential candidates frequently take their opponents' images into account when shaping their own. In 1976, Ford portrayed himself as a man of maturity and experience to counteract Carter's emphasis on being a "new face" and an outsider to the Washington scene. Four years later, as the incumbent president, Carter portrayed himself as a deliberate and moderate person who could be trusted to maintain his calm in a crisis, in contrast to his supposedly impetuous and irresponsible opponent, Reagan. Reagan, in turn, presented himself as a decisive leader who could overcome the nation's problems, as opposed to Carter, depicted as an uncertain, vacillating person overwhelmed by the burdens of the presidency and inclined to blame the country's difficulties on the "spirit of malaise" of the American people themselves. Bush redirected attention in 1988 to the candidates' character and values in response to the cold and colorless emphasis on "competence" that Dukakis had offered. In doing so, Bush was able to paint his own portrait of Dukakis, whose largely favorable public image, Bush's pollsters had discovered, was based on very little information.[25]

Bush tried the same tactic in 1992 by emphasizing his own experience and asking at the Republican convention and afterward, "Who do you trust in this election?"—a veiled reference to Clinton's alleged "character problems" that emerged during the nomination stage. "Trust and taxes" became the central focus of Bush's campaign as he argued Clinton was a tax-and-spend liberal who had dodged the draft while he was a college student. Clinton, much like Kennedy in 1960, emphasized how a "new generation of leadership" could bring about the change people seemed to want.

Besides molding their own images to balance those of their opponents, candidates also can attack directly the images of the opposition and so put them in a bad light. In 1976, for example, Ford described Carter as follows: "He wavers, he wanders, he wiggles, he waffles." He also charged that his opponent had a strange way of changing his accent: "In California he tried to sound like Cesar Chavez; in Chicago, like Mayor Daley; in New York, like Ralph Nader; in Washington, like George Meany; then he comes to the farm belt and he becomes a little old peanut farmer." Carter said that during the second debate Ford had shown "very vividly the absence of good judgment, good sense, and knowledge," all qualities expected of a president. In 1980, Carter suggested that a Reagan presidency would divide Americans "black from white, Jew from Christian, North from South, rural from urban" and could "well lead our nation to war." Reagan, in turn, impugned Carter's honesty, saying that the president's promise never to lie to Americans reminded him of a quotation from Ralph Waldo Emerson, "The more he talked of his honor, the more we counted our spoons."

At the urging of his campaign advisers, Bush unleashed one of the most negative strategies in modern presidential campaign history. In an effort to alter favorable public perceptions of his opponent, the Bush campaign portrayed Dukakis as a "card-carrying member of the ACLU" (American Civil Liberties Union), sympathetic to criminals (symbolized by the now infamous Willie Horton, a prison inmate who committed a rape in Maryland after fleeing from a Massachusetts prison furlough program), and of questionable patriotism, as indicated by the governor's veto of a bill that would have required students in Massachusetts schools to pledge allegiance to the flag in a daily exercise. Worse still, according to the Bush campaign, Dukakis was a "liberal," portrayed as someone who favored high taxes and big government except in national defense, where he would show his antimilitary colors. This strategy had been planned carefully using "focus group" research techniques in which small groups of Democrats who had supported Reagan in 1980 and 1984 but were leaning toward Dukakis in 1988 were asked to respond to new information about the Democratic front-runner's positions and record on a number of social issues. Those issues that elicited the desired effect—abandoning

Dukakis in favor of Bush—became cornerstones of the Bush campaign's advertising and media efforts. Dukakis, not hesitating occasionally to abandon the high road, sought to link Bush to the Iran-contra incident, to the illicit international drug activities of Panamanian leader Manuel Noriega, and to ethics violations committed throughout the Reagan years, but the effort was far less successful.[26]

In 1992, Bush charged Clinton with a "pattern" of deception throughout his life, but unlike Dukakis in 1988, the Clinton campaign was quick to respond to negative advertising, sometimes with negative ads of their own. Just as the Bush attacks on Clinton's character seemed to be achieving results, the Clinton campaign aired television ads that juxtaposed Bush's promises of economic performance with reality. Moreover, Bush's honesty came into question when the special prosecutor investigating the Iran-contra arms-for-hostages deal of the Reagan era released information that suggested Bush, as Reagan's vice president, had been far more aware of the policy than he had admitted previously. This disclosure came just four days before election day and clearly deflated the president's chances for a comeback victory.

Social Groups. Fairly early in life many Americans begin to think of themselves as members of ethnic, geographic, or religious groups. As they get older, they also begin to identify with groups associated with their occupations and to consider themselves as businesspeople or farmers or members of labor unions. Sometimes people relate politically to groups to which they do not belong. A well-to-do White liberal, for example, who sympathizes with the underdog in society, may favor programs that benefit poor African Americans. Responses to groups can also be negative: a self-made businessperson may have an unfavorable image of labor unions or social welfare organizations. Far from declining in significance, group identifications may be gaining importance as a guide to voter behavior. At the same time, partisanship appears to be losing significance.[27]

Both Republican and Democratic presidential candidates take these group attitudes into account in devising campaign appeals. Since the days of Franklin Roosevelt, the Democratic party has aimed its campaigns at certain groups thought to be particularly susceptible to its political overtures: among these are southerners, members of racial and ethnic groups, organized labor, Catholics, Jews, intellectuals, and big-city "bosses" and their political supporters (hence the quip that the Democratic party has more wings than a boardinghouse chicken). At the same time, the Democrats usually have tried to depict the Republicans as the party of "big business" and the rich.

Until recently, Republican candidates made little use of explicit group appeals in their presidential campaigns. In fact, in 1964, Sen. Barry

Goldwater conducted an antigroup campaign. The Republican candidate seemed to go out of his way to antagonize particular blocs, speaking in Knoxville against the Tennessee Valley Authority; in retirement communities against Social Security; and in Charleston, West Virginia, near the heart of Appalachia, against the Johnson administration's War on Poverty. (In writing off such groups as "minorities," Goldwater ignored the fact that an aggregation of minorities can make a majority.) In 1968, Nixon tried a different approach, aiming his campaign at the "forgotten Americans who did not break the law, but did pay taxes, go to work, school, church, and love their country." He thereby sought to establish a negative association between the Democrats and groups he considered to be outside the American mainstream, such as welfare recipients, atheists, and war protesters.

Since the Democrats' New Deal coalition began to come apart in the 1970s, Republican presidential candidates have been more inclined to seek the support of specific groups through targeted appeals. In 1972, the Committee to Reelect the President produced campaign buttons for almost thirty nationalities, provided copy for ethnic newspapers and radio stations, and made special appeals to Catholics, Jews, African Americans, and Mexican Americans. In his 1980 campaign, Reagan appealed to union members by pointing out that he had been president of a labor union for six terms; courted the Polish vote by meeting on Labor Day with Stanislaw Walesa, father of the leader of the strike against the Polish government; and wooed African Americans by arguing that their high unemployment rate was caused by the sluggish state of the economy. Four years later, the Reagan campaign set aside an "ethnic week" to court groups such as Polish Americans and Italian Americans (recall that the Democratic vice-presidential candidate, Geraldine Ferraro, was the first person of Italian background to run on a presidential ticket). Reagan also tried to appeal to Jews by criticizing Mondale for not repudiating remarks of Jesse Jackson that many perceived to be anti-Semitic. Bush's carefully targeted strategy in 1988 was designed to appeal to former Democratic voters who had supported Reagan in the two preceding elections, particularly southern Whites and Catholics. By naming the first Hispanic to a cabinet level post, the Reagan administration also sought to strengthen its appeal to a group whose votes are especially important in California, Texas, and Florida. And during the campaign, President Reagan made campaign appearances in Chicago, before a gathering of community leaders of Polish descent, and in Newark, at an Italian American Columbus Day celebration. Such attention is typical of the new Republican appeal for group support.[28]

Two other groups took on a special significance in all three presidential elections of the 1980s. Women were thought to be anti-Reagan because of his promilitary stance and his opposition to social programs and the Equal Rights Amendment. Democrats played on such fears by portraying Reagan as "trigger-happy" and as insensitive to the needs of economic and social underdogs; the Republicans tried to assure women that he was a man of peace who looked to the private sector and to state and local governments to provide assistance to the disadvantaged. Work and family issues, such as child care and parental leave, received prominent attention in 1988 as a way to address the concerns of women, who now constitute a majority of registered voters. The Republicans in 1984, 1988, and 1992 also appealed to fundamentalist Christians, particularly in the South, by advocating prayer in the public schools and by opposing abortion; Democrats tried to counter such appeals by arguing that prayers should be said in church and the home (not in school), and that the government had no right to interfere with a woman's private decision whether or not to carry a pregnancy to term.

Another group targeted by both political parties in 1984 and again in 1992 was young voters. Traditionally Democratic in their sympathies, college-age youth were wooed in 1984 by Republican promises of job opportunities in an expanding economy and appeals to love of country. The Democrats responded by urging young people to consider those less fortunate than themselves and to express their concern about the dangers of nuclear war. Both parties' candidates made many campaign appearances on college campuses (Mondale gave one of his best speeches at George Washington University), typically with supporters and hecklers alike in attendance. Clinton appeared on the *Arsenio Hall Show* in shades and playing his saxophone; he was the first of the three candidates to appear in a special MTV program answering questions from a youthful audience. Bush did likewise, but only late in the election and with great reluctance. Clinton also promised to create the new AmeriCorps program designed to encourage community service in a new generation of Americans, a close parallel to the Peace Corps initiative launched by Kennedy.

Issues and Events. Over the years, both major political parties have been associated with certain broad issues in American life. Democratic presidential candidates usually emphasize economic issues: by doing so they can link the Great Depression to the Republican president Herbert Hoover, who was in office at the time, and can draw on the voters' traditional preference for Democrats over Republicans to handle the economy. In contrast, Republican candidates historically have focused more on foreign policy issues because Democratic presidents were in power at the start of World War I, World War II, and both the Korean and Vietnamese conflicts, leading many voters to conclude that Republicans were better able to keep the peace than Democrats. More recently, the growth of massive budget deficits in the 1980s and the willingness of presidents Reagan and Bush to use military force in Lebanon, Grenada, Libya, Panama, and the Persian Gulf may have altered these traditional party images.

Circumstances surrounding particular elections can lead to changes in the traditional politics. In 1980, the poor economic record of the Carter administration led Reagan to focus on that issue; four years later, as the incumbent president, Reagan continued to emphasize the economy because inflation and interest rates had fallen since he took office. The Carter record continued to haunt the Democrats. In both 1988 and 1992, Bush warned Americans that the Democratic candidate would lead them down the same road of high taxes and poor fiscal management that Carter had, but Clinton was able to maintain the focus on Bush's own economic performance. Foreign policy declined in salience. Far from being a central concern of the electorate, international issues had become a distant concern in 1992 when both Clinton and Perot concentrated on Bush's poor stewardship of the economy. As the Republican candidate in the first post–cold war election, Bush derived little of the boost his predecessors had received from foreign policy issues.

Although candidates address major issues in U.S. society, they frequently do so only in very general terms. The party out of power often uses a catchy slogan to link the party in power with unfortunate political events. In 1952, for example, the Republicans branded the Democrats with "Korea, corruption, and communism." The party in power responds in the same way, as when the Democrats defended their record in 1952 by telling the voters, "You never had it so good." In 1976, the situation was reversed; Democrats talked about Watergate, inflation, and unemployment, which combined to form the "misery index," and President Ford's pardon of Nixon. (Carter refused to attack Ford on the issue, but his vice-presidential candidate, Mondale, did.) President Ford asserted that his administration had cut inflation by half, brought peace to the nation ("Not a single American is fighting or dying"), and restored faith, confidence, and trust in the presidency. In 1980, as in 1952, the Republicans attacked the Democratic incumbent: Reagan blamed President Carter for the nation's mounting economic problems and for allowing the United States to fall far behind the Soviet Union in military preparedness. At the same time the Democratic president pointed with pride to the signing of the Egyptian-Israeli peace accord, the ratification of the Panama Canal Treaty, and the development of an energy program.

This general sort of attack and defense characterizes most presidential campaigns. The party out of power blames all the ills of American life on the administration; the party in power maintains that all of the nation's blessings have resulted from its leadership. The candidate in the most difficult position is a nonincumbent nominee of the party in power, such as Nixon in 1960 and Humphrey in 1968. Both served as vice president in administrations whose policies they did not fully endorse. Nixon, for instance, did not believe Eisenhower was doing enough in space exploration and national defense. Humphrey opposed the bombing of North Vietnam when it was initiated in 1965. Yet each hesitated to criticize the administration in which he had served. Humphrey's inability to dissociate himself from the Johnson administration's Vietnam policy is considered one of the main reasons for his defeat in 1968.[29]

In sharp contrast, Bush stressed his commitment to continuing Reagan's policies into the future when he first ran in 1988. This was most memorably expressed in his acceptance speech at the Republican national convention on August 18, 1988. As Bush argued, "In 1940, when I was barely more than a boy, Franklin Roosevelt said we shouldn't change horses in midstream. My friends, these days the world moves even more quickly, and now, after two great terms, a switch will be made. But when you have to change horses in midstream, doesn't it make sense to switch to one who's going the same way?" Bush put a modest amount of distance between himself and Reagan on environmental and education policy, but continuity was more central to his campaign than change.

While addressing current issues in very general terms, presidential candidates typically make few concrete proposals for dealing with such issues.[30] In 1960, Kennedy urged that he be given the chance to "get the nation moving again," but he was very vague about what, specifically, he would do to achieve that goal. Nixon was even more indefinite in 1968; he refused to spell out his plans for dealing with the most important U.S. political issue, Vietnam. His excuse was that doing so might jeopardize the Paris peace talks then being held. At a general level, Clinton promised to usher in change and claimed that his economic plan to restore competitiveness, create jobs, and provide a middle-class tax cut, endorsed by an impressive number of Nobel laureates and professional economists, was the answer. Nonetheless, his plan underwent substantial modification following the election.

Vague promises do not always prevail. In 1972, McGovern proposed that the defense budget be cut by 30 percent; and early in his campaign he advocated that everyone, regardless of need, be given a $1,000 grant by the government. In 1980, Reagan advocated the passage of the Kemp-Roth tax plan, which called for reducing taxes by 10 percent each year over a period of three years. In 1984, Mondale unveiled a plan that called for cuts in defense, health, and agricultural expenditures and tax increases for upper-income earners and corporations so that by 1989 the budget deficit could be reduced by two-thirds. Bush in 1988 reiterated

Reagan's position against raising taxes in his now famous statement: "Read my lips—no new taxes!" In 1990, Republican loyalists unleashed a storm of complaints at President Bush when he abandoned this promise and accepted limited tax increases as part of a negotiated budget agreement with the Democratic-controlled Congress. This was the reversal that first Pat Buchanan and later Clinton repeatedly brought to the attention of voters, illustrating precisely why most presidential candidates are loath to make specific commitments.

In manipulating political appeals, candidates usually attempt to develop an all-encompassing theme that will give the voters an overall impression of the campaign. Sometimes the theme focuses on the candidates themselves, as did Humphrey's slogan, "He's a man you can trust"; the Carter-Mondale phrase, "Tested and trustworthy"; and Reagan's 1984 motto, "Leadership that's working." The Dukakis campaign began to pick up support in the closing days of the campaign when it shifted to a new theme, "He's on your side." Alternatively, the appeal can be to a broad group, such as Nixon's "forgotten Americans." At other times the theme may be directed at issues and political events ("Korea, corruption, and communism" or "peace and prosperity") or take the form of a general call to action, such as Kennedy's "We've got to get the nation moving again"; McGovern's "Come home, America"; Carter's promise to make the government as "truthful, capable, and filled with love as the American people"; and Reagan's 1980 invitation to a "new beginning." Clinton sought to tap several of these sources of appeal, promising a "New Covenant" between citizens and government, embracing the theme of "change" and promising to help the forgotten middle class. Once the campaign's theme is established, candidates try, by constant repetition, to get the electorate to respond to it emotionally. Their success in doing so depends on another important aspect of presidential campaigns: how political appeals are communicated to the American voter.

Communicating with the Public

Because the electorate is two to three times as large as the selectorate and the campaign for the election is much shorter than it is for the nomination, presidential candidates place even more emphasis on the mass media during this latter stage of the process. Advertising expenses are one measure of that emphasis. In the 1984 campaign, for example, Reagan and Mondale each spent more than half of their $40 million subsidy from the federal government on television, radio, and print advertisements. Of the three types of media, television is by far the most important. Watching takes much less effort than reading, particularly as watching can be combined with other activities but reading cannot.[31] In addition, polls indicate that people are more inclined to believe what they see on television than what they read in the newspapers or hear on the radio. As a result, since 1952, television has been the chief source of campaign information for most Americans.

Over the years presidential candidates have employed several television formats. In 1968, Nixon used sixty-second spot announcements during popular programs such as Rowan and Martin's *Laugh-In*. The Republicans also staged appearances of Nixon before panels of citizens who asked questions that he could appear to answer spontaneously. (Nixon's advisers carefully screened both the panels and the questions to avoid possible embarrassment or surprise.)

In the 1972 campaign, the candidates adopted new formats for their televised political communications. Although thirty-second spots remained popular (one of Nixon's, for example, showed a hand sweeping away toy soldiers and miniature ships and planes to symbolize McGovern's proposed cuts in defense), five-minute advertisements became more common. McGovern chose still longer programs to present his addresses on Vietnam and the issue of corruption. Semidocumentary formats, such as a candidate discussing issues with ordinary citizens, were used as well. McGovern was filmed interacting with workers and owners of small businesses, and Nixon's trips to China and the Soviet Union were choreographed carefully for television viewers.

In 1976, President Ford employed the medium more imaginatively than did Carter. The president held an informal television interview, for example, with television personality and former baseball player Joe Garagiola, who tossed him some "gopher-ball" questions: "How many foreign leaders have you met with, Mr. President?" to which Ford modestly replied, "One hundred and twenty-four, Joe." In the last stages of the campaign, the Ford forces also broadcast short television interviews with voters in Georgia who described Carter as "wishy-washy." Carter concentrated on short commercials in which he looked directly into the camera and talked about various issues in an effort to counteract Ford's portrayal of him and to present himself as a strong, positive leader with specific programs.

During the 1980 campaign, the television advertisements varied in length from thirty seconds to thirty minutes, but most were short messages designed to reach peak audiences. The Carter television commercials appeared in three separate stages: the first showed the candidate being presidential, meeting with foreign dignitaries and working late at night in the Oval Office; the second consisted of interviews with people "in the street" saying that Reagan "scared" them; the third showed Carter being praised by prominent party figures, such as Lady Bird Johnson and Edward Kennedy, and by rank-and-file Democrats—a farmer, a steelworker, and a worker in a rubber factory. Most of the Reagan television advertisements featured the candidate himself, whom the Republicans considered to be a superb communicator, looking straight into the camera. They stressed three themes: Reagan's record as governor of California; his stand on issues, especially the economy; and a recitation of the record of President Carter, illustrated with graphs of rising consumer prices.

In 1984, the Republicans aired a nostalgic, half-hour film of President Reagan riding his horse, walking on a hilltop with his wife, Nancy, speaking at the Normandy beaches, and taking the oath of office. Most of the Republican commercials, however, were thirty-second ones. The most famous, "It's Morning Again in America," showed the sun shining on San Francisco Bay, people hurrying to and from work, and a bride and groom kissing at a wedding while a mellifluous voice asked, "Why would we ever want to go back to where we were less than four short years ago?" The Democrats relied entirely on thirty-second spots. One showed a roller coaster climbing its tracks (suggesting what would happen in the future as a result of record U.S. deficits), with a voice intoning, "If you're thinking of voting for Ronald Reagan in 1984, think of what will happen in 1985." Another, positive commercial pictured a warm, dynamic Mondale talking to a group of students, urging them to "stretch their minds" and to live their dreams, telling them he wanted to help them be what they wanted to be.

The most controversial advertisement of 1988 was run by the National Security Political Action Committee as part of an independent campaign for the Bush-Quayle ticket. Widely criticized as racist, the ad featured a police photograph of Willie Horton, a furloughed African American convict who fled Massachusetts to commit additional crimes. The advertisement ran for twenty-five days on cable television before the Bush campaign disavowed it. Because the advertisement was filmed by a former employee of the Bush campaign's media expert, Democrats charged that there was a link between the committee's effort and the main Republican campaign.

The media closely monitored 1992 campaign ads in an effort to deter a repeat of 1988. Bush was portrayed at work in the Oval Office much as other incumbent presidents had done. Some of the most negative messages about Clinton were delivered by citizens interviewed in a diner who spoke about the Democrat's character and their own lack of trust. Clinton's record as governor of Arkansas was also called into question in an ad that featured a vulture perched in a tree overlooking a desolate wasteland—Arkansas—as the state's low ranking on a variety of measures was recited. Some of the best Clinton ads showed clips of the enthusiastic reception that the Democratic team enjoyed during their widely publicized bus trips through the nation's midsection. In a similar way, several ads drew from the biographical film on Clinton's life that was completed for the convention. Later ads emphasized the campaign's central theme, Bush's failed economic policies, by reminding viewers of Bush's promises and heralding Clinton's plan. The most novel presentations of the campaign were Perot's half-hour "infomercials." The first two focused on the national debt and the economy; the last two concentrated on Perot's life and family. Professionals were surprised at the wide attention given these efforts, particularly the first two, which featured Perot seated at a desk and explaining a series of charts with the use of a metal pointer. Because Perot traveled far less than the partisan candidates, most of his campaign was conducted electronically, and by waiting to restart his campaign until October 1, he was able to concentrate his spending during a very brief period of the campaign. Bush, who trailed badly throughout the race, relied heavily on nationally broadcast ads while the Clinton campaign, because it was comfortably ahead in a number of states, was much more selective in its strategy, actually buying television advertising in only twenty states.[32]

Presidential Debates. In six elections, televised debates between presidential candidates have been the most important communication source of the campaign.[33] The first occurred in 1960 between Nixon, at that time Eisenhower's vice president, and Senator Kennedy. In the first of four debates, Nixon's somewhat uncertain manner and his physical appearance (he had not fully recovered from a recent illness and television accentuated his heavy beard) was contrasted with Kennedy's confident demeanor and bright, alert image (he wore a blue shirt and dark suit that showed up well against the television studio background rather than fading into it as Nixon's light-colored clothes did). Also, unlike Nixon, Kennedy had prepared thoroughly for the debates. As a result, viewers perceived a victory for the young Massachusetts senator.[34] Contributing to that perception was the fact that people had not expected Kennedy to best Nixon, who had gained political prominence in part because of his debating skills in previous campaigns. From that point on, Kennedy's campaign assumed more enthusiasm, and the senator himself credited the debate for his close victory over the vice president.

Televised debates again played a major part in the 1976 campaign. In the second debate with former Georgia governor Carter, President Ford stated that he did not consider countries of Eastern Europe (in particular, Yugoslavia, Romania, and Poland) to be under Soviet domination. To make matters worse, the president refused to change his answer even after the startled questioner (a newspaper reporter) gave him the opportunity to do so; in fact, it was not until several days after the debate that the president's staff finally persuaded him to retract his statement. Many political observers considered that gaffe to be the turning point of the contest, the one that ended a dramatic decline in public support for Carter (and the increased support for Ford) that had characterized the previous month of the campaign.

In 1980, the League of Women Voters, sponsors of the debates, originally extended an invitation not only to President Carter and Reagan but also to independent candidate Anderson, whose standing in the public opinion polls then exceeded the 15-percent cutoff point established by the League. Carter refused to participate on the grounds that the debate would legitimize the Anderson candidacy, which he asserted was strictly a "creation of the media." In contrast, Reagan, who believed that enhancing Anderson's standing would help his own candidacy, accepted the League's invitation and criticized Carter for refusing to debate. Just a week before election day, with Anderson's public support in the polls now below 15 percent, a single debate was held between the two major candidates. Both men looked and handled themselves well, and neither made a serious mistake, but most observers concluded that Reagan won the debate—on style rather than substance. In his eagerness to focus on Reagan, Carter may have been too aggressive in his accusations; Reagan's responses were reassuring rather than "trigger-happy," and he conducted himself in a "presidential" manner.[35]

In 1984, the Mondale forces sought six separate presidential debates and a format in which the candidates could ask each other questions. The Reagan organization refused that request, and the sides ultimately agreed to two debates between Mondale and Reagan and one between the vice-presidential candidates, Bush and Ferraro, with members of the media asking the questions. Mondale scored a clear victory in the first debate, projecting himself as calm, bright, and confident, while the president appeared confused, inarticulate, and, in his summation, to have lost his train of thought altogether. When the president at one point used the signature line from his 1980 debate with Carter, "There you go again," Mondale turned pointedly to Reagan and asked, "Remember the last time you said that?" and then answered the question himself: "You said it when President Carter said you were going to cut Medicare . . . and what did you do right after the election? You went out and tried to cut $20 billion out of Medicare." The media and most observers (even Reagan supporters) agreed that the president had been defeated decisively, and the debate raised the issue of whether his age had slowed him down and made him incapable of handling the demands of the office for the next four years. The second debate, however, produced a far different result: Reagan prevailed on style, appearing more relaxed and coherent (although he again rambled in his closing remarks). Most important, the president defused the age issue when, in response to a question on the matter, he replied that he did not intend "to exploit my opponent's youth and inexperience," a clever retort that drew a broad smile even from Mondale.

There were two presidential debates and one vice-presidential debate during the 1988 campaign. All were sponsored by a new entity, the Commission on Presidential Debates, a nonprofit, bipartisan organization created in February 1987 with support from the Democratic and Republican national chairs. Party sponsorship was presented as a means to ensure that election-year debates would be held, and a plan was developed for four debates to be financed through private contributions. Long before he became the Democrats' nominee, Dukakis committed himself to the plan, but Bush delayed making a commitment until after the Republican nominating convention, leaving open the possibility that he would refuse to participate. Two of the debates planned for early September were canceled; dates for the remaining sessions had to be worked in around the Olympic Games (NBC eventually agreed to delay broadcast of the games rather than the debate), baseball playoffs, and the World Series.

Many observers considered the 1988 presidential debates less than riveting. Bush and Dukakis loyally echoed the major themes of their campaigns. Dukakis stressed the need for improving access to health care and housing, fighting drug use, and restoring economic health, while also touching on symbols of the family, strong leadership, and middle-class opportunity. Bush placed somewhat more emphasis on foreign policy and education than did his opponent but hammered away on symbols related to crime, Democrats, and liberalism, the focus of his controversial campaign ads.[36] Dukakis was widely viewed as having demonstrated mastery of substance in the first debate but as failing to project an attractive personality to his audience. His cold demeanor was painfully apparent at the outset of the second debate when he was asked a blunt question by journalist Bernard Shaw: "Governor, if Kitty Dukakis were raped and murdered, would you favor an irrevocable death penalty for the killer?" Instead of using his response to this horrible prospect as a means to project a more human side, Dukakis patiently and unemotionally repeated his lifelong opposition to the death penalty and proceeded to discuss the need for a stepped-up war on drugs. (Campaign aides later explained that Dukakis had been ill throughout that day and had slept during much of the afternoon.) The debates, in short, provided neither candidate with a "knockout." Dukakis, the trailer in the contest, was not able to reverse the campaign's momentum.

The vice-presidential debate offered the most dramatic moment of all three encounters. In response to the third question he was asked about what he would do if forced to assume the duties of president, Dan Quayle compared the length of his congressional service to that of former president Kennedy. Lloyd Bentsen, the Democrats' vice-presidential nominee, delivered his prepared response with withering directness: "Senator, I served with Jack Kennedy. I knew Jack Kennedy. Jack Kennedy was a friend of mine. Senator, you're no Jack Kennedy." Millions of viewers watched as hurt, anger, and astonishment flashed across the youthful features of the Republican candidate whose selection had been so controversial. Quayle's response—"That was really uncalled for, Senator"—sounded lame in comparison.

There were four televised debates in 1992 during a nine-day span in mid-October. For the first time, an independent candidate participated in the three presidential debates; Perot reactivated his campaign just as negotiations over the debate terms were being concluded, and he welcomed the opportunity to have his candidacy legitimized. The fourth debate included Perot's running mate, retired navy admiral James Stockdale, but he was so badly overmatched in the mud-wrestling between Quayle and Gore that he was barely noticeable. A major innovation was using three different formats for the presidential debates: a panel of journalists, a town meeting with citizens asking questions of the candidates, and a single moderator. The formats allowed for greater interaction and extemporaneous exchange among the contestants rather than the patented responses that have characterized so many of these meetings in the past. Perot's humor and homespun one-liners spiced up the first debate; Clinton's ease and command of issues shone forth in the second town-meeting format; Bush was most aggressive and effective in the third confrontation, although his advantage was not overwhelming. There were few truly memorable moments of drama between Bush and Clinton; Perot's criticism of the president reinforced Clinton's message on the economy, and Perot scored most consistently with humorous one-liners that suggested the party protagonists were "irrelevant," the adjective he used during the third debate to describe Clinton's experience as governor of Arkansas. Although integral to the process, this series of debates reinforced the overall dynamic of the race: Clinton held his lead over Bush, who was unable to score the knockout his campaign needed; Perot's criticisms and witticisms drew support from each, but polls taken during this period of the campaign suggest that Perot gained at Clinton's expense.[37]

Televised presidential debates have become the most important campaign events of modern presidential elections. Candidates have recognized the danger of making a mistake or an embarrassing gaffe on live television, a particular danger for incumbents. Challengers have sought to use the opportunity to demonstrate their knowledge of issues and their presidential qualities to a large nationwide audience. Kennedy in 1960, Reagan in 1980, and Perot in 1992 seem to have benefited the most from an opportunity to engage a more experienced opponent, at least in part because they were able to exceed performance expectations and dispel negative impressions. Most candidates prepare extensively prior to the meeting and follow a conservative plan of reemphasizing themes already made prominent during the campaign. As a result, the exchanges frequently seem wooden rather than extemporaneous, an impression heightened by the cautious rules approved by the respective camps. Although there may be good reason to prefer sponsorship by a nonpartisan rather than a bipartisan organization (the former may be better able to resist adopting procedures that help candidates more than voters), the question may be moot. The Commission on Presidential Debates assumed control in 1988 and introduced several valuable innovations in 1992. The new formats employed in 1992 are likely to be repeated in the future and promise to enliven this important feature of the modern selection process.

Media Coverage. Besides political commercials and debates, a third source of communication in presidential campaigns is the coverage provided by representatives of the mass media themselves, both the broadcast media (television and radio) and print media (newspapers and magazines). These representatives are not nearly as important in general election campaigns, however, as they are in the nomination stage. By the time of the fall election, the campaign is much more structured. The contest usually has come down to two candidates who by then are fairly well known to the electorate; in addition, the voters at this stage associate the candidates with their respective parties and evaluate them on that basis. Moreover, the candidates have more money to spend on campaign communications than they did in the nomination process; and debates, if held, are more focused (typically involving just two candidates) and reach a wider audience than any that occurred in the nomination campaign.

The media's coverage of the election campaign is similar to their coverage of the nomination stage. Reporters and commentators pay great attention to the election "game," that is, which party candidate is leading in the public opinion polls and by how much, the strategies being pursued by both camps, and the "hoopla" of campaign rallies and the like. The media also tend to focus on "campaign issues"—such as Carter's remark in the 1976 campaign that he "lusted after women in his heart" and Ford's comment about Eastern Europe—rather than policy issues. In 1984, the media zeroed in on the financial affairs of Ferraro and her husband. Quayle's service in the National Guard during the Vietnam era and his admission to law school despite a weak undergraduate record similarly attracted unusual and possibly excessive attention in 1988.

The principal departure in media coverage of the 1992 campaign was initiated by the candidates and welcomed by the public: widespread use of non-news television programming, often carried by cable stations, in what came to be called the "talk-show campaign." Circumventing the media is not a new campaign tactic, but candidates took advantage of what has become a highly fragmented media to deliver their message in new ways. Symbolizing the shift was Perot's candidacy, which was launched on the *Larry King Live* show carried by CNN two days after the New Hampshire primary. Pressed by King, Perot suggested he would run if his name were put on the ballot in all fifty states. Perot's unconventional campaign featured minimal travel and few interactions with traditional journalists; Perot relied more heavily on the "soft journalism" he encountered in talk-show formats. Throughout the year, Larry King alone had thirteen visits from the three major candidates, six from Perot, four from Clinton, three from Bush. During the general election period, the three candidates logged a combined forty visits on *CBS Morning News, Good Morning America, Today, Donahue,* and *Larry King Live.* Clinton led the way with twenty-four appearances (not including twenty-three during the nomination period); Perot made thirty-three appearances on these shows throughout the entire year.[38] Clinton used these outlets to revive his candidacy in May and June; discovering that voters regarded him as just another politician, a conscious effort was made to have Clinton appear as often as possible on the network morning shows and in other informal settings where viewers could get to know him better. Bush was least interested in these formats— at one point calling them "weird talk shows"—but was forced to make his share of appearances as well.[39]

Do all these efforts make a difference? Thomas Patterson's study of the 1976 election contest indicated that the voters became more aware of the candidates' positions on policy issues as the campaign progressed.[40] He attributes some of that increase to their familiarity with the policy tendencies of the Democratic and Republican parties. His analysis also shows that newspaper coverage of policy issues increased voters' awareness of them, particularly for voters who previously had not been highly interested in policy issues. In contrast, the short, superficial coverage of the issues by network news did not raise voters' awareness of the issues. More recent campaign studies, however, do not confirm the superiority of the print media. In their analysis of the 1980 campaign, Michael Robinson and Margaret Sheehan conclude that the broadcast networks covered the issues at least as well as the wire services.[41] Moreover, Patterson and Richard Davis found in their study of the 1984 campaign that only 4 of

114 newspaper articles they analyzed mentioned Mondale's charge that Reagan's tax cuts benefited the rich, and none mentioned Mondale's progressive tax plan.[42] Ironically, Patterson found that the public learns more about candidate policy positions through exposure to campaign advertising than through attention to television news.[43]

Despite the dominance of television in recent presidential contests, the other media continue to play a role in campaigns. Newspapers not only cover the issues in more detail than television but also are free to endorse candidates.[44] The print media are also available for advertisements stressing visual effects. In 1960, the Democrats used pictures of Kennedy and his attractive wife, Jacqueline, in many of their promotions. Radio also plays a role in presidential campaigns. It is less expensive than television and can be used in ways that television cannot, such as broadcasting appeals targeted at commuting drivers. Moreover, some radio networks, such as National Public Radio, cover presidential campaigns in much greater depth than does television.

The formats available in the various media therefore make it possible for candidates to emphasize different types of appeals and to reach disparate groups. Dan Nimmo distinguishes between two major types of audiences.[45] The first consists of the politically concerned and interested, who use the print media as well as television and radio to obtain information on presidential campaigns. The second comprises less politically involved voters who must be reached through television and sometimes through radio, particularly by means of spot announcements, such as those used by Nixon during his 1968 campaign.

During the 1988 election, there was renewed concern that campaign strategists might be able to control media coverage through adroit staging of events. As Patterson points out, "Since the candidates decide what they will say, and where they will say it, they frequently can direct the press's attention to what they want it to see." [46] *Sound bites* are brief, punchy lines developed for candidates to deliver with the intent of providing dramatic footage for television news broadcasts. Effective campaign managers seek to develop a theme for the day and stage events in which their candidate can deliver the pithy lines in time to make the evening news. Informal and even structured interaction with the press is minimized. One consequence of such a pattern is the trivialization of public issues and candidate positions.

During 1992, many of the traditional campaign journalists felt ignored as candidates favored talk shows in which they could interact with the audience rather than aggressive interviewers. In comparing reporters' questions with those asked by the public, Richard Berke of the *New York Times* found that "Reporters dwell on the process, asking about polls, tactical strategy, and, of course, the story of the day. Questions from the public are far less confrontational, and an overwhelming number of people ask candidates how they would solve problems that would affect the questioner." [47] The traditional media also made some changes in coverage: many conducted aggressive "ad watches" to ensure that candidate advertising was accurate; CNN initiated a daily 4:30 P.M. summary of campaign developments; CBS sought to increase the length of candidate sound bites to thirty-seconds; several newspapers sought to tailor their coverage to the concerns of their readers. Nonetheless, Philip Meyer argues that "the hegemony of the traditional mainstream media was forever altered" as King and others served as "passive mediators" between candidates and the citizenry. [48] Moreover, Meyer suggests that the new, faster pace of communication via cellular telephones, fax machines, satellite transmissions, and computer bulletin boards has created a "virtual newsroom" that may have restructured forever the ways in which campaigns are conducted and covered. We saw the first signs of these changes in 1992.

Clinton's 1992 campaign organization took advantage of these technological opportunities to perfect the art of "damage control," responding to an opponent's charges before they can become news or before the public comes to believe them. Aides in the "War Room," as Little Rock campaign headquarters came to be called, monitored Bush's speeches and ads, as well as journalists' reports, even intercepting them during satellite transmission to give themselves additional time to develop responses. They could put together quickly an ad of their own to be televised or draft responses that could be communicated via fax and telephone to news services and individual reporters. Their goal was to avoid a two-day story that could develop unless a credible refutation was provided immediately or unless they at least could get their rebuttal into the same story carrying the charge. [49] As these activities indicate, an effectively managed campaign can make the difference between victory and defeat, making it critical to understand how candidates construct a campaign team.

Campaign Organization and Workers

A modern presidential campaign requires the coordination of many aides with specialized skills. Media specialists design campaign ads; pollsters track the candidate's competitiveness in target states; schedulers and advance people coordinate the candidate's many trips; opposition research, speech writing, and rapid response are other assignments. Assembling a support staff, establishing lines of communication, and coordinating activities are critical tasks that the candidate cannot personally perform.

Presidential candidates typically start the general election campaign with a core of people who, in effect, constitute their personal organization, usually carried over from the nomination contest. John Kennedy put his brother Robert in charge of his 1960 campaign against Nixon, and Jordan continued as the head of Carter's 1976 fall campaign. Many who worked for the candidate in the primary and caucus-convention states also are available for the election campaign. Incumbent presidents frequently reassign key members of their administration to work on the fall campaign. In 1972, Nixon initially put his attorney general, John Mitchell, in charge of the Committee to Reelect the President and transferred others in the White House to assignments with the committee. Three important figures in the Carter administration, Robert Strauss, Jordan, and Gerald Rafshoon, played significant roles in the 1980 campaign. In August 1992, Bush called on James Baker to leave his post as secretary of state to become White House chief of staff and oversee the reelection effort. The move was widely regarded as the desperate act of a candidate who was trailing badly and whose organization received much of the blame. The reelection effort had gotten off to a slow start in 1991 and was further disrupted when John Sununu resigned as White House chief of staff in early December, replaced by Samuel Skinner. Baker was regarded as a campaign wizard after his performances in 1976 (with Ford), 1980 (with Bush and later Reagan), 1984 (with Reagan), and 1988 as a major figure in Bush's campaign. While he provided more discipline to the overall effort and settled on a coherent message, the task was greater than even his well-honed skills could perform. Robert Teeter, an experienced pollster, played a critical role as campaign strategist. Frederick Malek also served a vital function as campaign manager. Robert Mosbacher, a long-time fund-raiser who had served as secretary of commerce, specialized in raising soft money.

Clinton relied heavily on a group of political consultants: James Carville and Paul Begala had worked on Harris Wofford's Senate campaign in Pennsylvania and joined Clinton as strategists shortly after he declared his candidacy; Mickey Kantor, a Los Angeles attorney, served as campaign manager for the general election, and David Wilhelm, another consultant who served initially as chair of the nomination campaign, was Kantor's chief of staff (after Clinton's election, Wilhelm became chair of the Democratic National Committee and Kantor the special trade representative); George Stephanopolous served first as deputy campaign manager and later as the campaign's communication director; Robert Farmer and Rahm Emanuel were charged with directing financial affairs.

Because the electorate for the general campaign is so much broader than the selectorate, which participates in the nomination phase, presidential candidates must increase the ranks of their supporters in the fall to include people who had not been involved previously. One potential source of new recruits is political rivals who had sought the nomination themselves. In 1972, McGovern asked Humphrey to campaign for him; Humphrey did so out of personal friendship and party loyalty. In 1984, both Gary Hart and Jackson worked hard on Mondale's behalf in the fall campaign. In 1976, Ford and Reagan supporters cochaired the general election campaign in many states.[50] In several instances, however, personal loyalties and commitments to issues are so strong that it is not possible to recruit those who supported the other candidates for the nomination. In 1968, the Humphrey organization was not able to persuade many of Eugene McCarthy's supporters to work in the general election campaign after McCarthy lost the presidential nomination. In 1980, many who backed Edward Kennedy's unsuccessful bid for the Democratic nomination did not work for President Carter in the fall campaign; nor in 1984 did many of Hart's supporters campaign for Mondale. Jackson's role in 1988 was more limited than his supporters would have liked, a factor that may have contributed to the decline in turnout among African Americans.

Persons associated with the regular party organization are another potential source of campaign workers. Termed "organizational loyalists" by John Kessel, these are the people who owe their allegiance to the party instead of a particular presidential candidate or set of political issues.[51] Because of such loyalties, they are often willing to work in the fall campaign for whichever candidate wins their party's nomination, no matter what their personal feelings about the nominee may be. At the same time, because they are pragmatic and not ideological, party loyalists may not work hard for a presidential candidate they believe to be a loser who will hurt the chances of party candidates seeking other political offices. Many Republicans took this attitude toward Goldwater in 1964, as did some Democratic leaders toward Humphrey in 1968, McGovern in 1972, Mondale in 1984, and even Dukakis in 1988.

State and local political parties are another potential source of workers for the presidential general election campaign. For several reasons, however, problems traditionally have arisen in persuading these organizations to work for the presidential candidates. First, state and local races are more important than the presidential contest to local leaders, particularly those in patronage positions. Second, national, state, and local organizations compete for the same resources, such as visits by candidates and financial donations. Finally, the campaign finance legislation passed in the early 1970s to provide public funds for presidential campaigns prohibited state and local parties from spending money on such campaigns. The 1979 amendment to the campaign finance legislation, however, permitted state and local party organizations to spend money in presidential campaigns for any purpose except campaign advertising and hiring outside personnel. This legislation enabled both parties in 1980 to develop grassroots support for their presidential campaigns, although the Republicans clearly outdid the Democrats.

Democratic presidential candidates generally have benefited from another major source of campaign workers: those provided by organized labor. In 1968, the AFL-CIO said it had registered 4.6 million voters, printed and distributed more than a 100 million pamphlets, operated telephone banks in 638 localities, sent out 70,000 house-to-house canvassers, and provided almost 100,000 volunteers on election day to transport people to the polls.[52] This effort was extended on Humphrey's behalf and is credited with winning the votes of a large number of workers who initially planned to vote for George Wallace.

In contrast, the antipathy of Meany and other AFL-CIO leaders toward McGovern caused the organization to remain neutral in the 1972 presidential race and to concentrate its efforts instead toward helping Democrats win House seats and state and local offices. In 1976, the AFL-CIO returned to its traditional policy of supporting the Democratic presidential candidate and played an important role in registering its members and their families and in transporting them to the polls to vote for Carter. In 1980, although some of its principal leaders backed Senator Kennedy in the Democratic nomination struggle, labor generally did support President Carter; the National Education Association was especially active on his behalf. In 1984, except for the Teamsters, who backed Reagan, labor unions were united on behalf of Mondale, as they were for Dukakis in 1988.

One distinctive feature of the 1984 campaign was the extent to which both political parties sought to register new voters. Initially, observers thought that the Democrats would benefit most from this effort by registering traditionally low-voting groups such as African Americans, Hispanics, and the poor. Their registration effort ran into difficulties, however, because of rivalries among organizations attempting to register the same people and the reluctance of some political organizations to add new voters who would later share in deciding which candidates would prevail in Democratic primary contests for various offices. Moreover, the Republican party launched an all-out drive of its own to counteract the rival party's effort. Republicans registered a large number of White southerners, with the assistance of fundamentalist ministers. Key states, such as California, Texas, and Florida, were selected for special registration drives. Most observers considered the parties' 1984 efforts a standoff even though significant registration gains were made among some groups. For example, it is estimated that as many as two million new African American voters joined the rolls.[53] Registration efforts were more selectively targeted by the parties in 1988 (for example, Hispanics in Texas) and both parties seemed to devote more time to mobilizing voters, stressing persuasion over registration.

Campaign Finance

Since 1976, campaign reform legislation has significantly influenced general election campaigns. In 1976, both Ford and Carter accepted federal funds ($21.8 million each that year) and were therefore restricted to that figure for the entire campaign (in addition to another $3.2 million that each national committee could spend on behalf of its presidential candidate). As a result, both sides had to conduct more restricted campaigns than they did in 1972, when the Republicans spent $61 million and the Democrats $30 million. The equal public subsidy provided to both candidates meant that Ford had to forgo the traditional Republican advantage in campaign funds. As the incumbent president, however, he received a great deal of free publicity, and his Rose Garden strategy enabled him to reserve his financial resources for the last ten days of the campaign, in which he spent $4 million on television and radio broadcasting. All told, both candidates spent about half of their total campaign outlay on the mass media, particularly television, and therefore had limited funds available for organizing their grassroots campaigns. Largely missing from the 1976 contest were fund-raising activities and the buttons, bumper stickers, and yard signs used extensively in previous elections (under the law then in effect, state and local parties could not assist the presidential campaign by spending money for such purposes).

The 1980 campaign brought new developments in campaign finance. Again two major-party candidates accepted public financing, and each spent about $18 million of the $29.4 million in federal funds on the mass media, which again meant that they had limited funds available for grassroots activities. In 1980, however, the law permitted state and local parties to make expenditures for such activities. Figures provided by the FEC show that Republican state and local committees spent $15 million on grassroots efforts on Reagan's behalf compared with $5 million spent by Democratic organizations for Carter.

Also of increased importance in the 1980 campaign were the actions of independent groups in support of Reagan. In the summer of 1980, several organizations announced plans to spend as much as $70 million on media efforts for the Republican candidate. A citizens' interest group, Common Cause, together with the FEC and the Carter-Mondale Presidential Committee, challenged such expenditures on the grounds that the groups were not truly autonomous, as some of their leaders had been closely associated with Reagan in past political campaigns. Although these challenges were unsuccessful, they did impede the fund-raising efforts of the independent groups and forced them to cut back on their original plans. Eventually, independent organizations spent approximately $10.6 million on Reagan's behalf. Although much less than originally antici-pated, these expenditures were nonetheless significant: independent groups were estimated to have spent only $28,000 for President Carter, about one-quarter of 1 percent of the amount spent for Reagan.[54]

Total independent expenditures increased for 1983–1984 to nearly $17.5 million, with $15.83 million spent in efforts favoring the Republican candidates and $800,000 supporting the Democratic ticket. The overall total declined in 1988, but the party imbalance widened. Total expendi-tures of $14.13 million were reported to the FEC for 1987–1988; $10.54 million was spent in support of the Republican cause and $568,000 for the Democrats. Spending to *oppose* a ticket rose dramatically from $831,000 in the previous election to $3.5 million in 1988, of which all but $150,000 was directed against the Democrats.[55] According to the FEC, these expendi-tures declined in 1991–1992 to $3.4 million in behalf of Bush and $0.5 million in behalf of Clinton.

In 1984, both presidential candidates again spent a major portion of their federal funds ($40.4 million plus $6.9 million for the national com-mittee) on the mass media. Both parties also expended considerable sums of money on voter registration and get-out-the-vote efforts, making use of a loophole in the campaign finance laws that allows money to be raised and spent for "party building" activities. The Republicans funneled much more money to state parties to assist in the campaign than did the Democ-rats, a gap that was narrowed substantially in 1988 when it was reported that Republicans spent $69 million and Democrats $60 million on such efforts. Many observers are concerned about the growth in these soft money expenditures (referred to as "sewer money" by critics) since there are no limits on the amounts that individuals, corporations, and labor unions may contribute, and the funds can be channeled into areas critical to the presidential election with only a nominal separation from the presi-dential campaigns. Reportedly, 270 contributions of $100,000 or more were received by the Republicans in 1988 and the money was clearly tar-geted, as was the Democrats', to critical state contests.[56] Moreover, the par-ties' efforts to raise soft money were coordinated by the chief fund-raisers for each presidential candidate, Robert A. Farmer, finance chair of the Dukakis nomination campaign, and Mosbacher, Bush's finance chair, roles reprised by both of these men in 1992.[57] Herbert Alexander and

TABLE 3-2 General Election Funding Sources for Major Presidential Candidates, 1992 (in millions of dollars)

Source	Bush	Clinton	Perot
Federal grant	55.2	55.2	n/a
Accounting and legal costs	4.3	6.0	n/a
Coordinated party expenditures	10.3	10.3	n/a
Independent expenditures	2.0	0.5	n/a
Labor/corporate	2.5	36.0	n/a
Privately raised	n/a	n/a	68.4
Soft money	15.6	22.1	n/a
Total	89.9	130.1	68.4

SOURCES: Herbert E. Alexander and Anthony Corrado, *Financing the 1992 Election* (Armonk, N.Y.: M.E. Sharpe, 1995), Table 5.2; The Federal Election Commission, *The Presidential Public Funding Program* (Washington, D.C.: Federal Election Commission, 1993), Chart 4-1, 31; F. Christopher Arterton, "Campaign '92: Strategies and Tactics," in Gerald M. Pomper, ed., *The Election of 1992: Reports and Interpretations* (Chatham, N.J.: Chatham House, 1993), Table 3.1, 84.

NOTE: N/a indicates not applicable.

Anthony Corrado argue that Bush and Clinton benefited from $18.9 million and $23.6 million in 1992 soft money, respectively, although others estimate the amounts may have been twice as much.[58] The growth in soft-money contributions, solicited openly by the candidates and solicited by members of their campaign staffs, has reopened the door to the influence of big money; Republicans claimed 198 individuals contributed $100,000 or more in 1992 soft money and the Democrats surpassed those totals with 375 who gave or raised $100,000.[59]

An estimate of total funds spent by the three candidates for the presidency in 1992 is found in Table 3-2.[60] As Alexander points out, the Democrat outspent the Republican candidate for the first time in the twentieth century in 1988 and duplicated that achievement in 1992. The principal difference is the significant advantage that Clinton enjoyed in expenditures of organized labor on his behalf. These are spent in communications to their members and in nominally nonpartisan activities. Compared to earlier elections, Democrats have been more successful in raising funds for both party-coordinated expenditures and soft money, while at the same time the gap in independent expenditures has narrowed. Both the Republicans and Democrats conducted significant party advertising campaigns that could also have helped the presidential candidates.

Perot's spending total matched the $65.5 million in campaign funds available to the party nominees through the federal grant and coordinated party expenditures, but fell short in not having the party and interest group support enjoyed by major-party nominees. Perot contributed

$63.3 million of his own money and received the balance in individual contributions. At the time he withdrew from the race, Perot had spent $12.3 million of his own money and had received another $2.5 million in contributions as part of the effort to get his name on the ballot in all fifty states, build grassroots organizations, and mount a national campaign. He had assembled a campaign staff headed by experienced presidential strategists from both political parties (Ed Rollins, Republican, and Jordan, Democrat) but had rejected their recommendations on how to mount a national campaign. Despite his apparent withdrawal, Perot continued to maintain organizations and offices as a way to remain on the ballot and gain access to several other important states such as New York. He may have spent as much as $7 million during the time that his campaign was ostensibly suspended.[61]

Both the rules of the game and the campaign strategies and resources developed by the opposing candidates shape the outcome of presidential campaigns. The campaign, however, is only one influence on the way people vote. Chapter 4 examines other influences, as well as patterns of voting in presidential elections.

Notes

1. During the 1988 election, approximately 36.5 million persons participated in primaries or caucuses as part of the nomination process and 91.6 million voted in the general election. Harold G. Stanley and Richard G. Niemi, *Vital Statistics on American Politics,* 2d ed. (Washington, D.C.: CQ Press, 1990), Tables 3-1, 3-2, 3-3, 3-4, 3-5, 3-6.
2. Max Farrand, *The Framing of the Constitution of the United States* (New Haven: Yale University Press, 1913), 160.
3. Neal Peirce, *The People's President: The Electoral College in American History and the Direct-Vote Alternative* (New York: Simon and Schuster, 1968), 430.
4. Lucius Wilmerding, *The Electoral College* (New Brunswick, N.J.: Rutgers University Press, 1958), chap. 8.
5. John Roche, "The Founding Fathers: A Reform Caucus in Action," *American Political Science Review* 55 (December 1961): 811.
6. Lawrence Longley, "Minorities and the 1980 Electoral College" (Paper delivered at the annual meeting of the American Political Science Association, Washington, D.C., August 28–31, 1980).
7. The 270 electoral votes constitute a majority of the total number of 538, which is the sum of 435 electoral votes representing members of the House of Representatives, 100 representing the senators from the fifty states, and 3 representing the District of Columbia.
8. As part of the settlement in a lawsuit filed against the Census Bureau, a postcensus survey of 165,000 households was conducted to determine the extent of undercounting. Preliminary survey findings suggested that the size of eight state delegations could be adjusted. July 15, 1991, was the deadline for making

adjustments in the original census count. On that date, Secretary of Commerce Mosbacher announced that no adjustment would be made.

9. Wallace, however, may have affected the results of the Truman-Dewey contest in some states; Wallace's winning 8 percent of the popular vote in New York probably drained enough votes away from Truman to allow Dewey to defeat him by about 1 percent of the popular vote in that contest.

10. Although presidential candidates are free to refuse public funds, no major-party nominee has done so in the general election, perhaps because of the difficulty of raising money under the limitations on contributions from individuals and political action committees. Candidates may also think that the American public favors the use of public rather than private funds in the presidential general election. Perot ran for president in 1992 using virtually all his own money (he received $4 million in contributions) and repeatedly claimed that the American people applauded the use of his own funds.

11. *New York Times,* November 12, 1988, A8. Also see Thomas Weko and John H. Aldrich, "The Presidency and the Election Campaign: Framing the Choices in 1988," in *The Presidency and the Political System,* 3d ed., ed. Michael Nelson (Washington, D.C.: CQ Press, 1990).

12. Although campaign activities are carried in the national media, local media give special publicity to the candidate and thus affect the immediate audience. Moreover, some voters are flattered by the fact that a candidate takes the time and effort to come to their locality to campaign. Attention to local media was expanded considerably in the past two elections.

13. Lewis Chester, Godfrey Hodgson, and Bruce Page, *The American Melodrama: The Presidential Campaign of 1968* (New York: Viking, 1969), 620.

14. Sometimes, however, presidential candidates venture into states thought to belong politically to their opponents as a way to force the opposing campaign to act defensively. This was true of Carter in 1976, who forced Ford to spend time and money in states he expected to carry, and Clinton in 1992, who forced Bush to increase his efforts in Texas and Florida as a result of Democratic campaign efforts. Martin Schram, *Running for President 1976: The Carter Campaign* (New York: Stein and Day, 1977), 247. Carter in 1980 and Mondale in 1984 also visited California, in part to require Reagan to use some resources to protect his home state.

15. Kessel reports the comment made during the 1972 campaign that "McGovern could not carry the South with Robert E. Lee as his running-mate and Bear Bryant as his campaign manager." John Kessel, "Strategy for November," in *Choosing the President,* ed. James D. Barber (Englewood Cliffs, N.J.: Prentice-Hall, 1974), 109.

16. Robert D. Loevy, *The Flawed Path to the Presidency 1992* (Albany, N.Y.: SUNY Press, 1995), 241–242. Each candidate also visited other states during this period, but the tier of seven states was heavily represented in the list of destinations.

17. This carefully thought-out plan is to be contrasted with the pledge Nixon made at the 1960 Republican national convention to visit all fifty states personally. In the closing days of the campaign, Nixon took precious time to fly to Alaska, which he had not previously visited, while his opponent, Kennedy, was barnstorming through heavily populated Illinois, New Jersey, New York, and the New England states.

18. F. Christopher Arterton, "Campaign '92: Strategies and Tactics of the Candi-

dates," in *The Election of 1992: Reports and Interpretations*, ed. Gerald M. Pomper (Chatham, N.J.: Chatham House, 1993), 87. See also the discussion in Paul R. Abramson, John H. Aldrich, and David W. Rohde, *Change and Continuity in the 1992 Elections* (Washington, D.C.: CQ Press, 1994), 48–49.

19. Thomas Cronin, "The Presidential Election of 1984," in *Election '84: Landslide Without a Mandate*, ed. Ellis Sandor and Cecil Crabb Jr. (New York: Mentor, 1985), 49.

20. Loevy, *The Flawed Path to the Presidency 1992*, 199.

21. The approval measure has become standard. It reflects responses to the common question, "Do you approve or disapprove of the way Ronald Reagan is handling his job as president?" In contrast, Humphrey was trying to succeed a disheartened and discredited Johnson whose approval rating in September 1968 stood at 42 percent (with 51 percent disapproval). Eisenhower's ratings were strong in 1960, although they slipped during the year from 68 percent positive and 21 percent negative in March to 58 percent positive and 31 percent negative in mid-October. James A. Barnes, "Aging Well," *National Journal*, October 8, 1988, 2562.

22. Paul J. Quirk, "The Election," in *The Elections of 1988*, ed. Michael Nelson (Washington, D.C.: CQ Press, 1990), 76.

23. David Broder, "The American Political Scene Could Turn Upsidedown," *Wilmington News Journal*, January 29, 1989, J1.

24. In 1980, the Republicans handled the potential problem of an even older Reagan, who was almost seventy at the time of the fall campaign, in a very different way: he was depicted as an unusually vigorous man for his age. This image was helped considerably by Reagan's full head of hair, as opposed to Eisenhower's bald pate.

25. Marjorie Randon Hershey, "The Campaign and the Media," in *The Election of 1988: Reports and Interpretations*, ed. Gerald Pomper (Chatham, N.J.: Chatham House, 1989), 78.

26. Hershey, "The Campaign and the Media," 80–83; Quirk, "The Election," 75–76; Weko and Aldrich, "The Presidency and the Election Campaign," 273–275.

27. Martin P. Wattenberg, "From a Partisan to a Candidate-Centered Electorate," in *The New American Political System*, 2d ed., ed. Anthony King (Washington, D.C.: AEI Press, 1990).

28. Dick Kirschten, "The Gipper's Last Campaign ... A Mix of Wit and Harsh Rhetoric," *National Journal*, October 15, 1988, 2609.

29. A variant of this problem plagued Mondale in 1984. Although he was not the incumbent vice president, he did hold that office from 1977 to 1981 and was associated with the policies of the Carter administration, some of which he did not endorse (for example, placing an embargo on grain shipments to the Soviet Union).

30. One political scientist calls "position issues" those that "involve advocacy of governmental action from a set of alternatives," in contrast to "valence issues," which "merely involve linking of the parties with some condition that is positively or negatively valued by the electorate." Donald Stokes, "Special Models of Party Competition," in *Elections in the Political Order*, ed. Angus Campbell, Philip Converse, Warren Miller, and Donald Stokes (New York: Wiley, 1966), 170–171.

31. Marshall McLuhan, *Understanding Media: The Extensions of Man* (New York: McGraw-Hill, 1964), chap. 1.

32. Loevy, *The Flawed Path to the Presidency 1992*, 212.
33. A problem in holding presidential debates is a provision of the Federal Communications Act of 1934 requiring the networks to provide equal time to *all* candidates, including those of minor parties. In 1960, Congress temporarily suspended the provisions of the act to allow the Nixon-Kennedy debates. In 1976, 1980, and 1984, the debates were sponsored and paid for by the League of Women Voters. The networks supposedly covered them as "news events," a legal fiction that was exposed when the first Carter-Ford debate in 1976 was interrupted for twenty-eight minutes until an audio failure could be repaired.
34. This was especially true of people who watched the first Nixon-Kennedy debate on television. Those who heard that same debate on the radio, however, thought the two candidates came out about equally. Theodore White, *The Making of the President, 1960* (New York: Pocket Books, 1961), 348.
35. Albert Hunt suggests that Reagan convinced many viewers of the debate that he was sufficiently smart to go head-to-head with the president and not crumble. President Carter, however, did not meet the greater expectations the viewers had of his debate performance, namely, that he explain why things had not gone very well in the previous four years and how he would do better in a second term. Albert Hunt, "The Campaign and the Issues," in *The American Elections of 1980*, ed. Austin Ranney (Washington, D.C.: AEI Press, 1981), 170–171.
36. For press reports of these events see *Los Angeles Times*, October 4, 1988, 23; October 5, 1988, 14; October 6, 1988, 20; October 7, 1988, 19. See also *Washington Post*, October 4, 1988, 15, 18; and *Christian Science Monitor*, November 7, 1988, 14. See the content analysis of debate transcripts in Hershey, "The Campaign and the Media," 90.
37. Abramson, Aldrich, and Rohde, *Change and Continuity in the 1992 Elections*, 56–61.
38. Based on research completed by Dirk Smillie of The Freedom Forum Media Studies Center and reported by W. Lance Bennett, "The Cueless Public: Bill Clinton Meets the New American Voter in Campaign '92," in *The Clinton Presidency: Campaigning, Governing, and the Psychology of Leadership*, ed. Stanley A. Renshon (Boulder, Colo.: Westview Press, 1995), 106.
39. F. Christopher Arterton, "Campaign '92," 89–93.
40. Thomas Patterson, *The Mass Media Election: How Americans Choose their President* (New York: Praeger, 1980), chap. 13.
41. Michael Robinson and Margaret Sheehan, *Over the Wire and on TV: CBS and UPI in Campaign '80* (New York: Russell Sage Foundation, 1983), 166.
42. Thomas Patterson and Richard Davis, "The Media Campaign: Struggle for the Agenda," in *The Elections of 1984*, ed. Michael Nelson (Washington, D.C.: CQ Press, 1985), 116.
43. Thomas E. Patterson, "Television and Presidential Politics: A Proposal to Restructure Television Communication in Election Campaigns," in *Presidential Selection*, ed. Alexander Heard and Michael Nelson (Durham, N.C.: Duke University Press, 1987).
44. Over the years, endorsements have clearly favored Republican candidates, except in 1964, when the press favored Johnson over Goldwater. As a group, newspaper owners and editors, who decide on endorsements, tend to be conservative, possibly because much of their advertising revenue comes from large corporations. Political reporters, by contrast, are widely perceived to be

liberal. In 1988, the number of newspaper endorsements fell to the lowest point since *Editor and Publisher* began to track them in 1932. This was taken as an expression of dissatisfaction with the quality of the campaign conducted by the two major-party nominees.

45. Dan Nimmo, *The Political Persuaders: The Techniques of Modern Political Campaigns* (Englewood Cliffs, N.J.: Prentice-Hall, 1970), 117–118.
46. Patterson, "Television and Presidential Politics," 312.
47. Richard Berke, "Why Candidates Like Public's Questions," *New York Times* August 15, 1992, 7, as cited in Philip Meyer, "The Media Reformation: Giving the Agenda Back to the People," in *The Elections of 1992*, ed. Michael Nelson (Washington, D.C.: CQ Press, 1993), 100–101.
48. Meyer, "The Media Reformation," 90–91.
49. Loevy, *The Flawed Road to the Presidency 1992*, 196; Arterton, "Campaign '92," 85.
50. Jonathan Moore and Janet Fraser, *Campaign for President: The Managers Look at 1976* (Cambridge, Mass.: Ballinger, 1977), 133.
51. John Kessel, "Strategy for November," in *Choosing the President*, ed. James D. Barber (Englewood Cliffs, N.J.: Prentice-Hall, 1974), 179.
52. Theodore White, *The Making of the President, 1968* (New York: Bantam, 1969), 453–454.
53. Rhodes Cook, " '88 Vote: Stress Persuasion Over Registration," *Congressional Quarterly Weekly Report*, October 1, 1988, 2704.
54. Herbert E. Alexander, *Financing the 1980 Election* (Lexington, Mass.: D.C. Heath, 1983), 387.
55. The data for 1983–1984 and 1987–1988 may include minor expenditures made during the nomination stage, although the bulk of spending occurred during the general election. *Statistical Abstract of the United States*, 1990, Table 447.
56. An example of coordination between party expenditures and presidential campaigns was the Democrats' funneling of more than half the $15.8 million raised from August through October 1988 into California, Illinois, Texas, Pennsylvania, and Michigan—key targets of the Dukakis campaign. *National Journal*, December 17, 1988, 3219. For a discussion of coordination in the Illinois campaign during 1988, see *New York Times*, September 29, 1988, A1.
57. *National Journal*, October 8, 1988, 2516–2517.
58. Alexander and Corrado, *Financing the 1992 Election*, chap. 5, Table 5.1; The Federal Election Commission, *The Presidential Public Funding Program* (Washington, D.C: Federal Election Commission, 1993), 31; Arterton, "Campaign '92," 84, 105.
59. Alexander and Corrado, *Financing the 1992 Election*, chap. 5.
60. There are different ways to compute these figures, and we have relied heavily on the computations of Alexander and Corrado of the Citizens Research Foundation, acknowledged experts on these issues, who set July 1, 1992, as the dividing line between prenomination and general election campaigns for the party nominees. Perot faced no such distinction in his effort. Other analysts include larger totals of "soft money" spent by state party committees, not limiting it to the six month period. See, for example, the discussion by Arterton, "Campaign '92," 84.
61. Alexander and Corrado, *Financing the 1992 Election*, chap. 5; Abramson, Aldrich, and Rohde, *Change and Continuity in the 1992 Elections*, 56.

Selected Readings

Abramson, Paul R., John H. Aldrich, and David W. Rohde. *Change and Continuity in the 1980 Elections.* Washington, D.C.: CQ Press, 1982.

___. *Change and Continuity in the 1984 Elections.* Rev. ed. Washington, D.C.: CQ Press, 1987.

___. *Change and Continuity in the 1988 Elections.* Rev. ed. Washington, D.C.: CQ Press, 1990.

___. *Change and Continuity in the 1992 Elections.* Rev. ed. Washington, D.C.: CQ Press, 1994.

Chubb, John, and Paul Peterson. *The New Direction in American Politics.* Washington, D.C.: Brookings Institution, 1985.

Nelson, Michael, ed. *The Elections of 1984.* Washington, D.C.: CQ Press, 1985.

___. *The Elections of 1988.* Washington, D.C.: CQ Press, 1989.

___. *The Elections of 1992.* Washington, D.C.: CQ Press, 1993.

Patterson, Thomas E. *Out of Order.* New York: Vintage, 1993.

chapter four

Voting in
Presidential Elections

RIVAL CAMPAIGNS SPEND MILLIONS of dollars and untold hours pursuing two objectives: to motivate people to vote on election day and to win support for their candidates. A combination of factors other than campaign appeals will help determine who votes and how they will vote. The ultimate choice voters make among candidates depends on their long-term political predispositions, such as political party loyalties and social group affiliations, and their reactions to short-term forces, such as the particular candidates and issues involved in specific elections.

The first two sections of this chapter explore participation in presidential elections and the various factors that shape the voters' choice of candidates. The final section shifts to other important aspects of presidential elections—their effects on the political party system and on policy making in the United States.

Participation in Presidential Elections

True to the Constitution, members of the electoral college make the official selection of president. Nonetheless, important developments in U.S. politics have altered substantially the selection process. With the formation of rival political parties in the 1790s, electors began to vote the presidential preferences of the electorate instead of exercising independent judgment. Moreover, state legislatures that were granted power by the Constitution to determine how the electors should be chosen soon began to vest that right in the general electorate. In the process, the U.S. presidential election system became less "elitist" and more "democratic."

This development was highly significant, but it left an important question unanswered. Who should be entitled to vote for the presidential electors? The Constitution leaves that decision to the individual states, so that it is possible for some states to allow particular groups to vote for president while other states prevent them from doing so. As a consequence, the federal government has sometimes found it necessary to take action in order to force all states to allow certain groups of people to participate in the selection of the chief executive.

An early state barrier to participation in presidential elections was the requirement that voters own *property*. Many legislatures took the position that only property owners would have enough of a stake in society to interest themselves in its political affairs. Some legislators also were concerned that the poor would sell their votes to unscrupulous politicians or, worse, use their votes to choose candidates who would proceed to redistribute the wealth of property owners. However, as more and more people acquired property and redistribution of wealth did not happen, state legislatures began to drop the property qualification for voting in presidential and other elections. By the early 1840s, such qualifications had generally disappeared at the state level. Thus, the first major expansion of the presidential electorate took place without federal intervention—in contrast to later battles over the composition of the presidential electorate.

The most bitter franchise struggle involved the right of African Americans to vote in elections, including presidential contests. At the end of the Civil War, as part of a concerted program to bring liberated slaves into the mainstream of American life, the Fifteenth Amendment was passed. It stated that "the right of the citizens of the United States to vote shall not be denied or abridged by the United States or by any state, on account of race, color, or previous condition of servitude." For a short time, African Americans did participate in presidential and other elections, but when federal troops withdrew from the South in the 1870s, a systematic disenfranchisement of African Americans began. It took many forms, including physical violence; economic coercion; and legal devices, such as excluding African Americans from participating in primaries of the dominant Democratic party, assessing poll taxes (which also disenfranchised many poor White citizens), and selectively administering literacy tests.

The federal government has taken action on many occasions to force states to extend the right to vote to African Americans. The earliest pressure came from the federal courts. In a 1915 decision, *Guinn v. United States*,[1] the Supreme Court invalidated the "grandfather" clause of the

Oklahoma constitution, which exempted persons from a literacy test if their ancestors were entitled to vote in 1866; the Court viewed this as a deliberate (and not too subtle) attempt to avoid the Fifteenth Amendment's prohibition against denying certain citizens the right to vote. Ultimately, the Court in 1944 also outlawed "White" primaries, ruling in *Smith v. Allwright* [2] that a primary was a *public* function and not the business of a private organization—the Democratic party—as had been held in 1935 in *Grovey v. Townsend*.[3] Hence, "White" primaries were forbidden under the Fifteenth Amendment.

The two other branches of the national government lagged behind the courts in helping African Americans to win the right to vote. Democratic presidents Franklin D. Roosevelt and Harry S. Truman both favored enfranchisement for African Americans, but they were unsuccessful in persuading Congress, dominated by southern committee chairs who could readily block legislation, to move against poll taxes or even to enact an anti-lynching law. Not until 1957, during the Republican administration of Dwight D. Eisenhower, did Congress finally pass legislation giving the attorney general of the United States the right to seek judicial relief against persons violating the right of individuals to vote. Many southern election officials easily circumvented the law; they continued to harass African Americans who tried to vote and destroyed records to cover up their actions. In 1960, Congress passed additional legislation that strengthened the enforcement of voting rights by authorizing courts to appoint voting referees to register persons deprived of the right to vote because of race or color and by making it a crime to destroy election records.

Building on these modest beginnings, Congress in the 1960s initiated the Twenty-Fourth Amendment outlawing the use of the poll tax in presidential and congressional elections; the states ratified the amendment in early 1964.[4] The following year, Congress enacted the Voting Rights Act of 1965, which suspended literacy tests and authorized appointing federal examiners to supervise electoral procedures in areas in which such tests were in use and in which less than one-half the voting-age population was registered to vote or had voted in 1964. The act subsequently was amended in 1970 to cover areas in which a similar situation existed in November 1968. In 1975, the act was extended for seven years, and its provisions were expanded to cover the voting rights of other minorities, including Hispanics, American Indians, Asian-Americans, and Alaskan Natives. In 1982, after some initial difficulties,[5] the act was extended for twenty-five years with provisions requiring certain areas of the country to provide bilingual election materials until 1992.

The national government also has taken action to expand the electorate to include two other major groups: women and young people. Even though some states had acted on their own to enfranchise both groups, Congress ultimately decided to require all states to do so. In 1920, the states ratified the Nineteenth Amendment, which forbade the federal government and the states from denying a U.S. citizen the right to vote "on account of sex." Young people won a major victory in the early 1970s when Congress first passed a law granting eighteen-year-olds the right to vote in national, state, and local elections. After the Supreme Court ruled that a national law could affect voting only in national elections, the Twenty-Sixth Amendment was enacted to extend the right to state and local elections.

Congress has initiated other actions to expand the presidential electorate. The Twenty-Third Amendment, ratified in 1961, grants residents of the District of Columbia the right to vote in presidential elections, a privilege they had been denied since the capital was located there in 1800. The 1970 act that lowered the voting age to eighteen also provides that people may vote in presidential elections if they have lived at their current residence for at least thirty days.

Thus, the number of people eligible to vote in presidential elections has increased greatly over the years. The right to vote and the actual exercise of that right are, however, two separate matters.

General Trends in Voter Turnout

Recent presidential elections have highlighted a central irony: as more and more citizens have acquired the right to vote, a smaller and smaller proportion of them have exercised that right. As Table 4-1 indicates, the estimated number of people of voting age has more than doubled since Franklin Roosevelt was first elected to office in 1932. After reaching a peak in 1960, however, the percentage of eligible voters who actually went to the polls declined in the next seven presidential elections, except for a modest increase in 1984. In 1988, only 50.1 percent of eligible voters went to the polls, the second lowest turnout recorded for a presidential election in the twentieth century. The most pronounced drop—more than 5 percent—occurred between the 1968 and 1972 elections after eighteen-year-olds were granted the vote. In 1992, however, observers were heartened when a record 104.4 million voters participated in the presidential election, 55.2 percent of the eligible voting age population.

The long-term decline in voter participation ran counter to theories of why people fail to vote. Restrictive laws, particularly those pertaining to registration and voting, frequently are said to prevent citizens from going to the polls. Yet many states had eased such restrictions in recent years, and the Congress facilitated voting in presidential elections for new resi-

TABLE 4-1   Participation of General Public in Presidential Elections, 1932–1992

Year	Estimated population of voting age (in millions)	Number of votes cast (in millions)	Number of votes as percentage of population of voting age
1932	75.8	39.7	52.4
1936	80.2	45.6	56.0
1940	84.7	49.9	58.9
1944	85.7	48.0	56.0
1948	95.6	48.8	51.1
1952	99.9	61.6	61.6
1956	104.5	62.0	59.3
1960	109.7	68.8	62.8
1964	114.1	70.6	61.9
1968	120.3	73.2	60.9
1972[a]	140.8	77.6	55.1
1976[a]	152.3	81.6	53.6
1980[a]	164.6	86.5	52.6
1984[a]	174.5	92.7	53.1
1988[a]	182.8	91.6	50.1
1992[a]	189.0	104.4	55.2

SOURCE: U.S. Bureau of the Census, *Current Population Reports,* Series P-25, No. 1085 (Washington, D.C.: U.S. Government Printing Office, 1994).

[a] Elections in which persons eighteen to twenty years old were eligible to vote in all states.

dents, so that generally it was easier for a person to register and to vote for president in 1992 than it was in 1960. A person's lack of education also is often cited as a reason for not voting; however, the level of education of U.S. citizens consistently rose during the period that participation declined. Lack of political information is yet another frequently cited explanation; however, because of increased use of the mass media, and particularly because of televised presidential debates, more Americans than ever have been made aware of the candidates and their views on public issues (more than 100 million tuned in to the 1980 debate). Finally, close political races are supposed to stimulate people to get out and vote because they think their ballot might make a difference in the outcome. Pollsters forecast that the 1964 and 1972 elections would be landslides and that the 1968, 1976, and 1980 elections would be close contests, but a smaller percentage of people voted in 1968 than in 1964, and participation also declined in 1976 and 1980 despite close contests. In 1984 there was a slight increase (one-half of one percentage point) in participation even though the outcome was hardly in doubt, while participation declined in 1988, a closer contest.

It is possible to attribute some of the decline in voter turnout to the extension of the right to vote to eighteen-year-olds, which first took effect in the 1972 presidential election. Analyses of participation in that election by age group showed that eighteen- to twenty-year-olds did not vote as much (proportionately to their number) as did people twenty-one and older. (See Table 4-2.) Therefore, some of the overall 5 percent decline in voter turnout between 1968 and 1972 was caused by the addition of people to the potential electorate who were less inclined to vote. This factor, however, does not help to explain the decline in participation between 1964 and 1968 and again in 1976, 1980, and 1988. Moreover, analyses of the 1972 election indicate that people twenty-one and older did not participate as much (proportionately) as they did in 1968.

It is difficult to determine why voting has declined in presidential elections in recent years. Paul Abramson, John Aldrich, and David Rohde, who analyzed this decline in *reported* turnout in all presidential elections from 1952 through 1980, link it to two major factors.[6] The first is an erosion in the strength of the political party identification of many Americans (the next section contains a discussion of that matter), which may result in less psychological involvement in politics. The second factor is a decline in the sense of political efficacy: over the years, fewer and fewer people have thought that public officials cared about their opinions, and many have felt that as citizens they had little to say about how the government operated. These attitudes, in turn, relate to public disaffection with the government's policies on issues such as race relations, Vietnam, and the Watergate scandals, as well as a general feeling that government has failed to solve the country's economic and social problems.

No single factor explains the increased participation rates in 1992. Neither the decline in party identification nor in the perception of political efficacy changed significantly in 1992. Abramson, Aldrich, and Rohde point to the evidence that the presence of Perot in the 1992 election contributed to the increased turnout; 14 percent of Perot voters indicated in exit polls that they would not have voted if the Texan had not been on the ballot. That would translate into just fewer than 3 million voters and account for one-third of the increased turnout.[7] Neither major party made a concerted effort to register new voters, although there were some nonpartisan turnout efforts, including MTV's "Rock the Vote" feature aimed at youth voters, the group with the lowest turnout rates. Among party identifiers, Democratic turnout increased more than Republican, possibly evidence of how Clinton's candidacy and the prospect of success brought Democrats out to the polls. Moreover, as the election came to a close, national polls indicated that Clinton's lead was narrowing and that the outcome was in doubt, although state-by-state polls used by the campaigns offered a very different picture.

TABLE 4-2   Participation of Various Groups in Presidential Elections, 1972–1992 (in percent)

Group characteristic	Year					
	1972	1976	1980	1984	1988	1992
Male	64.1	59.6	59.1	59.0	56.4	60.2
Female	62.0	58.8	59.4	60.8	58.3	62.3
White	64.5	60.9	60.9	61.4	59.1	63.6
African American	52.1	48.7	50.5	55.8	51.5	54.0
Age						
18–20 years old	48.3	38.0	35.7	36.7	33.2	38.5
21–24 years old	50.7	45.6	43.1	43.5	38.3	45.7
25–43 years old	59.7	55.4	54.6	54.5	48.0	53.2
35–44 years old	66.3	63.3	64.4	63.5	61.3	63.6
45–64 years old	70.8	68.7	69.3	69.8	67.9	70.0
65 and over	63.5	62.2	65.1	67.7	68.8	70.1
Residence						
Northeast	n/a	59.5	58.5	59.7	57.4	61.2
Midwest	n/a	65.1	65.8	65.7	62.9	67.2
South	55.4	54.9	55.6	56.8	54.5	59.0
West	n/a	57.5	57.2	58.5	55.6	58.5
School year completed						
Grade 8 or lower	47.4	44.1	42.6	42.9	36.7	35.1
Grade 9 to 11	52.0	47.2	45.6	44.4	41.3	41.2
Grade 12	65.4	59.4	58.9	58.7	54.7	57.5
College						
1–3 years	74.9	68.1	67.2	67.5	64.5	68.7
4 years or more	83.6	79.8	79.9	79.1	77.6	81.0

SOURCE: *Statistical Abstract of the United States,* 1994, Table 448 (Washington, D.C.: U.S. Government Printing Office, 1994).

NOTE: Data are based on estimated population of voting age. The percentages are based on those *reporting* that they voted and are higher than those who actually voted. N/a = Not available.

Thus, we cannot be certain what caused the reversal. It is important to note, however, that the 1992 turnout was still well below that for 1960 and that neither of the long-term causes noted previously has been reversed.

Group Differences in Voter Turnout

As shown in Table 4-2, participation in presidential elections varies among groups. African Americans and young people—two groups who historically participate the least—were formerly denied the franchise. One possible reason for this pattern is that some of the "newly" enfranchised may still be affected by the public attitudes that originally denied them the right to vote. Non-Whites, especially older people who grew up in the South where formerly they could not vote, may feel that they are not able to make good choices. Some eighteen- to twenty-year-olds may also feel that they are too immature to exercise the right to vote intelligently. In all probability, however, the voting patterns of these two groups can be attributed to other factors. As a group, African Americans have completed fewer years of education, which, as Table 4-2 shows, is linked to low voting participation. Many eighteen- to twenty-year-olds have not yet settled down and become involved in community affairs, another factor related to voter turnout. It is significant to note that women, another group that traditionally had a comparatively low rate of participation, now vote more than men, a development probably linked to the increased level of education now achieved by women. (In recent years, women have begun to outnumber men among college students.)

Group differences in voter turnout are rooted in psychological feelings that affect all kinds of political participation, including voting. Well-educated people are more likely to be aware of political developments and their significance than poorly educated people. In addition, well-educated people tend to feel politically efficacious. They have a sense of confidence about the value of their opinions and believe that people in public office will listen to them; therefore, they think that what they do has an important effect on the political process. Poorly educated persons, however, are likely to feel that political officials do not care about them or their opinions. General attitudes about other people also affect voting behavior; those who trust people are more likely to cast their ballots than those whose cynicism and hostility toward others make them feel alienated in general.

The influence of a group is frequently important. Thus, if individuals belong to a business organization or labor union whose members talk a lot about political affairs, they may develop their own interests in such matters. If so, their political interests probably will lead them to make the effort to vote. Moreover, even if people are not interested in politics, they may feel that it is their duty as citizens to vote. This attitude is much more likely to exist in the upper and middle classes than in the lower classes.

The reasons that prompt some people to vote and lead others to remain at home on election day are, indeed, varied; yet the factors that shape preferences between competing groups of presidential candidates are even more complex.

Voting Preferences in Presidential Elections

Long-term political dispositions that voters begin to acquire early in life, such as party affiliation and social-group loyalties, affect how they vote in presidential elections. So do short-term forces, such as the particular candidates and issues involved in specific elections. Over the years, however, these separate factors have exerted varying degrees of influence in different elections.

Party Affiliation

Analyses of presidential elections in the 1950s by a group of researchers at the University of Michigan indicated that the single most important determinant of voting at that time was the party affiliation of the voter.[8] This general psychological attachment, shaped by family and social groups, tended to intensify with age. For the average person looking for guidance on how to vote amid the complexities of personalities, issues, and events of the 1950s, the party label of the candidates was the most important reference point. In this era—which voting analyst Philip Converse refers to as the "Steady State" period[9]—partisanship was also fairly constant. When asked, about 45 percent of Americans in 1952 and 1956 said they thought of themselves as Democrats, and about 28 percent said they thought of themselves as Republicans, for a combined total of nearly three-fourths of the adult electorate. When asked to classify themselves further as "strong" or "weak" partisans, both Republicans and Democrats tended to divide equally between those two categories. Independents in 1952 and 1956 averaged about 23 percent of the electorate.

In the mid- to late-1960s, however, partisan affiliation in the United States began to change. (See Table 4-3.) In 1964, party affiliation among the voters rose about 5 percent for the Democrats but fell about 3 percent for the Republicans; the Independents' share of the electorate also declined slightly. Beginning with the 1968 election, the number of Independents began to increase, primarily at the expense of the Democrats, until they constituted one-third of the electorate in 1972. Even those voters who stayed with the Democrats were increasingly more inclined to say they were weak rather than strong party members. Moreover, since 1968, more people have identified themselves as Independents than as Republicans. This trend progressed one step further in 1988, when some polls found that Independents outnumbered Democrats for the first time, a pattern that extended into 1992 when 38 percent of the electorate declared themselves to be Independents with 36 percent declaring themselves Democrats and 25 percent Republicans.

TABLE 4-3   Party Identification, 1952–1992 (in percent)

Party	1952	1956	1960	1964	1968	1972	1976	1980	1984	1988	1992
Strong Democrat	22	21	20	27	20	15	15	18	17	18	18
Weak Democrat	25	23	25	25	25	26	25	23	20	18	18
Total	47	44	45	52	45	41	40	41	37	36	36
Strong Republican	14	14	16	11	10	10	9	9	10	14	11
Weak Republican	13	15	14	14	15	13	14	14	15	14	14
Total	27	29	30	25	25	23	23	23	25	28	25
Independent	22	24	23	23	30	35	37	34	34	36	38

SOURCE: *Statistical Abstract of the United States,* 1994, Table 446 (Washington, D.C.: U.S. Government Printing Office, 1994).

Another indication of the declining importance of political party identification in presidential elections is the increase in recent years in the number of "switchers," that is, people who vote for one party's candidate in one presidential election and for another party's candidate in the following election. Analyses of presidential voting from 1940 to 1960 show that approximately one-eighth to one-fifth of the electorate switched from one election to the next.[10] From 1968 to 1980, the proportion ranged from one-fifth to one-third.[11] A similar phenomenon has occurred in split-ticket voting, that is, voting for candidates of more than one party in the same election. In 1952, some 13 percent of the Americans who voted cast a split ticket in presidential-House races; by 1972, 30 percent did. The number of split-ticket voters declined to 26 percent in 1976, rose to 35 percent in 1980, and declined to 25 percent in 1984. It remained at that point in 1988 and declined slightly to 22 percent in 1992.[12] Still more significant, even voters who identify with one of the major parties have increasingly displayed partisan disloyalty by switching and ticket-splitting.

Thus, independence from political parties, whether measured by voters' expressed attitudes toward the parties themselves or by reports of their actual behavior in the voting booth, has increased in recent years in the United States. This rise in Independents is not, however, spread evenly across the voting population.[13] It has occurred primarily among young people, particularly those who entered the electorate in 1964 or later. New voters who came of age since that time are much more likely to be political Independents than are voters of earlier political generations. For example, in 1992, among voters under 34 years of age, 46 percent were self-declared Independents, while among voters 66 to 81 years old, only 28 percent were Independents.

Independents in the United States not only have grown dramatically in numbers but also have changed in character. In the 1950s, Independents tended to be less knowledgeable about political issues and candidates and to participate less in the political process than partisans.[14] Since the early 1960s, however, they have shown themselves to be just as knowledgeable about political matters as Democrats and Republicans.[15] Furthermore, although not as likely to vote as are party identifiers, Independents do participate at least as much as partisans in other political activities, such as writing to political officials and voting on referendums. Thus, nonpartisanship, rather than general political disinterest, characterizes many of the younger Independents, particularly those with a college education. A new type of Independent seems to have joined the ranks of nonpartisans prevalent in the 1950s.

Observers of voting behavior have suggested several possible reasons for the decline in partisanship among U.S. voters. One is a decrease in the transfer of partisanship from one generation to the next; beginning in the late 1960s, younger groups became less likely than earlier generations to retain their family partisan affiliation.[16] Two political "shock" periods, as Converse calls them, also weakened partisan loyalties.[17] The first, which began in 1965 and stemmed from the Vietnam War and racial unrest, affected voters of all ages, Democrats somewhat more than Republicans. The second, which began in 1972, and was precipitated by Watergate and the disclosure that led to Vice President Spiro Agnew's resignation, had a distinct impact on older Republicans.

As shown in Table 4-3, however, the decline in partisanship reached its peak between 1972 and 1976. The proportion of Independents has not changed significantly in the four presidential elections since then. Since 1980, modest Republican gains of roughly 5 to 10 percent have been offset by Democratic losses of the same size. Considered in light of their enormous success in winning presidential elections, Republican gains have been limited, although they may still have had an impact on election results. Although the trend away from party affiliation appears to have stopped, the parties have been unable to reestablish firm loyalties with the public. Overall, the picture has remained remarkably stable since 1972, with just less than two-thirds of the citizenry expressing a party identification.

Social Groups and Social Class

Analysts of the presidential elections of 1940 and 1948 found that a fairly close association existed between voters' social group membership and social status and their support for one of the two major parties.[18] Democrats received most of their support from southerners, African Americans, Catholics, and people with limited education, lower incomes, and a working-class background. Republican candidates were supported by northerners, Whites, Protestants, and people with more education, higher incomes, and a professional or business background.

Table 4-4 shows how various groups voted in presidential elections from 1952 through 1992. Comparisons need to take into account Perot's unusually strong showing as a third candidate. The support of many groups for their traditional party's candidates declined over the forty-year period. Especially noticeable for the Republicans was their loss of votes from white-collar workers through 1984 (comparable figures are unavailable for 1988 and 1992) and the initial decline followed by resurgent support among Protestants. The most significant drop for the Democrats came in the southern vote in the 1968 and 1972 elections. The party regained this vote in 1976, when Jimmy Carter of Georgia headed the ticket, but lost it again in 1980, 1984, 1988, and 1992, even though there were two southerners on the ticket. Loss of support has been concentrated among southern Whites; by 1988, only one in three White votes in the South went to Dukakis and Clinton did only marginally better with 38 percent of the southern White vote in 1992.[19] The only group that significantly increased its support for its traditional party candidate over the thirty-six-year period was non-Whites, who have been more firmly in the Democratic camp since 1964 than they were in 1952 with the exception of the three-way race in 1992.[20]

Table 4-4 also shows that the circumstances of particular elections can greatly alter group voting tendencies. In 1964, when the very conservative Barry Goldwater was the Republican standard-bearer, all groups, including those that typically support the GOP, voted predominantly for the Democratic candidate, Lyndon Johnson. In 1972, when the very liberal George McGovern ran on the Democratic ticket, all of the groups that usually sympathize with that party, except for non-Whites, voted for the Republican candidate, Richard Nixon. In 1984, when Walter Mondale, a traditional, New Deal Democrat, ran against the highly popular Republican president, Ronald Reagan, the Democrats won overwhelming support only from non-Whites and eked out a narrow victory among voters with a grade school education and members of labor unions, traditional elements of the New Deal coalition.

Michael Dukakis did better than Mondale among several traditionally Democratic groups. Dukakis won increased support from labor, Catholics, and the less educated, but lost ground among non-Whites, although the Democratic margin in this last group remained enormous. Dukakis even

TABLE 4-4　Group Voting Patterns in Presidential Elections, 1952–1992 (in percent)

Group	1952		1956		1960		1964	
	Stevenson	Eisenhower	Stevenson	Eisenhower	Kennedy	Nixon	Johnson	Goldwater
Sex								
male	47	53	45	55	52	48	60	40
female	42	58	39	61	49	51	62	38
Race								
White	43	57	41	59	49	51	59	41
non-White	79	21	61	39	68	32	94	6
Education								
college	34	66	31	69	39	61	52	48
high school	45	55	42	58	52	48	62	38
grade school	52	48	50	50	55	45	66	34
Occupation								
professional,								
business	36	64	32	68	42	58	54	46
white collar	40	60	37	63	48	52	57	43
manual	55	45	50	50	60	40	71	29
Age								
under 30	51	49	43	57	54	45	64	36
30–49	47	53	45	55	54	46	63	37
50 and								
older	39	61	39	61	46	54	59	41
Religion								
Protestant	37	63	37	63	38	62	55	45
Catholic	56	44	51	49	78	22	76	24
Region								
East	45	55	40	60	53	47	68	32
Midwest	42	58	41	59	48	52	61	39
South	51	49	49	51	51	49	52	48
West	42	58	43	57	49	51	60	40
Members of								
labor union								
families	61	39	57	43	65	35	73	27
National	44.6	55.4	42.2	57.8	50.1	49.9	61.3	38.7

SOURCE: Excerpted from CNN/*USA Today*/Gallup Poll, October 30–November 2, 1992.
NOTE: N/a = not available.

TABLE 4-4   (continued)

	1968			1972		1976			1980			1984		1988		1992	
Humphrey	Nixon	Wallace	McGovern	Nixon	Carter	Ford	Carter	Reagan	Anderson	Mondale	Reagan	Dukakis	Bush	Clinton	Bush	Perot	
41	43	16	37	63	53	45	38	53	7	36	64	44	56	41	37	22
45	43	12	38	62	48	51	44	49	6	45	55	48	52	46	38	16
38	47	15	32	68	46	52	36	56	7	34	66	41	59	39	41	20
85	12	3	87	13	85	15	86	10	2	87	13	82	18	77	11	12
37	54	9	37	63	42	55	35	53	10	39	61	42	58	43	40	17
42	43	15	34	66	54	46	43	51	5	43	57	46	54	40	38	22
52	33	15	49	51	58	41	54	42	3	51	49	55	45	56	28	16
34	56	10	31	69	42	56	33	55	10	34	66	n/a	n/a	n/a	n/a	n/a
41	47	12	36	64	50	48	40	51	9	47	53	n/a	n/a	n/a	n/a	n/a
50	35	15	43	57	58	41	48	46	5	46	54	n/a	n/a	n/a	n/a	n/a
47	38	15	48	52	53	45	47	41	11	40	60	37	63	40	37	23
44	41	15	33	67	48	49	38	52	8	40	60	45	55	42	37	21
41	47	12	36	64	52	48	41	54	4	41	59	49	51	46	39	15
35	49	16	30	70	46	53	39	54	6	39	61	42	58	41	41	18
59	33	8	48	52	57	42	46	47	6	39	61	51	49	47	35	18
50	43	7	42	58	51	47	43	47	9	46	54	51	49	47	35	18
44	47	9	40	60	48	50	41	51	7	42	58	47	53	44	34	22
31	36	33	29	71	54	45	44	52	3	37	63	40	60	38	45	17
44	49	7	41	59	46	51	35	54	9	40	60	46	54	45	35	20
56	29	15	46	54	63	36	50	43	5	52	48	63	37	n/a	n/a	n/a
43.0	43.4	13.6	38	62	50	48	41	51	7	41	59	46	54	n/a	n/a	n/a

won a majority of votes in one region—the East—something that neither Carter nor Mondale had been able to do in the two previous elections. Despite these improvements among major elements of the Democratic coalition, Dukakis lost because the Democrats' base had shrunk appreciably, because there were higher rates of desertion among its identifiers, and because nonvoting was especially prevalent among African Americans and the poor, two of the party's major constituencies. One cannot conclude, however, that a higher turnout would have produced a Democratic victory. One study analyzed the partisan and policy preferences of nonvoters for 1988 and concluded "there is no reasonable scenario under which increased turnout would have altered the outcome of the presidential election." Democrats, the study concludes, suffer from low support more than low turnout.[21]

Bill Clinton received overwhelming support from members of only two groups that were part of the New Deal coalition: African Americans and Jewish voters. The final Gallup poll revealed 77 percent support among non-Whites and, according to exit polls conducted by Voter Research and Surveys (VRS), 82 percent of African American voters supported Clinton. As a result of the strong support of African Americans, they constituted about one-fifth of Clinton's total vote, even though they were only 8 percent of the total electorate.[22] The exit polls also provide separate data on Jewish and Hispanic voters: 78 percent of Jews who comprised 4 percent of the electorate supported Clinton; Hispanics comprised 3 percent of the electorate and supported the Democrat with 62 percent of their vote, though they are not part of the New Deal Coalition. Two traditional parts of that coalition were supportive but not in overwhelming numbers: members of union households, a figure not available from Gallup, provided Clinton with 55 percent support, and he led Bush among Catholics 47 to 35 in the Gallup poll and more narrowly by 44 percent to 36 percent in the VRS exit polls. Geographically, Clinton ran strongest in the East (12 percent over Bush), and the West (10 percent margin); results for the Middle West differ between Gallup and the exit polls, with the latter placing Clinton's margin at only 5 percent; both polls agree that Clinton lost to Bush in the South, though the Gallup margin of 7 percent was considerably greater than that found in the exit polls (43 percent to 42 percent).[23] Thus, Clinton's support exceeded Bush's in several components of the New Deal coalition even if the levels of support were not sufficient to consider the coalition "reassembled."[24]

Party identification and group affiliation have not meant as much in recent presidential voting as they once did, but their effects may not have disappeared completely. With a large part of the electorate having lost their partisan *anchor,* other forces, such as candidates, issues, events, and presidential performance have gained importance in the political world of the American voter.

Recent Trends in Race and Gender

Since 1964, African American voters have become a mainstay of the Democrats' presidential electorate. African American voters have consistently supported the Democratic presidential candidate in overwhelming numbers. In 1988, African American voters bucked the trend among other traditionally Democratic groups and gave Dukakis less support than Mondale received in 1984. African American support for Dukakis was estimated at 86 percent in the CBS News/*New York Times* exit poll and 90 percent in the National Election Study (NES) survey. Support for Clinton in 1992 may also have declined; the VRS exit poll placed it at 82 percent but the NES survey found 92 percent support for Clinton, a very slight rise over 1988. Abramson, Aldrich, and Rohde found that African Americans gave both Dukakis and Clinton a large majority across the board—that is, regardless of differences in social class, income, or other politically significant social categories.[25] Approximately 12 percent of African American voters supported Bush in 1988 and 11 percent in 1992, an increase over Reagan's support in 1984 but only slightly more than the level of African American support received by every Republican presidential candidate since Goldwater in 1964. Turnout among both African Americans and Whites dropped in 1988, but it decreased more among African Americans—down 11 percentage points from 1984. Some African Americans reportedly stayed away from the polls because Jesse Jackson and his supporters felt slighted at the Democratic convention and because Jackson was not included on the Democratic ticket. African American turnout increased a modest 2.5 percent in 1992 compared to a 4.5 percent increase among White citizens, a difference possibly related to the absence of an African American candidate in the primary contest for the first time since 1984. Overall, it is estimated that there was at least a 10-percent difference in turnout between African American and White voters in 1992, and the gap may have been even greater.[26]

During the period following World War II, the Democratic party actively pursued civil rights reform despite considerable opposition from the party's southern wing. The consequences of this support were substantial: regional challenges were mounted to the national ticket in 1948 and 1968, and southern White citizens have converted to Republican allegiance in massive numbers, first in presidential elections and more recently in congressional elections. The Republican party has recently stepped up its efforts to win African American support, especially as the party has continued to make inroads with other groups that traditionally have supported the Democratic party. In 1977, the Republican National Committee (RNC), under the direction of Bill Brock, attempted to expand the party's base by initiating an outreach program aimed at African Americans. The firm of Wright-McNeill and Associates was awarded an initial $257,300 contract and, subsequently, more than $1 million over the following three years to run the committee's Black Community Involvement Division.[27] But, even in the 1980 and 1984 Reagan victories, African American support for the Democratic party candidate remained the strongest of all of the traditional Democratic voting groups. President Bush and the RNC sought to gain support through the appointment of African Americans to jobs in the administration and in the party apparatus. As Pearl T. Robinson suggests, the success of the Republican party in securing the support of African American voters will depend on whether conservative Republican ideology can accommodate the economic interests of the African American middle class and can offer support for civil rights.[28] Otherwise, the weak performance of the GOP among African Americans since 1964 is likely to continue.

In the past four presidential elections, gender has become an important group difference. During the 1980s, men were more likely to vote Republican than were women, a phenomenon labeled *the gender gap*. This gap was prominent in the 1992 election as well, with Clinton clearly benefitting. One explanation offered for the differences in voting behavior between women and men in 1980 was Reagan's perceived "macho" stand on many issues. Throughout Reagan's term in office, men consistently reported a higher presidential approval rating than women. Although he initially led Bush among women in 1988, Dukakis lost votes to both genders, though by only a single percentage point among women. In 1992, women comprised 54 percent of the electorate, a very significant voting bloc. Immediately after the Democratic convention, Clinton held a huge lead over Bush among women (58–33 percent), an advantage similar to that of Dukakis at the same time in 1988 (58–34). Unlike Dukakis, however, Clinton held on to the advantage among women, securing 46 percent support, and also won a 41 percent plurality among men. (Bush received 37 percent of women's votes and Perot 17 percent. Among men, Bush received 38 percent and Perot 21.)[29] Female college graduates made up 20 percent of the electorate, and 49 percent supported Clinton while he received only 40 percent support among male college graduates. In a similar way, among voters without a high school diploma, Clinton received 58 percent of the women's vote and 49 percent of the men's.[30] Clinton's appeal to women was not without reservations. On the one hand, election-year polls showed that charges of marital infidelity were important to women, especially the college-educated, but on the other hand, his clear pro-choice position on abortion was probably even more important for this group.[31] Michael Carpini and Ester Fuchs also noted that attitudes toward violence, defense spending, social welfare programs, health care, and the environment—on which Democrats' positions were closer to most women's positions—may have contributed to women's voting decisions. In 1984, the difference between male and female support for Reagan was 9 percent, a gap that narrowed to only 4 percent in 1988 and 5 percent in 1992.

Another potentially important difference may emerge in the next decade. Abramson, Aldrich, and Rohde's analysis of the 1988 NES survey and the CBS News/*New York Times* exit poll found clear behavioral differences between married and single women in 1984 and 1988.[32] Married women were more likely to vote for Bush in 1988 than were single women. In the same way, married men were more likely to vote for Bush. Again in 1992, there was 69 percent support for Clinton among women who had never married versus 46 percent among those who were married. The gap was narrower among men who had never married compared to those who were or had been married (53 percent for Clinton versus 37 percent).[33] These findings suggest that marital status may well become a factor in presidential elections in the 1990s—a *marriage gap*.

Candidates

The precise influence of candidates on the outcome of elections is difficult to determine. It is easier for observers to focus on the specific qualities of a particular candidate, such as Eisenhower's personal warmth, John Kennedy's youth and Catholicism, and Johnson's expansive style, than it is to compare candidates systematically over a series of elections.[34]

Recognizing these limitations, scholars nonetheless have made overall comparisons of voters' reactions to candidates from 1952 through 1992. Each presidential election year, the University of Michigan Center for Political Studies asked people whether there was anything about the major candidates that would make them want to vote for or against that person. The total number of favorable and unfavorable comments were tabulated for each candidate; the more numerous the favorable comments about a candidate, the more positive the score. The overall scores, positive and negative, of the Republican and Democratic party candidates can be compared with one another to determine the relative appeal of the nominees in each election year. (See Figure 4-1.)

Three significant findings are revealed in Figure 4-1. First, voters' attitudes toward the candidates are highly variable. The differences in candi-

FIGURE 4-1   Appeal of Presidential Candidates, 1952–1992

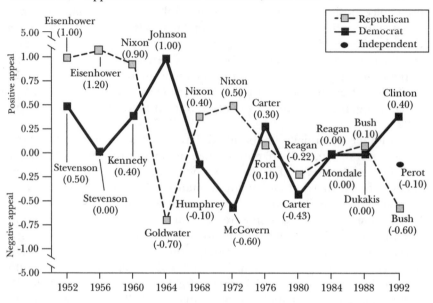

SOURCES: *American National Election Studies Data Sourcebook, 1952–1986* (Cambridge: Harvard University Press, 1987), Table 2.42; 1988 and 1992 data provided by the Center for Political Studies, University of Michigan.

NOTE: 5.00 and –5.00 are the greatest possible positive and negative scores because 5 is the maximum number of comments tabulated over the election series. The numbers in the figure are the candidates' composite scores.

date appeal were much less pronounced in 1952, 1960, 1968, and in the past four elections than they were in 1956, 1964, and 1972. Second, except for elections in 1964, 1976, and, surprisingly, 1984, voters evaluated the Republican candidate more favorably than the Democratic candidate. It is somewhat surprising to find that voters evaluated Nixon more highly than Kennedy in 1960, and far more surprising to find that Reagan did not hold a substantial advantage over Mondale in 1984. This leads to the third finding: candidate appeal is generally declining with even the winning candidates in three of the past four elections having less appeal for voters than was true in previous contests. Both Reagan and Carter received negative scores in 1980, the only time this has occurred since the surveys began; the appeal of Reagan and Mondale was neutral in 1984; Bush eked out a bare preference over Dukakis in 1988 but trailed both his challengers in 1992.

Herbert Asher has suggested that the advantage often enjoyed by Republican candidates may stem from several factors. As the minority party, Republican hopes for success have hinged on nominating attractive candidates who have also been advantaged by the nature of the times. Democratic candidates in 1952 and 1968 were forced to defend their party's record on the Korean and Vietnam wars while hostilities had been concluded or had virtually disappeared when the Republicans were the incumbent party in 1956 and 1972.[35] In 1980, the Democratic administration was beset with the Iranian crisis and high inflation caused by rising oil prices. More difficult to explain is the general decline in candidate appeal. One possible explanation is the decline in the importance of parties as a structure that mediates voters' relations with politics: with fewer citizens having a strong relationship to the parties, voters may now scrutinize candidates more directly and evaluate them more harshly.[36]

A 1988-election-day poll asked voters about positive and negative characteristics of the candidates that influenced their vote. Bush's experience and competence were widely cited—97 percent of the people who said that experience was important to them voted for the vice president. Voters who wanted a more caring president and one more likely to introduce change disproportionately supported Dukakis. On the negative side, voters citing Dukakis as too liberal went overwhelmingly for Bush, as did those who saw the Democrat as "too risky." Dukakis was supported disproportionately by voters who commented on candidates running a dirty campaign. Among voters who cited the vice-presidential candidates as a reason for their ticket choice, 86 percent supported Dukakis. Their support contributed an estimated 7 percent of Dukakis's vote total.[37] Overall, Bush seems to have derived greater benefit from candidate characteristics, but members of the Democratic ticket derived some advantages as well.

Issues, Events, and Presidential Performance

Michigan researchers in the 1950s suggested that issues influence a voter's choice only if three conditions are present.[38] First, the voter must be aware that an issue or a number of issues exist. Second, issues must be of some personal concern to the voter. Third, the voter must perceive that one party better represents his or her own thinking on the issues than the other party does.

When these three conditions were applied to U.S. voters in the 1952 and 1956 presidential elections, researchers found that these criteria existed for relatively few voters. About one-third of the respondents were not aware of *any* of the sixteen principal issues about which they were questioned. Even the two-thirds who were aware of one or more issues frequently were not personally concerned about them. Finally, a number of those who were aware and concerned about issues were not able to perceive differences between the two parties' positions on them. The conclusion of the analysis was that issues determined the choice of no more than one-third of the electorate. (The proportion who actually voted as they did because of the candidates' stances on issues could have been, and probably was, even less.)

Studies of political attitudes in the 1960s[39] and 1970s[40] revealed that issues had become more important to voters. In this period the number and types of issues of which voters were aware increased. Voters during the Eisenhower years had exhibited some interest in traditional domestic matters (welfare, labor-management relationships) and in a few foreign policy issues (the threat of communism, the atomic bomb); beginning with the 1964 election, however, voters' interests broadened to include concerns such as civil rights and Vietnam. Vietnam in particular remained a prominent consideration in the 1968 and 1972 contests and was joined by new matters such as crime, disorder, and juvenile delinquency (sometimes referred to collectively along with race problems as the "social issue").

The connection between voters' own attitudes on issues and their perceptions of where the parties stand on them has grown closer since the early 1960s. Gerald Pomper's analysis of voters' attitudes on issues from 1956 through 1972 shows that beginning with the 1964 presidential election, attitudes became more aligned with partisan identification.[41] Democrats were more likely to express the "liberal" position on economic, civil rights, and foreign policy issues than were Republicans. Also, voters in the 1960s perceived more clearly than voters in the 1950s the differences between the general approaches the two parties take on issues. During this decade a consensus developed that the Democratic party takes a liberal stand and the Republican party takes a conservative one. With these developments, the potential for voting on the basis of issues has increased in recent years. Correlations of voters' attitudes on issues with the way they voted in presidential elections in the 1960s and 1970s show that this potential for issue-voting was converted into reality.

Recent analyses also reveal a change in the way the Americans think about politics. When voters in the 1950s were asked to indicate what they liked or disliked about the candidates and the parties, only about one in ten responded in ideological terms by linking personal attitudes on such matters to political issues or by mentioning such general concepts as "liberal" or "conservative" to describe differences between candidates and parties. Far more people made references to group benefits—such as Democrats helping the worker, Republicans helping business—or to the nature of the times, linking Democrats to foreign wars and Republicans to economic downturns and depressions. More than one-fifth of the voters in the 1950s gave replies that had no issue content at all, such as "I just like Democrats better than Republicans" or "Ike's my man." In the 1960s and early 1970s, however, the number of "ideologues" increased considerably, to as much as one-third of the electorate in 1972, for example.[42] Particularly noticeable was a movement away from the perception of politics, primarily from the vantage point of group benefits and toward a broader view of issues and general political ideas.

In addition to this broadening of the conceptualization of politics, voters increasingly related political issues to one another as liberal or conservative. Studies of the electorate in the 1950s showed that voters were inconsistent in this respect; that is, people who took the "liberal" position that government should take an active role in providing welfare for the needy did not necessarily think it should assume a similar role in encouraging racial integration in the schools. Nor were voters' attitudes on either of these domestic matters related to their opinions on the foreign policy issue of what stand the U.S. government should take toward the threat of communism in the world. Beginning with the 1964 election, however, voters' attitudes were more often correlated, showing consistency among domestic issues as well as between domestic and foreign issues.[43]

Many observers assumed that the decline in the social unrest produced by the U.S. involvement in Vietnam and the racial tensions of the late 1960s and early 1970s would mean a return to a less ideological and issue-related presidential election in 1976. A study of that election by political scientists Arthur Miller and Warren Miller indicates, however, that this did not occur.[44] Using the same criteria that were used to discern the development of ideological thinking in the earlier period—voters' liberal and conservative attitudes on issues, their perceptions of party differences on such matters, and a correlation among their attitudes on issues—Miller and Miller concluded that ideological thinking declined only slightly between 1972 and 1976. Economic matters were much more important to the electorate in 1976 than social or cultural issues; Democrats in particular were concerned over the rise in unemployment before the election. Because many people believed that the Democratic party would do a better job than the Republican party in dealing with unemployment, and because Carter emphasized economic issues over noneconomic ones in his campaign, many voters distinguished between the two parties and their respective candidates on economic grounds. As Miller and Miller stated, the results of the 1976 election ultimately turned on "incumbent performance   [Ford's] versus partisan ideology [Democratic]."

Analysis of the 1980 election shows that economic issues were again more important to the electorate than were social and cultural issues, with inflation being the most important concern for many voters. Arthur Miller attributes President Carter's defeat primarily to voter dissatisfaction with his performance in office, particularly his perceived inability to deal with the economy and, to a lesser extent, with a perceived decline in U.S. prestige in the world.[45] On the whole, it seems dissatisfaction with Carter was more important than ideological considerations in explaining his loss in 1980.[46]

The economy was again on the minds of the U.S. electorate in 1984, although government spending had replaced inflation as the major source of concern, and Reagan's perceived success in coming to grips with this issue was a major reason for his overwhelming victory over Mondale. The voters were generally more satisfied with their family's financial situation and with national economic conditions than they were in 1980, and they credited President Reagan with bringing about those positive changes. In fact, there was an optimistic feeling about the general state of the nation, which again was attributed to the president's leadership. As in 1980, the performance of the incumbent significantly influenced the voting decisions of the electorate, but in 1984 the incumbent's performance was the primary reason for *retaining* rather than *removing* the president from office.

The electorate also evaluated the candidates' policy positions differently in the 1984 and the 1980 elections. In 1980, voters generally approved of Reagan's conservative policies, but in 1984, voters were actually closer to the liberal views of Mondale on desired policy *changes* than they were to the conservative views of the president (especially on cutting defense spending, increasing government aid to women, and avoiding involvement in Central America).[47] At the same time, the electorate was in general agreement with the *current* policies of the Reagan administration. Between 1980 and 1984, it seems that the Reagan administration shifted government policies in the direction of increasing spending for defense and reducing domestic programs, and by 1984 the electorate had decided that the shift had gone far enough and should not be continued.

In 1988, economic concerns again preoccupied the electorate and were cited by 45 percent as the most important problem, but this represented a significant decline from 1976 when 76 percent had identified them as most important. For the first time since 1972, social issues regained prominence, being named by more than one-third; foreign and defense problems were identified as most important by only 10 percent of the electorate.[48] Budget deficits and government spending, drugs, and homelessness were the leading issues of public concern. Unlike the situation in 1984, however, a majority (56 percent) of respondents in the University of Michigan's National Election Study thought the government was doing a poor job in handling the most important problem, a level of negative evaluation approaching that suffered by the Carter administration in 1980, when 61 percent felt the government's performance was poor.[49] Unlike 1980, however, when the Republicans established themselves as a viable alternative, Democrats were unable to convince voters that they were likely to perform better. In fact, a majority of respondents (54 percent) felt there was no difference in how the parties would perform in handling the most important problem with the remainder dividing almost evenly between the two alternatives. In a similar way, neither party gained an advantage from voter perceptions of their stands on the issues. Abramson, Aldrich, and Rohde found that "the average citizen was almost exactly halfway between the two candidate placements" on six issues, with the average respondent closer to Bush on three and closer to Dukakis on three.[50] Even though voters perceived a clear choice between the candidates and roughly half could place both themselves and the candidates on an issue scale, neither party benefited.

Two factors seem to account most fully for Bush's victory in 1988: evaluations of Reagan's performance and shifts in the partisan preferences of the electorate. At the time of the election, 60 percent of the electorate approved of the way Reagan was handling his job and Bush was regarded as the candidate most likely to continue the Reagan policies.[51] Voters, in other words, were moved by a subtle combination of retrospective and prospective evaluations—judgments about past performance and likely action on policy promises, respectively. In addition, gains made by Republicans in party identification among Whites, approximately 10 points between 1982 and 1988, were probably critical: had Bush confronted the same electorate that Reagan did in 1980, his share of the popular vote would probably have been 5 percentage points less, placing him behind Dukakis with 47 percent of the popular vote.[52] This view of the outcome is not inconsistent with Pomper's "ideological interpretation" of the 1988 election, according to which Bush served as "the champion of traditionalist values" now broadly associated with the Republican party.[53]

Public perception of Bush's performance changed dramatically in 1992, as did the election's outcome. Fifty-seven percent of respondents in the NES survey disapproved of the way Bush had handled his job, only slightly below the level of disapproval suffered by Carter in 1980. Connected to this widespread disapproval was dissatisfaction with how the government was performing on its most important problem (69 percent said poor) and the view that the Republican party would perform less effectively in addressing that problem than the Democratic party (13 percent versus 39 percent). Finally, 64 percent of the public identified economics as the most important problem, the highest level since 1976; social issues were a distant second at 28 percent; and foreign/defense issues were at only 3 percent. Ironically, Bush's success in foreign policy may have contributed to his demise; having presided over a successful conclusion to the cold war, Bush lost one of the major advantages enjoyed by Republican candidates in the period following World War II. Walter Dean Burnham points out that "in 1992 foreign policy issues and public concerns about them played the smallest role in any American presidential election since 1936." [54] Thus, the 1992 election can be viewed as a retrospective judgment on Bush's performance as president, particularly his performance on the economy, and the evaluation was overwhelmingly negative. As Abramson, Aldrich, and Rohde conclude, "In 1992, Bush lost because of the far more negative evaluations of his administration and of his party than had obtained in any other recent elections except 1980." [55]

Many forces, therefore, influence voting behavior in presidential elections. Over the years, the two major parties have developed different characteristics, and voters associate candidates with those characteristics. Democratic candidates have been favorably regarded for their party affiliation, their attitudes toward social groups, and their stands on domestic issues. In contrast, Republicans have benefited from their positions on foreign policy issues, their party philosophy, their perceived ability to manage the government, and a generally favorable assessment of them as candidates. Although the mix of these factors varies significantly from election to election, Republican victories in five of the past seven presidential elections (two by landslides) and in seven of the past twelve have raised questions about the Democrats' capacity to compete successfully.

Consequences of Presidential Elections

The most immediate and obvious consequence of a presidential election is the selection of a leader of the country for the next four years. As the following discussion indicates, presidential elections have other political effects as well.

Effect on the Political Party System

Angus Campbell and his associates categorized presidential elections according to three clusters of electoral factors.[56] A *maintaining election* is one in which the long-term partisan orientation of the electorate keeps the traditional majority party in power. The majority party candidate wins primarily because the people vote according to their traditional party loyalties. Short-term forces, such as candidates and issues, are present, but instead of determining which party wins, they contribute to the size of the majority party's victory. When they favor the majority party, as they did in 1964 when Goldwater was the Republican nominee, the vote margin separating the two major candidates is larger than usual. If short-term forces are in balance, as they were in 1948, the vote division approximates the proportion of voters who identify with the two parties.

A *deviating election* occurs when short-term forces benefit the minority party and override the long-term partisan preferences of the electorate. An especially appealing candidate or an outstanding issue, event, or type of presidential performance allows the minority party candidate to win with the support of some majority party members, Independents, and a good share of new voters. The electorate does not, however, change its basic party preferences. Examples of deviating elections are those of 1952, 1956, 1968, and 1972: they were won by the Republican candidates, Eisenhower and Nixon, but the commitment of many voters to the majority party—the Democrats—was unaltered.[57]

An election that brings about major political change is a *realigning election*. Such elections entail a major realignment of electoral support among blocs of voters that switch their traditional party affiliation. An unusually large number of new voters may also enter the electoral arena and cast their ballots disproportionately for one party's candidate. Unlike the deviating election, the effects of the realigning election persist in the form of durable loyalties to the advantaged party. Political historians usually include five elections in the realigning category: 1800, 1828, 1860, 1896, and 1932.

Immediately after the 1980 election, many observers concluded that the decisive Reagan victory (51 percent of the popular vote to 41 percent for Carter), plus the unexpected Republican capture of the Senate and their gain of 33 seats in the House of Representatives, 4 governorships, and more than 200 state legislative seats, meant that 1980 was a realigning election. Moreover, social groups that traditionally voted Democratic—including Catholics, blue-collar workers, and voters with no college education—cast their ballots for the Republican nominee, giving further credence to the contention that the liberal New Deal era in U.S. politics was over and a new Republican majority had been formed.[58] When President Reagan embarked successfully on a series of major policy changes, and when by mid-1981 the percentage of voters declaring themselves to be Republicans equaled that of Democrats, some observers became even more convinced that a party realignment had taken place.

Subsequent events, however, indicated that the 1980 election was not a realigning one. As President Reagan began to have problems with Congress and the economy took a downturn, the number of voters identifying with the Republican party declined, and those declaring themselves to be Democrats rose again until the gap between the two major parties approached its traditional 5:3 ratio. In the 1982 elections, the Democrats picked up 26 seats in the House of Representatives, a net gain of 7 governorships, and some 160 additional seats in state legislatures, showing that many Democrats had not permanently deserted their traditional party.

Although we now have three additional presidential elections to provide perspective on a possible realignment, the situation remains unclear. The results of the 1984 presidential election, in which President Reagan captured 59 percent of the popular vote (compared with Mondale's 41 percent) and the electoral votes of forty-nine states (Mondale carried only his home state of Minnesota and the District of Columbia), suggested that 1984 was the long-awaited realigning election. Several developments were evident in the middle of the 1980s that one would expect to find if a realignment of significant magnitude were occurring: younger voters and newly registered ones tended to be Republicans; many traditional Democrats were deserting the party because they agreed more with the Republicans on issues such as economic growth and opportunity, the necessity of building up the national defense, and social concerns (prayer in the public school, abortion, busing); and the number of political Independents appeared to have leveled off or even declined.[59]

Other developments of the mid-1980s, however, did *not* point in the direction of a realigning election. Although President Reagan won by a large margin in the 1984 election, the Republican party actually lost two seats in the Senate, and the fourteen seats it picked up in the House of Representatives did not compensate for the twenty-six it lost in the 1982 elections. Moreover, despite the presidential landslide, Democrats still controlled thirty-four of the nation's fifty governorships and both houses of the legislature in twenty-eight states, compared with eleven for the Republicans. In late 1985, a Gallup poll found that the Democrats were on the rise again; 40 percent of the American public identified with that party compared with 33 percent who said they were Republicans.[60] Finally, in the 1986 congressional elections, the Democrats unexpectedly picked up eight seats in the Senate to regain control of that body by a 55–45 margin and added five seats in the House of Representatives.

Indications were similarly mixed after 1988. Bush's 7.7-percentage point margin of victory over Dukakis was smaller than Reagan's 9.7 percent margin over Carter in 1980 and far smaller than the 18.2 point victory over Mondale in 1984. "The victory was broad, but shallow," concludes Pomper; Bush won seven states by less than 5 percent and five more by margins of 5 to 10 percent. Moreover, the magnitude of Bush's win compares poorly with other Republican victories in the twentieth century.[61]

It was also the first time since 1960 that the party winning the presidency simultaneously lost seats in the House of Representatives (a loss of three placed the party balance at 260–175 in favor of the Democrats); the Republicans also lost one seat in the Senate (enabling the Democrats to regain a 55–45 margin) as well as one governorship. On the other hand, this was the third Republican victory in a row, the first time either party had achieved such success since 1952. Republican gains among White voters had been steady so that they could claim a majority of those declaring a partisan identification. Support was even stronger among young party identifiers.[62]

The 1992 elections added even further confusion to the picture. Clinton's margin of victory in the popular vote was the third lowest since 1832; only Abraham Lincoln and Woodrow Wilson had registered lower levels in a winning effort. Clinton won popular majorities only in Arkansas and the District of Columbia. The Democrats maintained their strength in the Senate but lost ten seats in the House of Representatives, the second consecutive presidential election year that this had happened. Moreover, a true electoral earthquake occurred in the 1994 mid-term elections when Republicans gained majorities in both the Senate and the House—the first time since 1954 that there was a House Republican majority.

Hovering in the background of the political landscape was Perot. In contrast to Clinton's mediocre results, Perot's 18.9 percent of the popular vote was the third-best showing in history of a non-major-party candidate behind Theodore Roosevelt's 27.4 percent in 1912 and Millard Fillmore's 21.5 percent in 1856. Unlike these predecessors, however, Perot had not previously served as president nor previously been the nominee of a major party. Perot's support reflected the declines in partisanship that had occurred since 1964. He won a 41 percent plurality of "pure" Independents who lean toward neither of the parties (Clinton received 37 percent of this vote and Bush 22), a larger share than either George Wallace in 1968 or John Anderson in 1980 was able to secure. Perot also won more than one-fourth of Independents who lean toward supporting one of the parties as well as substantial portions of Weak Democrats and Weak Republicans. Finally, many of Perot's voters were dissatisfied with government performance and lacked confidence that either party had the answers to national problems.[63]

Political analysts have differed over how to characterize the period that began in the late 1960s. Kevin Phillips terms the era one of "split-level" realignment.[64] The Republican party became the dominant party in presidential elections, winning five of the six contests between 1968 and

1988, three of them (1972, 1980, and 1984) by substantial margins. Meanwhile, the Democrats became the permanent majority party in the House of Representatives. Only the Senate could properly be termed a "two-party" institution.

Burnham characterized the recent era as one of party "decomposition" or "dealignment." [65] Traditional loyalties of the American public to political parties declined greatly, and therefore the party affiliation of candidates is no longer the principal factor in voting decisions, as it once was. Instead, short-term forces, such as the candidates themselves, issues, events, and incumbent performance, shape how people cast their ballots. As a result, voters switch their votes in presidential elections from one party's candidate to another and split their ballots for different party candidates running for separate offices in the same election. As Burnham explains, "Electoral disaggregation carried beyond a certain point would, after all, make critical realignment in the classical sense impossible." [66]

Everett Carll Ladd has suggested that contemporary developments do not represent an either/or situation; rather, the best description of the "post–New Deal system" is a combination of realignment and dealignment, with the latter a feature of the new partisan alignment.[67] In this view, we should not expect the next (or current) realignment to be just like the last one. Instead, the adjustments are likely to take different forms and manifest themselves in different ways.

In previous realigning elections (1800, 1828, 1860, 1896, and 1932), the new majority party captured not only the presidency but also both houses of Congress. With the exception of the first instance (1800), the emerging party controlled the House of Representatives in the session preceding the key presidential election, suggesting that 1996 could potentially become the realigning election. Moreover, two years after the presidential race, the new majority party maintained control of both houses of the Congress in what one writer calls "cementing" elections.[68] Finally, voting participation generally increased in past realigning elections. This clearly did not happen from 1980–1988, but the recovery of participation in 1992 from its lowest level in more than half a century could presage a further increase, particularly since passage of the Motor Voter bill in 1993 made electoral registration much easier by tying it to getting a driver's license. Early evidence indicates that the surge in registration could add large numbers of new voters in 1996, perhaps as many as 20 million, introducing the possibility of a surge in participation during the next presidential election. Thus, none of the elections between 1980 and 1992 met the criteria of a realigning election, but the electoral landscape is highly unstable, opening the possibility for important changes in the near future.

Effect on Policy Making

The strongest influence voters in presidential elections can exercise on policy making in the United States is to send the winning candidate a clear message that identifies the issues they believe to be most important and that specifies the policies the candidate should follow in dealing with those issues. Such a message is called a *mandate*—a set of instructions to the new president on how to govern the nation. Mandates, however, may result as much from the content of the campaign that the victorious candidate wages as from the public's collective voting decisions.

For many reasons presidential elections may not meet the requirements of a mandate. As discussed in preceding sections, issues often have little to do with a voter's choice of candidate. Some people vote according to traditional loyalties—they simply choose the candidate who represents the political party with which they identify. Others base their decision on the personal qualities of the competing presidential candidates; they vote for the candidate whose qualities they like or for the opponent of a candidate they dislike (the lesser of two evils).

Even when voters choose a candidate because of issues, the election may not produce a mandate. Voters differ on the particular issues in which they are interested: some may be concerned over the state of the domestic economy; others, the U.S. position in the world community. Thus, a candidate may garner a plurality of the votes cast by issue-conscious voters, without any single issue having majority support. Moreover, it is one thing for voters to be interested in an issue and quite another for them to be able to suggest specific policies to deal with it. Finally, individual policies favored by voters may conflict with one another. Voters may favor, for example, increased government expenditures for national defense but also support a tax cut and a balanced budget. In the same way, voters may wish to minimize taxes but hope to maintain the benefits derived from government programs, even when costs continue to increase. If it proves to be impossible to carry out all these policies simultaneously (as was true during Reagan's presidency), the electorate may provide no clear message on which policy has the highest priority.

The failure of a presidential election to produce a mandate does not mean that the election has no effect on the making of public policy in the United States. Elections are in effect a "retrospective" judgment on the performance of the incumbent.[69] When voters reelect the office holder, they are showing their general satisfaction with the way the administration has been handling the principal issues facing the country. Evaluation of past performance may also shape their expectations of a president's future performance.[70] In 1984, for example, supporters of President Reagan approved of the way he had handled major problems (especially the economy) and assumed he would continue to handle those problems successfully in the next four years. Yet they gave little guidance on the specific policies the administration should follow, something that should not be surprising given the nature of that campaign, in which the president made few specific promises about how he would address the major economic issue (the budget deficit), except to say that he would raise taxes only as a "last resort." Thus, a vote to keep a president in office is primarily a favorable judgment on his past performance and promised goals, not an assessment of the *means,* that is, the specific policies, necessary to reach those outcomes.

In the 1968 election, for example, the voters did not instruct Nixon to follow any particular course of action in extricating the nation from Vietnam, but they did give him the message that he should somehow reach that goal. The electoral message also may suggest that the new president should not continue to follow the policies of his predecessor on the issue, a reasonable interpretation of the public's message in 1992 on the economy.

Aside from the question of what policy directions (if any) presidential elections offer successful candidates, presidents themselves frequently interpret the election results as a mandate to pursue the policies they favor. As presidential adviser George Reedy put it, "President Johnson and most of his close advisors interpreted the election result [the 1964 landslide victory of Johnson over Goldwater] as a mandate from the people not only to carry on the policies of the Johnson administration but any other policies that might come to mind." [71] The same tendency can apply when the candidate of the party out of power wins an election. When Reagan assumed the presidency after his victory over Carter in 1980, he claimed a mandate from the people to embark on a broad range of conservative policies, some of which—such as reduced rates of government expenditures on health, education, and environmental protection and opposition to the Equal Rights Amendment and abortion—ran counter to voters' preferences.

The indefinite guidance the electorate offers the winner of presidential elections gives the president great freedom in initiating public policies. In recent years new presidents often have sought to enact the pledges made in their party platforms. [72] Johnson and Nixon acted on more than half of the promises they made in campaign speeches in 1964 and 1968, [73] as did Eisenhower and Kennedy on the promises they made in their 1952 and 1960 campaigns. [74] A positive relationship does exist, therefore, between what presidential candidates say they will do if elected and the policies they actually follow after they assume office, whether or not the electorate has supported them for that reason.

At the same time, U.S. presidents must strive to keep their policies in line with the preferences of the voters. If their new policies go further than their supporters intended, or if the favored policies do not succeed, presidents face the possibility of being removed from office at the next election. As political scientist V. O. Key points out, "Governments must worry, not about the meaning of past elections, but about their fate at future elections." This means that "the electorate can exert a prospective influence if not control" over government policy.[75]

The elections of 1984, 1988, and 1992 illustrate how the conduct of a campaign can contribute to or detract from an election's policy significance. As Thomas Weko and John Aldrich point out, the candidates' campaign strategies, in framing the choices that confront voters during an election, also shape the choices that confront members of Congress after the election.[76] Presidents who run a campaign devoid of issues will have difficulty framing a legislative agenda once in office, a fate that befell Reagan in his second term, Bush in January 1989, and Clinton after his inauguration. In 1988, the voters sent a blurred message on their preferences for the future; by locating themselves between the two candidates and identifying about evenly with their respective issue positions, the voters precluded simple interpretations. Moreover, the campaign contributed to a mixed retrospective judgment: a majority of the electorate regarded the Republican administration as doing a poor job on major problems, but the challenger was not viewed as likely to provide a significant improvement. Bush's victorious campaign emphasized areas in which the president's powers are limited—crime and punishment are principally state and local concerns. The clearest commitment Bush made in 1988 was to hold the line on taxes, a position he abandoned in 1990.

Clinton has experienced similar problems. Running on a platform of change and complaining of Bush's failed economic policy, Clinton laid out few specific answers to the nation's problems and seemed to abandon one—a middle-class tax cut—soon after the election. Clearly, he promised to pursue economic policies substantially different from Bush's, and he promised to address health care; developing an economic stimulus package, job creation, and "investing" in America would be important goals, but they remained remarkably vague. The result was uncertain direction at the administration's outset and a Congress that resisted administration proposals; few believed there had been a mandate, a reasonable conclusion given the weak plurality victory that followed a modestly programmatic campaign.[77]

Thus, waging a "framing"—one that clearly frames the voters' choices—campaign can have advantages after the votes have been counted. Unless an agenda is spelled out during the campaign, the victor can make only minimal claims to having received a mandate. The problem is exacerbated when the electorate speaks with two voices, choosing a president from one party and a Congress dominated by the other, a condition faced by all Republican presidents since Eisenhower and now by a Democrat for the first time since Truman.

Notes

1. 38 U.S. 347 (1915).
2. 321 U.S. 649 (1944).
3. 295 U.S. 45 (1935).
4. In *Harper v. Virginia State Board of Elections*, 383 U.S. 663 (1966), the Supreme Court eliminated the payment of a poll tax as a requirement for voting in state elections by ruling that it violated the equal protection clause of the Fourteenth Amendment.
5. A major issue was whether voting rights violations should require actual proof of the "intent" to discriminate (as favored by the Reagan administration), or whether it was sufficient that an election law or procedure merely "result" in discrimination (as favored by civil rights groups). Senator Dole (R-Kan.) led in developing an acceptable compromise on the issue.
6. Paul R. Abramson, John H. Aldrich, and David W. Rohde, *Change and Continuity in the 1980 Elections* (Washington, D.C.: CQ Press, 1982), chap. 4.
7. Paul R. Abramson, John H. Aldrich, and David W. Rohde, *Change and Continuity in the 1992 Elections* (Washington, D.C.: CQ Press, 1994), 120.
8. Angus Campbell, Philip Converse, Warren Miller, and Donald Stokes, *The American Voter*, abr. ed. (New York: Wiley, 1964).
9. Philip Converse, *The Dynamics of Party Support: Cohort-Analyzing Party Identification* (Beverly Hills: Sage Publications, 1976), 34.
10. V. O. Key, Jr., *The Responsible Electorate: Rationality in Presidential Voting* (Cambridge, Mass.: Belknap Press, 1966).
11. Based on data provided by the University of Michigan Center for Political Studies.
12. Harold G. Stanley and Richard G. Niemi, *Vital Statistics on American Politics*, 4th ed. (Washington, D.C.: CQ Press, 1994), Table 4-7, 146. One possible reason for the high percentage of ticket-splitting between presidential and House races in 1980 was the presence of independent Anderson in the presidential contest that year. In most states, Anderson's supporters did not have the option of voting for an independent House candidate. Of course, this factor should have been even more powerful in 1992 with the Perot candidacy but was not.
13. Norman Nie, Sidney Verba, and John Petrocik, *The Changing American Voter* (Cambridge, Mass.: Harvard University Press, 1979), chap. 4.
14. Campbell et al., *The American Voter*, 83–85.
15. Gerald Pomper, *Voter's Choice: Varieties of American Electoral Behavior* (New York: Dodd, Mead, 1975), chap. 2.
16. Nie, Verba, and Petrocik, *The Changing American Voter*, 70–72.
17. Converse, *The Dynamics of Party Support*, chap. 4.
18. For the 1940 election, Paul Lazarsfeld, Bernard Berelson, and Hazel Gaudt,

The People's Choice (New York: Columbia University Press, 1944); for the 1948 election, Paul Lazarsfeld, Bernard Berelson, and William McPhee, *Voting* (Chicago: University of Chicago Press, 1954).

19. Gerald M. Pomper, "The Presidential Election," in *The Election of 1988: Reports and Interpretations,* ed. Gerald M. Pomper (Chatham, N.J.: Chatham House, 1989), 136; and Abramson, Aldrich, and Rohde, *Change and Continuity in the 1992 Elections,* 133.

20. Another group whose significance in national politics has increased greatly is White fundamentalist or evangelical Christians. This group has become solidly Republican, and in 1988 comprised nearly as large a proportion of the voting population as African Americans (9 percent versus 10 percent). See poll results reported in Pomper, "The Presidential Election," 134.

21. Paul R. Abramson, John H. Aldrich, and David W. Rohde, *Change and Continuity in the 1988 Elections* (Washington, D.C.: CQ Press, 1990), 111. See also polling data reported by Pomper, "The Presidential Election," 136, indicating that Bush was favored over Dukakis among nonvoters by 50 percent to 34 percent.

22. As reported in the *New York Times,* November 5, 1992.

23. The NES survey found that approximately 40 percent of Clinton's southern votes came from African Americans. Abramson, Aldrich, and Rohde, *Change and Continuity in the 1992 Elections,* 150.

24. Abramson, Aldrich, and Rohde, *Change and Continuity in the 1992 Elections,* 160.

25. Abramson, Aldrich, and Rohde, *Change and Continuity in the 1988 Elections,* 122–123, and *Change and Continuity in the 1992 Elections,* 136.

26. ———, *Change and Continuity in the 1992 Elections,* 106.

27. Pearl T. Robinson, "Whither the Future of Blacks in the Republican Party?" *Political Science Quarterly* 97, no. 2 (Summer 1982): 217.

28. Ibid., 231.

29. Results of national exit polls conducted by VRS, published in the *New York Times,* November 5, 1992.

30. Michael X. Delli Carpini and Ester R. Fuchs, "The Year of the Woman? Candidates, Voters and the 1992 Elections," *Political Science Quarterly* 108, no. 1 (1993): 36.

31. *The Gallup Poll Monthly,* August 1992, 2–5.

32. Abramson, Aldrich, and Rohde, *Change and Continuity in the 1988 Elections,* 126.

33. Abramson, Aldrich, and Rohde, *Change and Continuity in the 1992 Elections,* 137.

34. Warren Miller and Teresa Levitin, *Leadership and Change: The New Politics and the American Electorate* (Cambridge, Mass.: Winthrop, 1976), 42.

35. Herbert Asher, *Presidential Elections and American Politics: Voters, Candidates and Campaigns since 1952* (Homewood, Ill.: Dorsey, 1976), chap. 5.

36. Martin P. Wattenberg, "From a Partisan to a Candidate-Centered Electorate," in *The New American Political System,* 2d ed., ed. Anthony King (Washington, D.C.: AEI Press, 1990).

37. Pomper, "The Presidential Election," 143. The results of this CNN/*Los Angeles Times* poll can also be found in *National Journal,* November 12, 1988, 2854.

38. Campbell et al., *The American Voter,* chap. 7.

39. Pomper, *Voter's Choice.*

40. Nie, Verba, and Petrocik, *The Changing American Voter.*
41. Pomper, *Voter's Choice,* chap. 8.
42. Nie, Verba, and Petrocik, *The Changing American Voter,* chap. 7.
43. Philip Converse, "The Nature of Belief Systems in Mass Publics," in *Ideology and Discontent,* ed. David Apter (New York: Free Press, 1964). Norman Nie and Kristi Anderson, "Mass Belief Systems Revisited: Political Change and Attitude Structure," *Journal of Politics* 36 (August 1974): 540–591.
44. Arthur Miller and Warren Miller, "Partisanship and Performance: Rational Choice in the 1976 Presidential Election" (Paper delivered at the annual meeting of the American Political Science Association, Washington, D.C., September 1–4, 1977).
45. Arthur Miller, "Policy and Performance Voting in the 1980 Election" (Paper delivered at the annual meeting of the American Political Science Association, New York, September 3–6, 1981).
46. Abramson, Aldrich, and Rohde, *Change and Continuity in the 1980 Elections.*
47. Paul R. Abramson, John H. Aldrich, and David W. Rohde, *Change and Continuity in the 1984 Elections,* rev. ed. (Washington, D.C.: CQ Press, 1987), chap. 6.
48. Abramson, Aldrich, and Rohde, *Change and Continuity in the 1988 Elections,* 157.
49. Ibid., 183–184.
50. Ibid., 161–162. Bush was closer to the median position identified by respondents on the issue scales of government spending and services, jobs and standard of living guarantees, and aid to minorities. Dukakis was closer on defense spending, health insurance, and the role of women. Respondents were almost precisely located at the midpoint between the candidates' perceived positions on relations with the Soviet Union.
51. Ibid., 193, 195. Pomper reads the results somewhat differently. As he reports, Bush received overwhelming support from those who wanted "to continue Reagan's policies," minimal support from those who wanted to "change these policies," and a comfortable majority (57 percent) among those who claimed that Reagan's policies had not influenced their vote. Pomper, "The Presidential Election," 140, 151 n. 19. The data he cites are from a CBS News/*New York Times* exit poll.
52. Abramson, Aldrich, and Rohde, *Change and Continuity in the 1988 Elections,* 222.
53. Pomper, "The Presidential Election," 144–150.
54. Walter Dean Burnham, "The Legacy of George Bush: Travails of an Understudy," in *The Election of 1992: Reports and Interpretations,* ed. Gerald M. Pomper (Chatham, N.J.: Chatham House, 1993), 21.
55. Abramson, Aldrich, and Rohde, *Change and Continuity in the 1992 Elections,* 216. See their discussion of prospective and retrospective voting in chaps. 6 and 7.
56. Campbell et al., *The American Voter,* chap. 16.
57. Analysts refer to an election following a deviating period as a *reinstating* one, because it reinstates the usual majority party. Examples are the 1960 and 1976 elections, when the Democrats returned to power after the two Eisenhower and the two Nixon victories. A reinstating election, therefore, is like a maintaining one in that long-term partisan factors determine the result. It would be difficult to describe the 1992 election as "reinstating," even though it did reassemble components of the New Deal coalition.

58. See, for example, Kevin Phillips, *The Emerging Republican Majority* (New Rochelle, N.Y.: Arlington House, 1969).
59. Thomas Cavanaugh and James Sundquist, "The New Two-Party System," in *The New Direction in American Politics*, ed. John Chubb and Paul Peterson (Washington, D.C.: Brookings Institution, 1985), chap. 2.
60. *The Gallup Report*, October–November 1985, 42–44.
61. Pomper, "The Presidential Election," 132.
62. Abramson, Aldrich, and Rohde, *Change and Continuity in the 1988 Elections*, 206–207. Among White identifiers 18–24 years of age, 65 percent were Republicans in 1988.
63. Abramson, Aldrich, and Rohde, *Change and Continuity in the 1992 Elections*, Table 8-9, 245.
64. This term is used in Phillips's biweekly newsletter, *The American Political Report* (January 11, 1985), as cited in Abramson, Aldrich, and Rohde, *Change and Continuity in the 1984 Elections*, 287.
65. Walter Dean Burnham, *Critical Elections and the Mainsprings of American Politics* (New York: Norton, 1970), chap. 5.
66. Ibid., 91–92.
67. Everett Carll Ladd, "On Mandates, Realignments, and the 1984 Presidential Election," *Political Science Quarterly* 100, no. 1 (Spring 1985): 1–25; Ladd, "The 1988 Elections: Continuation of the Post–New Deal System," *Political Science Quarterly* 104, no. 1 (Spring 1989): 1–18. On the concept of realignment more generally, see David G. Lawrence and Richard Fleisher, "Puzzles and Confusions: Political Realignment in the 1980s," *Political Science Quarterly* 102, no. 1 (Spring 1987): 79–92.
68. Gerald Pomper, with Susan Lederman, *Elections in America: Control and Influence in Democratic Politics*, 2d ed. (New York: Longman, 1980), 212.
69. Key, *The Responsible Electorate*.
70. Anthony Downs, *An Economic Theory of Democracy* (New York: Harper and Row, 1957); and Morris Fiorina, *Retrospective Voting in American National Elections* (New Haven: Yale University Press, 1981).
71. George Reedy, *The Twilight of the Presidency* (New York: New American Library, 1970), 66.
72. Pomper, *Elections in America*, chap. 8.
73. Fred Grogan, "Candidate Promise and Presidential Performance" (Paper delivered at the annual meeting of the Midwest Political Science Association, Chicago, April 21–23, 1977).
74. Arnold John Muller, "Public Policy and the Presidential Election Process: A Study of Promise and Performance" (Ph.D. diss., University of Missouri-Columbia, 1986).
75. Key, *The Responsible Electorate*, 77.
76. Thomas Weko and John H. Aldrich, "The Presidency and the Election Campaign: Framing the Choice in 1988," in *The Presidency and the Political System*, 3d ed., ed. Michael Nelson (Washington, D.C.: CQ Press, 1990), 279.
77. John H. Aldrich and Thomas Weko, "The Presidency and the Election Campaign: Framing the Choice in 1993," in *The Presidency and the Political System*, 4th ed., ed. Michael Nelson (Washington, D.C.: CQ Press, 1995), 251–270. Clinton, it should be pointed out, reintroduced a version of his middle-class tax cut in December 1994, an initiative that figured prominently in his 1995 State of the Union address as well.

Selected Readings

Campbell, Angus, Philip Converse, Warren Miller, and Donald Stokes. *The American Voter.* Abr. ed. New York: Wiley, 1964.

Fiorina, Morris P. *Retrospective Voting in American National Elections.* New Haven, Conn.: Yale University Press, 1981.

Kessel, John H. *Presidential Campaign Politics: Coalition Strategies and Citizen Response.* 3d ed. Chicago, Ill.: Dorsey , 1988.

Key, V. O., Jr. *The Responsible Electorate: Rationality in Presidential Voting.* Cambridge, Mass.: Belknap Press, 1966.

McCubbins, Matthew. *Under the Watchful Eye.* Washington, D.C.: CQ Press, 1993.

Nie, Norman, Sidney Verba, and John Petrocik. *The Changing American Voter.* Cambridge, Mass.: Harvard University Press, 1979.

Summary and Assessment of Presidential Contests

OVER TIME, NUMEROUS CHANGES have been made in the way Americans choose their president. In some cases changes have been made through formal mechanisms (constitutional amendments and federal statutes); in others they have emerged through informal changes in party practices and public expectations. This final chapter reviews recent concerns about the presidential selection process and assesses several proposals for reform.

Although critics have focused on many different features of the present selection process, nearly all of the critics have sought ways of making the process *more democratic* or *more effective*. Although disagreement naturally exists over the definition of these criteria and how they relate to one another, a widely accepted concept of democracy underlies several of the important proposals for reform. According to this concept, any process that involves broader participation by the public is more democratic.

There is less agreement about what would constitute greater effectiveness. For some, eliminating the possibility of having the system malfunction would make it more effective. For others, selecting candidates with the best chances of winning or those best qualified to serve as president would represent greater effectiveness. Unfortunately, reforms designed to enhance democracy may not necessarily improve effectiveness, however it is defined.

The chapter's first section focuses on the nomination stage of the presidential contest; the second section targets the general election stage.

The Nomination Process

As discussed in Chapter 1, parties have used a variety of means to select their candidates for the general election contest. Influence over the nomination shifted first from party leaders in Congress to local and state party figures, and finally to party and candidate supporters among the general public. These changes have made the selection process progressively more democratic in the sense that decisions have come to be made through ever broadening participation. National conventions, developed as a means to aggregate local concerns and produce a nominee, continue to prevail today, although they have been altered significantly by the spread of presidential primaries. Although the public's role has been enhanced over time, its influence remains *indirect*; participants in primaries and caucuses determine the composition of the national convention, at which time the presidential candidate is officially named.

The changes that occurred from the early days of the nation's history until the mid-1960s, a span of nearly two centuries, were gradual; those that have occurred since then have been abrupt. From 1968 to 1980, what political scientist Byron Shafer calls a "quiet revolution" took place in the process by which the parties (especially the Democrats) chose their presidential candidates.[1] Alterations in the rules of the game during those years transferred the choice of candidates from caucus-conventions dominated by elected and party officials to popular primaries in which an increasing number of rank-and-file voters choose delegates to the national convention, delegates pledged to support specific presidential candidates. In addition, the private financing of nomination campaigns by large contributors gave way to a system of government subsidies that match the donations of small donors. New political elites also emerged during this period of flux: political amateurs, mobilized to campaign for candidates, and members of the media replaced governors, senators, House members, and state party leaders as the most influential forces in the nomination of presidential candidates. Moreover, as Shafer points out, the new political elites within the Democratic party spoke for a white-collar electorate, in contrast to the older rank-and-file of blue-collar voters represented by the party professionals.[2]

No one is fully satisfied with the nomination process that has emerged. Several areas of continuing concern and several possible solutions are reviewed in the following sections.

Restoring Peer Review

The 1980s witnessed a partial, short-lived "counterrevolution" in nomination politics. Between 1980 and 1984, six states abandoned presidential primaries in favor of caucus-conventions. As a direct consequence, the proportion of Democratic convention delegates chosen in primaries fell from almost three-fourths to slightly more than half. These actions reflected a consensus that the democracy-enhancing reforms of the previous decade had gone too far. One of the major casualties was *peer review,* the opportunity for knowledgeable politicians to assess the relative merits of contestants and select as the party's nominee the person most likely to win or best qualified to serve as president. Complementing the retreat from primaries, professionals were brought back into the nomination process in the form of superdelegates, who constituted one of seven delegates at the 1984 Democratic national convention. In the battle over the 1988 rules, a balance was struck: the professionals once again prevailed over the amateurs by winning an increase in the number of superdelegates attending the convention, but at the same time the Democrats returned to relying on primaries as the principal method for selecting 1988 convention delegates. Although an agreement reached in 1988 to reduce the number of superdelegates at the 1992 convention fell through, the spirit of participatory reform that arose following 1968 remains dominant in the Democratic party. In 1996, superdelegates will constitute roughly the same percentage of the overall convention that they did in 1988.

The result of this revolution, counterrevolution, and response—created over two decades of continual reform in the Democratic party—is a mixed nomination system. It selects delegates by both the primary and caucus-convention methods. Its participants include professionals representing blue-collar constituencies, such as organized labor, as well as amateurs who speak largely for white-collar constituents. The 1984 nomination process vividly reflected these differences: Walter Mondale generally was favored by party professionals, Democratic loyalists, blue-collar workers, and older people; Gary Hart was supported by amateurs, political independents, white-collar workers, and younger voters. With Hart's early departure from the 1988 race, Jesse Jackson remained the principal candidate of nonprofessionals, but the battle lines within the party were less clearly drawn than in the past. Seeking to break their string of defeats, Democratic party officials went to great lengths in 1992 to reduce internal conflict and unite all factions behind a common candidate. Brown provided some appeal to "amateurs," but so did Clinton, thereby reducing the potential conflict.

One of the unfortunate features of this ongoing internal dynamic has been the tendency for Democratic rules to be *candidate-driven*—adopted as a means to facilitate the chances of one candidate over another.[3] As a consequence, the Democrats have suffered even greater intraparty conflict than the selection process would ordinarily generate. With the emergence of relative stability after 1988, the party faithful hoped that struggles over rules would become subordinate to finding ways to win general elections, a dream that was realized in 1992.

The mixed nomination system has a number of desirable features, notably its blend of political amateurs, who are primarily concerned with the candidates' stands on issues, and party professionals, who bring distinctive "peer" perspectives to bear on the candidates' ability to work effectively with the other officials with whom they will govern the nation. Professionals are in a position to assess how successful candidates are likely to be in shaping compromises among the many increasingly assertive groups in U.S. society. Yet presidential primaries place a premium on candidates who possess the personality and communications skills needed to attract the support of rank-and-file voters, skills especially important for modern presidents, who find it increasingly necessary to pursue their goals by "going public" rather than through the traditional vehicle of bargaining among elites.[4] The variegated nomination process may be especially important for the Democrats, the more heterogeneous party, for whom it is critical "to dampen conflict and resolve tensions among the elements of their coalition."[5]

Not all features of the mixed system are likely to prove permanently beneficial. Democrats, in creating and maintaining the system of superdelegates, may be playing with political fire. Making up just 16 percent of the convention delegates, these restored professionals can determine the party's nominee only if the convention reaches an impasse. At a deadlocked convention—one in which the nomination has *not* been decided by the time the party convenes and in which a first-ballot nomination is unlikely—uncommitted superdelegates probably would play a critical role. Although such a deadlock has not occurred in either party since 1952, despite the presence of a larger pool of candidates to divide party preferences, a nominee chosen by an old-style "open convention" rather than "by the people" (as the process has operated recently) runs the risk of having the legitimacy of his or her candidacy called into question much as Hubert Humphrey's was in 1968. Of the two major parties, the Democrats, with their system of superdelegates, are closer to that possibility. At its foundation, the nomination system remains one of *indirect* public participation even though the public's role has increased and has proved decisive since 1968. In running the risk of violating new public expectations, today's system is susceptible to a *nomination misfire* in much the same way as the electoral college is susceptible to a *general election misfire*.

The Schedule of Competition

The election calendar has been another source of continual dissatisfaction and adjustment. The 1992 nomination contest lasted sixteen weeks, a grueling period that many regard as too long since it primarily tests candidates' endurance and the public's attention span. Another recurrent complaint has been the privileged position of Iowa and New Hampshire, which are able to influence party decisions far more than their size would merit simply because they hold their caucus-convention and primary contests earlier than any of the other states. This special standing has been sanctioned by the Democratic party and is justified as giving lesser known, poorly financed competitors a chance to compete in the labor-intensive, small state contests. Although the electorates of both states are grossly unrepresentative of the nation and even of the parties, winners of the Iowa and New Hampshire contests receive a boost of media attention, the label of being a "winner," and the associated benefits in raising funds.

Several challenges have been mounted against the present calendar. In 1988, southern Democrats sought to enhance their own impact and hoped to boost the chances of moderate candidates by creating the first true *regional primary*. However, "Super Tuesday," the day in early March 1988 when twenty states concentrated in the South and Middle West held their state primaries or caucuses, proved far more important for the Republican contest, enabling George Bush virtually to sew up his party's nomination by burying his principal opponent, Bob Dole. The Democratic vote, in contrast, was divided three ways. A number of southern states responded to this disappointment by withdrawing from a common date in 1992 only to discover that the pared-down "Super Tuesday" accomplished its original purpose, giving Bill Clinton the boost he needed after New Hampshire to go on to the nomination.

Full-scale regional contests, long advocated by many critics of the presidential nomination process, do not appear likely. Instead, there has been a scramble among states to move their delegate selection contests to the early weeks of the schedule, each hoping to claim a larger share of the publicity and influence now enjoyed by Iowa and New Hampshire. The Democrats continue to sanction a "window" that provides very few exceptions to the March-through-June timetable, but the early weeks of March are becoming increasingly crowded. After California moved up in the process from June to March (March 26, 1996), New York felt compelled to leap-frog to an earlier spot, as well, March 7, 1996. Having these "megastates" actively involved in the early stages is likely to help better-financed candidates offset the advantages that lesser-known candidates have sometimes gained in Iowa and New Hampshire, but it is also likely to settle the contest quite early.

Robert Loevy has termed the present schedule "the manipulated sequential primary and caucus system" because dates are manipulated to help particular candidates and enhance a state's political impact.[6] In its place, Loevy recommends a Model Calendar that would shorten the process to ten weeks, establish five dates when all contests other than Iowa and New Hampshire would be held, leave two weeks between each date, and "back load" the system with large states selecting on the last date. Although the proposal has much merit, it would require that states coordinate their delegate selection decisions to a far greater degree than has ever been achieved before, making it an unlikely development.

The final schedule of contests for 1996 will not be known until late in 1995; at that time candidates will adjust their strategies accordingly. (The 1996 schedule as it stood in June 1995 can be found in Appendix A.) Prospective candidates apparently believe that a massive war chest must be amassed well before the beginning of 1996 in order to survive the glut of early contests. In contrast to 1992 when there were remarkably few "early birds"—aspirants who "announced their candidacy by the end of February in the year preceding the national convention"[7]—there was an early stir among Republican candidacies in 1995, although only one declared in February. Until 1992, each contest since 1972 had seen at least one such candidate, and three had gone on to garner the nomination (all Democrats). By the end of February 1991, no such candidates had emerged— Paul Tsongas was the first to declare on the last day of April. Phil Gramm declared his candidacy in February 1995 with Lamar Alexander, Arlen Specter, Pat Buchanan, Alan Keyes, Dole, and Robert Dornan declaring before April 15; Richard Lugar declared later in April and Pete Wilson is on the way, as well. Thus, a crowded field of challengers has emerged early to compete for the opportunity to run against President Clinton. Democrats continued to discuss the possibility of challenges being mounted by Sen. Bill Bradley (N.J.), House Minority Leader Richard Gephardt, and former presidential candidate Jackson, though the latter could also run as an independent.

Campaign Financing

The system of public funding for presidential campaigns has received lukewarm public support, particularly if we look at the public participation rates. Republican leaders have become especially critical of the system over the past decade. Nonetheless, partial federal funding for primary campaigns has continued and a critical problem—insolvency—was averted. At the end of 1990, only $115 million remained in the fund used to partially support the nomination campaign, to provide a convention subsidy, and to finance the general election. In 1988, sixteen candidates received a combined $67.5 million in matching funds, and total spending rose to $178 million, an increase of almost 35 percent over 1984 and far more than was available for 1992. While expenditures rose, the percentage of taxpayers participating in the checkoff system had steadily declined from a high of 28.7 percent in 1980 to 19.8 percent in 1990 and 17.7 percent in 1992. Moreover, because the payments to candidates are indexed for inflation but contributions are not, the matching-funds ceiling had steadily increased but the checkoff had remained at one dollar since being introduced in 1976.

Several proposals were developed to deal with the impending shortfall, projected to be most severe in 1996 but already dangerously close in 1992. One proposal for 1992 would have set aside the funds needed to finance conventions (projected at $11 million each), and major-party nominees (projected at $55 million each), leaving only $15 million for the primary election stage, a total that would prove a disadvantage to the Democrats far more than to the Republicans since President Bush expected little competition within his own party for the nomination.[8] As it developed, such draconian measures were unnecessary and Congress addressed the problem of long-term solvency by approving a new checkoff level of $3 in August 1993 when it appeared that there would be no funds available for the primary stage in 1996.

Of the many reforms introduced over the past quarter-century, the public-financing provisions possibly have been the most beneficial. The reforms, in essence, democratized campaign financing by providing public funds and encouraging broad-based contributions. The demise of this system would once again open the presidential race to the highest bidder and damage public trust. Thus, efforts to preserve the system are critical even though the system is not perfect.

Media Coverage

Dissatisfaction persists over mass-media coverage of the nomination process. The media continue to concentrate on the "horse race" aspect of the campaign and devote little effort to providing in-depth information on the issues of the campaign or on the records of candidates in previous office. This is particularly bothersome to the many observers who believe that "the news media have assumed the parties' traditional function of assessing candidates and selecting issues"[9] as the contest has come to accentuate appeals for broad public support. Thus, in the view of some, "judgment by peers is yielding to an 'audition' by the media."[10] The contest has shifted "from smoke-filled rooms to rooms filled with the bright lights of ever-present television cameras."[11]

Evidence of the media's substantial influence may never have been greater than in the 1988 contest, from which two prominent Democratic contenders, Hart and Joseph Biden, withdrew before the race began. Hart entered 1987 as the front-runner; Biden was carefully honing a message that he hoped would inspire a new generation of Democrats. Each soon confronted a storm of controversy over purported character flaws. Hart exacerbated his problems by challenging reporters to look into his personal life, but many questioned whether the press overstepped its role by staking out the candidate's private residence; Biden's problems were triggered when John Sasso, campaign manager for Michael Dukakis, provided the press with a videotape of public statements by Biden containing unattributed passages from the speeches of British Labour party leader Neal Kinnock. In each instance, the media-created controversy derailed the candidate's campaign. Clinton survived a similar storm of controversy during the New Hampshire primary in 1992 when revelations regarding his draft record and a possible extra-marital relationship dominated media coverage.

Doris Graber reports that the three major television networks (still the chief source of campaign information for most citizens) provided 1,543 election stories during the period from January 1 through the party conventions in 1992. An estimated one-third to one-half of the stories provided information on the candidates or policy issues, with emphasis on the candidates. The remainder of the stories (one-half to two-thirds of the total) dealt with trivia information (providing the human touch) or campaign information (novel developments in the competition).[12] A disproportionate share, perhaps as much as 40 percent, of the total nomination coverage is devoted to New Hampshire. Moreover, some argue that the media provide "discretionary" rather than "objective" journalistic coverage of campaigns, allowing their political preferences and professional biases to color their stories. The media declare front-runners, identify the "real" winners of nomination contests (sometimes by providing survey data that contradict the poll results), and generally "keep conjuring up ways to take control of the campaign and campaign issues."[13] In short, the media's collective concern may be less to help voters make better choices than to enhance their own influence.

Media coverage of the campaign, however, can be helpful, as illustrated by the recent proliferation of debates among the competing candidates, a development that was especially important for the Republicans in 1980 and the Democrats in 1984, 1988, and 1992. Such encounters enable the voters to judge the candidates' ability to think on their feet and to see how the participants handle common questions (in regular campaign speeches, the candidates frequently talk past one another). Dukakis, for example, engaged in thirty-nine televised debates during the 1988 nomination contest.[14] While such encounters force candidates to take stands on many controversial issues, they may also help to sow the seeds of party discord in November and could thereby prove to be counterproductive.

Summary of Recent Changes in the Nomination Process

Although the current nomination process is far from ideal (for example, most observers consider it too long), it has undergone substantial change, probably for the better. Moreover, there is little one can do about some of the remaining problems, such as the way the media in a free society choose to cover the campaign. Finally, as the recent record of the Democratic party demonstrates, there is real danger in constantly revising the rules of the game: unintended and unfortunate consequences can result from such changes.[15] Everyone has benefited from the hiatus over the past three elections in the quest for perfection in the presidential nomination process.

How effectively has the system functioned in selecting nominees? Are we finding candidates qualified to serve as president? And have recent changes in the selection process produced different kinds of nominees? John Aldrich argues that the nomination system established since 1968 has not changed the *kinds* of candidates who run but has changed *how* they run. Candidates are still drawn from the ranks of governors, senators, and vice presidents, as they have been historically.[16] As a group, these candidates are probably no more or no less qualified than those who have pursued the office under the old rules. Looking at the pool of successful candidates, Richard Rose has compared American presidents to heads of government in three major European parliamentary systems. According to Rose, the system used to select the former "gives too much weight to learning to campaign, and too little to learning to govern."[17] In short, the selection process rewards persons possessing the skills needed to win election but not necessarily those needed to govern effectively. As a consequence, presidents customarily enter office knowing how to mobilize public support but have far less experience than their parliamentary counterparts in managing the party and the legislature and in overseeing national security and economic policy. Despite the many recent changes in the nomination process, this bias against extensive governmental experience persists, but one also needs to recognize that by rewarding campaign skills, the process may produce presidents with greater ability to mount public appeals—a quality needed in the media age.[18]

One measure of campaign effectiveness is victory, and until 1992, Democrats were disappointed that their nominees did not go on to become winners. A party suffering electoral defeats is naturally more inclined to seek additional changes in the selection process in hopes of finding the way to produce a winner, a pattern true of the Democrats over the past two decades. But it is worth noting that the Republicans, to a large degree, have had to conduct their nominations by the same rules as the Democrats and have been rewarded by an impressive string of victories. Thus, the Democrats' fascination with changing the process may be misdirected effort.

As the nomination process has become longer and more complex, support has grown for a simpler method of selecting party nominees. Sixty-five percent of the public favored holding a single, nationwide primary in 1988 that would completely bypass the traditional party conventions.[19] Such a plan offers the advantages of simplicity and directness but would remove peer review altogether and weaken the mixed character of the present nomination process. Moving the selection of nominees fully into the hands of the public through a national primary might seem to be the next logical step in making the nomination process more democratic, but it would result in serious damage to the national party structures. Presidential nominating conventions have long functioned as the central mechanism for creating nationwide coalitions. Removing this *raison d'être* would do irreparable harm to these already fragile structures. Moreover, part of the difficulty that modern presidents have faced in working with Congress probably stems from the fact that neither institution plays a role in the other's selection. Superdelegates—though they may pose certain risks and may appear to represent a step backward in the democratization of the selection process—ultimately may contribute to greater cooperation between the executive and legislative branches. Because strong parties and legislative-executive harmony are essential to democracy, the proposal for a national primary would do greater harm than good.

One novel proposal would draw on several elements of the "mixed" system. Thomas E. Cronin and Robert D. Loevy have proposed a National Pre-primary Convention Plan in which all states would select delegates to a national convention using the caucus-convention method. Up to three candidates would be nominated by the conventions to appear on a national primary ballot to be held on a single day in September. The candidates receiving a plurality of votes in the primary voting would be the party nominees for the November ballot.[20] Such a system, Cronin and Loevy argue, would strengthen political parties, make the conventions truly deliberative assemblages, rationalize the timetable, retain a critical role for the public, and reduce the impact of the media. Loevy has also suggested an alternative: holding a mini-convention attended by elected officials of each party in January of the election year at which the contenders would be ranked even before the traditional selection of delegates begins.[21]

The present system evolved over the past quarter century and is at least broadly understood by the public. It is reasonable to wonder whether adoption of such dramatically different phases of the process would disrupt public confidence. Such proposals, moreover, may be trying to solve the wrong problem; procedure may be less at fault than more fundamental issues such as the "decline of political parties as representative institutions." [22] Thus, such attempts to rationalize a process that has emerged naturally over time need to demonstrate how they will do more good than mischief before it seems wise to endorse them.

The General Election Process

Recent changes in the election of the president have not been as sweeping as the changes in the nomination process; however, two in particular have had a significant effect on the general election process. The first has to do with the financing of presidential contests; the second pertains to the increased use of candidate debates in the fall campaign.

Public Financing of Presidential Elections

When originally introduced, reformers expected the public financing of presidential elections to provide two major advantages: to equalize the resources available to the two major-party candidates and to spare them the potential abuses associated with raising funds from large contributors. However, resource disparities have never been removed fully and presidential candidates have again become active fund-raisers. Political observers have been especially concerned about two loopholes allowed under the present financing rules: *independent expenditures* and *soft-money contributions*. Under current campaign finance laws, groups and individuals are permitted to spend as much as they wish on behalf of or in opposition to a candidate. However, such efforts must be independent of the favored candidate's campaign. Across the three presidential campaigns of the past decade—1980, 1984, and 1988—independent expenditures averaged more than $15 million, with efforts on behalf of Republican candidates far outdistancing those for Democrats. Independent expenditures sharply decreased in 1992 to $3.4 million from $14.3 million in 1988. The partisan imbalance also declined from 18:1 in 1988 to roughly 5:1 in favor of the Republican. During the 1988 election, the tone of such efforts had also changed dramatically: the proportion of expenditures used to deliver negative messages surged with nearly 25 percent of 1988 expenditures devoted to efforts targeted *against* candidates (including the notorious Willie Horton commercial), a five-fold increase over the previous two presidential elections. These expenditures also declined in 1992 when only $541,406 was devoted to negative messages directed against Bush or Clinton versus more than $3.5 million in 1988.[23]

Of greatest concern today is the competition between the national parties, assisted by their presidential candidates and their campaign organizations, for soft money, contributions made to the political parties and ultimately shared with the state party organizations. These contributions have escalated dramatically in recent election cycles and once again opened up opportunities for so-called "fat cats"—because of their ample wallets—to enjoy privileged access to candidates. Most of these efforts are concentrated during the general election phase of the contest, rather than the nomination phase when candidates raise funds to support their own efforts.

Beyond the $55.2 million in public funds received by Bush and Clinton for the fall election and the $10.3 million that the parties were permitted to raise and contribute to the candidate's efforts, each party raised and spent close to $20 million in soft money. These totals compare to estimates of $9 million in comparable funds raised by the Republicans and $4 million by the Democrats in 1980. Contributions to so-called "party building activities" are not subject to the annual limit of $25,000 on donations to federal candidates and committees. Thus, many of the contributions come in denominations of $100,000 or more, and, because many are made to state party organizations, they are not reported. Such funds— used for buildings, equipment, staff salaries, and the development of computerized voting lists—were strategically coordinated with presidential campaign efforts during 1988 and 1992. Bush and Clinton's finance aides responsible for helping them raise sufficient funds to secure the nomination were also put in charge of the soft money efforts. Herbert Alexander and Anthony Corrado report that 198 contributors gave $100,000 or more to the Republicans and 375 gave or raised $100,000 for the Democrats.[24] Many observers fear that soft money solicitations could once again open up the presidential contest to the highest bidders, the select group of wealthy individuals and interests able to seek influence through large contributions.

Finally, the existing finance system disfavors minor candidates (such as John Anderson in 1980) who must wait until after the election to determine whether they will receive any public subsidy. A third-party or independent candidate must win at least 5 percent of the popular vote to qualify for matching funds, a requirement that makes it difficult for them to raise money when it is most needed—during the campaign itself. Some observers contend that the law should be changed to provide public funds for candidates who reach a certain level of support in the public opinion polls (such as 15 percent) at some designated time during the campaign. These provisions, of course, did not leave Ross Perot at a disadvantage; his personal wealth enabled him to be independent of the finance rules.

Recent trends in both independent expenditures and soft-money contributions are undesirable. Establishing a system of public financing for presidential elections was one of the few developments of the 1970s that succeeded in countering the growing cynicism and distrust of public officials. By failing to place limits on soft-money contributions, failing to enforce rigorous guidelines for independent expenditures, and allowing presidential candidates to engage openly in the solicitation of soft money, the Federal Election Commission (FEC) may have placed these advances in jeopardy. It is essential that these developments be carefully tracked and evaluated over future election cycles.

Presidential Debates

On the whole, presidential debates have been a beneficial development in recent elections. Televised debates provide the public with direct exposure to the candidates and thereby stimulate interest among members of the electorate, particularly those less attentive to other campaign efforts. The encounters help to acquaint viewers with the candidates' views on a variety of political issues and enable the vast audience to reach conclusions on the participants' personal qualities. Nielsen ratings for the three presidential debates in 1992 revealed increased public attention and interest.[25] On the other hand, some observers feel that these events encourage the media as well as voters to focus on style more than substance, to wait breathlessly for a single slip of the tongue that might doom a campaign to failure, and to become fixated on the question of who won the contest as though it were a sporting event. The most severe critics suggest that "debate" is an inappropriate term for what usually amounts to little more than a joint press conference in which the two major-party nominees mouth campaign slogans, a criticism widely applied to the meetings between Bush and Dukakis in 1988. Several departures in debate format pioneered in 1992 are successful experiments that should be continued in the future.

First, the debate rules allowed for greater face-to-face exchanges among the candidates rather than restricting communication to members of a panel asking questions. For years, candidates and their advisers had worried that direct exchanges would increase the chances of a blunder or allow the opponent to gain some advantage, but voters are most interested in observing the candidates and evaluating their relative merits, a task made easier by direct exchanges. Both the single moderator and town-meeting formats used in 1992 provided more flexible and less formalized exchanges. This was true despite the fact that sponsorship had passed from the League of Women Voters to the Commission on Presidential Debates—a creation of the Democratic and Republican parties—which some had feared would preclude more open interaction. (The Commission, in fact, had recommended that the single-moderator format be used exclusively.) It is hoped that this pattern will continue in the future.

Second, progress was made in allowing persons other than journalists to question the contenders; the second debate employed a single moderator who directed questions from an audience of uncommitted voters to the candidates. The manner and substance of the questions seemed to connect with many viewers. This change does not exhaust the possibilities, however; other knowledgeable persons, such as economists, political scientists, and public officials, could help direct candidates' and viewers' attention to substantive concerns. Again, candidates are likely to oppose such a change, as they are more accustomed to dealing with journalists and may fear the technical expertise of others.

Third, participation in the debates should be mandatory rather than optional for major-party candidates receiving public funding. Presidents Lyndon Johnson and Richard Nixon refused to debate on the grounds that it might hurt their candidacies, but Gerald Ford established a precedent of incumbent participation that was followed by his successors. Jimmy Carter opted not to participate in the first 1980 debate, which took place between Ronald Reagan and Anderson, and Bush engaged in lengthy debates *over* the debates before agreeing to a series of contests in 1988 and 1992. Creation of the Commission on Presidential Debates was supposed to have resolved the issue of participation, as both national parties endorsed the new structure, but Bush's delayed commitments put the guarantee into question. Because the major purpose of presidential debates is to educate the electorate, and not to strengthen or weaken a particular candidacy, participation in the debates should be made a condition for the receipt of federal campaign funds.

Fourth, sponsorship of the debates by a bipartisan commission rather than a nonpartisan organization (such as the League of Women Voters, which sponsored the 1976, 1980, and 1984 presidential debates) or a truly public commission could be a problem. On the positive side, under present conditions, party sponsorship increases the likelihood that the debates will take place. The cost, however, is that the candidates' list of conditions are likely to be defended by their party's representative, thereby preventing the encounters from reaching their full potential. The performance of the Commission in 1992 was a pleasant surprise; it placed resolute pressure on Bush to participate and it is hoped that it will do likewise to Clinton in 1996.

Fifth, there is a related concern about participation by a major third-party candidate. There was reason to fear that sponsorship by a bipartisan commission would exclude an independent candidate from participating in the centerpiece of modern campaigns. The competitive conditions that contributed to Perot's participation in the 1992 debates may not be repeated in the future. Both Bush and Clinton had courted Perot's support before he reentered the race and both were willing to bet that Perot would hurt his opponent more than himself. In the future, these calculations may not be so uncertain. The nation could well have a repeat of 1980 when Carter's pollsters told him that Anderson was damaging the president's reelection chances more than Reagan's; thus, Carter refused to participate if Anderson did. This remains a difficult problem, as is the question of how much public support an independent candidate should have in order to qualify for participation. This could become a major issue if Perot's success spawns a spate of independent candidacies in the future.

Electoral College Misfires

The most serious problem in electing the president continues to be a latent one. The electoral college was devised as a means of allowing knowledgeable elites in the states to choose a "continental" character for president, but this purpose was altered with the rise of political parties. (See Chapter 1.) The present system enables voters to register a nationwide verdict but suffers from several weaknesses and potential dangers. Many proposals have been made to reform the system. Most reformers have claimed that their changes would remove an undemocratic feature of the presidential selection process and make the process more effective.

The electoral college as it operates today violates important tenets of political equality central to our contemporary understanding of democracy. Presently, each citizen's vote does not count equally: the influence one has in the election of the president depends on the political situation in one's state. For the many Americans who support a losing candidate in their state, it is as though they had not voted at all; under the general-ticket system, all the electoral votes of a state go to the candidate who wins a plurality of its popular votes. Other citizens who live in populous, politically competitive states have a premium placed on their votes because they are in a position to affect how large blocs of electoral votes are cast.

Three possibilities for an electoral college misfire remain, although the Twelfth Amendment (ratified in 1804) removed an important loophole. (See Chapter 3.) The electoral college still does not ensure that the candidate who receives the most popular votes will win the presidency: John Quincy Adams in 1824, Rutherford B. Hayes in 1876, and Benjamin Harrison in 1888 went to the White House even though they trailed their respective political opponents, Andrew Jackson, Samuel Tilden, and Grover Cleveland in the total popular vote. In 1976, Carter nearly became the first twentieth-century victim of such an electoral college misfire: if some 9,000 voters in Hawaii and Ohio had shifted their ballots to President Ford, Ford would have edged out Carter 270–268. It is possible that Dukakis's campaign consciously pursued a "wrong winner" strategy; polls showed in the closing weeks of the 1988 campaign that Dukakis could not win a popular vote plurality but might be able to eke out razor-thin victories in enough states to give the Democratic candidate the electoral vote victory. If fewer than 1 percent of the nation's voters located in eleven states had shifted their support, Dukakis would have won in the electoral college despite a 5.8 million vote plurality for Bush.[26]

If no candidate wins an electoral college majority, selection of the president will be thrown into the House of Representatives. This occurred in the elections of 1800, 1824, and 1876, and it has come dangerously close to being repeated several times over the past fifty years. In 1948, Harry S. Truman defeated Thomas Dewey by more than two million popular votes, but if just 12,000 people in California and Ohio had voted for Dewey rather than Truman the election would have been decided by the House of Representatives. The same would have occurred in 1960 if some 9,000 people in Illinois and Missouri had voted for Nixon instead of John F. Kennedy, and again in 1968 if approximately 42,000 people in Missouri, New Jersey, and Alaska had cast their ballots for Humphrey rather than President Nixon.[27] Permitting the House of Representatives, voting by states, to select the president of the United States is not consistent with the "one person, one vote" principle that has become a central tenet of modern American democracy.

The 1968 election also illustrates another danger of the electoral college system: an elector need not cast his or her ballot for the candidate who wins the plurality of votes in the elector's state. This problem of the *faithless elector* occurs occasionally (most recently in 1988 when one elector from West Virginia cast her presidential vote for Lloyd Bentsen rather than Dukakis) and is not particularly dangerous when individual electors refuse to follow the result of their state's popular vote. But the possibility of widespread desertion from the popular choice is another matter. If the outcome of the popular vote had made it clear in 1968 that Nixon was unlikely to win a majority of the electoral votes in 1968, third-party candidate George Wallace would have been in a position to bargain with Nixon before the electoral college balloting took place. Wallace could have asked his forty-five electors to cast their ballots for Nixon, which would have given Nixon enough electoral votes to gain victory.[28] (Wallace's forty-five electoral votes would have made little difference for Humphrey, who would not have had a majority even if he had carried the close contests in Missouri, New Jersey, and Alaska, but the Alabama governor could have tried to bargain with Humphrey by offering to influence southern members of the House of Representatives to choose Humphrey over Nixon.)

Proposals to Reform the Electoral College

Over the years, actual and potential problems have created a great deal of dissatisfaction with the electoral college. The sentiment for changing it has increased recently, particularly after the near misfires of 1948, 1960, 1968, and 1976. Although agreement on the need to change the electoral college is widespread, there is marked disagreement over what form that change should take. Five plans have been suggested as substitutes for the present system.

The *automatic plan*, designed to eliminate the possibility of "faithless electors," would make the least change in the present system. A state's electoral votes would automatically be cast for the popular-vote winner in that state. If no candidate received a majority of the electoral votes, a joint session of Congress would choose the winner. Each representative and senator would have one vote.

Under the *district plan*, states would return to the method used early in the nation's history. This method, used since 1972 by Maine and adopted for 1992 by Nebraska, awards one electoral vote to the presidential candidate who wins the plurality vote in each House district, with the remaining two electoral votes going to the statewide popular winner. If no candidate received a majority of the electoral votes, senators and representatives, sitting jointly and voting as individuals, would choose the president from the three candidates having the highest number of electoral votes. Members of Congress and private groups from rural areas have been the principal supporters of this plan, which would, if adopted, shift attention to the most politically competitive congressional districts in which the two major parties traditionally divide the vote 55 to 45 percent.

The *proportional plan* would divide each state's electoral votes in proportion to the division of the popular vote in the state: a candidate receiving 60 percent of the popular vote would receive 60 percent of its electoral votes. A plan of this type was passed by the Senate in 1950 but not by the House. It would eliminate the present advantage enjoyed by the large states, which are able to throw all their electoral votes to one candidate. Proportional division of the electoral votes, if fairly evenly split between the two major candidates, increases the possibility that neither candidate would receive a majority; hence, there would be a greater likelihood that an election would enter the House for decision, particularly in a year such as 1992 when there was a strong third-party candidate who drew support in all regions of the country.[29]

This possibility would be removed if the president were chosen through *direct popular election*. In 1969, the House passed a constitutional amendment providing that the president (and vice president) be elected by a minimum of 40 percent of the popular vote and, if no candidate received so large a vote, that a runoff be held between the two leading contenders. The Senate failed to pass the amendment, however, despite the efforts of its major sponsor, Birch Bayh (D-Ind.). After Carter's narrow electoral college victory, Bayh introduced the same measure in 1977, but it failed to clear the Congress that year. No such proposal has been enacted since.

Finally, a proposal advanced by the Twentieth Century Fund, a research group, is known as the *national bonus plan*.[30] It would award the nationwide popular winner 102 "bonus" votes (two for each state plus two for the District of Columbia), which would be added to the electoral votes received under the present state-by-state system. To win the election a candidate would have to receive a majority of 640, the new total number of electoral votes (the former total of 538 plus the 102 bonus votes). If no one received 321 electoral votes, a runoff would be held between the two front-runners. Thus, the proposal retains the electoral college system but ensures that the total electoral vote will better reflect the nationwide popular vote. It also allows the voters, rather than the House of Representatives, to make the final choice of the president if no candidate receives a majority of the electoral votes.

Conclusions

As argued in this chapter, proposed reforms of the nominating and election processes share a general concern with extending democracy and enhancing effectiveness, despite disagreements over how to define and balance these goals. Americans now select the president through a doubly indirect process: the popular will is mediated by the convention delegates who select the party nominees and by the electors who determine the winner of the general election. Democracy, some argue, would be better served by removing these mediating elites through a system of national primaries or a direct popular election plan. Moreover, because each stage of the present process is susceptible to a misfire that might thwart the people's will, reform might also improve system effectiveness.

Perhaps the most powerful argument is offered by advocates of direct popular election who argue that "the electoral college is morally wrong. It is undemocratic and therefore indefensible." [31] The entire focus of reform throughout American history has been toward democratizing the political process by giving citizens a greater role in directing public affairs. Moreover, emergence of a "wrong winner" would have disastrous consequences by denying the victorious candidate anything approximating a popular mandate, an essential ingredient for legitimacy and success in the modern era. Despite their apparent attractions, these arguments are not wholly convincing.

Although misfires are possible in both stages of the selection process, the system has evolved over the past four decades so that first-ballot nominations have become routine. Over the past century electors have validated the outcome of the popular vote. It is possible, of course, that the selection process could break down during any election, a possibility that is of greater concern in the general election, where the danger of violating popular preferences has been more narrowly averted. Nonetheless, it is difficult to regard any of the plans designed to replace the electoral college or the mixed nominating system as optimal solutions. None of the plans currently under consideration is foolproof. Moreover, their adoption would sacrifice an important quality provided by the present "flawed" system: continuity with the past. Despite their problems, the present nomination and election processes confer a degree of legitimacy on their outcomes, something that may be lost in the process of change. The Democrats' experience in redesigning their delegate selection procedures is instructive in this regard. Advocates of reform might point out that the new "mixed system" represents a distinct improvement over its predecessor. On the other hand, opponents of reform can point to the disruption (often unintended) and loss of legitimacy occasioned by reform proposals advanced to favor or obstruct particular candidates. Although it leaves open the possibility of repeating a past failure, remaining true to the traditional system brings with it the strength of continuity.

One unintended consequence likely to flow from adopting a system of direct election of the president is encouragement of splinter parties and charismatic candidates. As the system now stands, coalitions must be created before the election, a structural feature that encourages compromise and broad-based appeals. Any system of direct election would include a run-off provision to ensure that the winner receives at least 40 percent of the popular vote. Such a rule is likely to encourage multiple candidacies that will challenge the fundamental logic and stability of the traditional selection system. Groups will be encouraged to offer narrowly focused candidates in hopes of making the second round, and candidates, operating in a more crowded field, are more likely to offer more extreme solutions and grandiose promises as a way to distinguish themselves from their opponents. Although the arguments encouraging popular notions of democracy are appealing, Americans would do well to consider fully the consequences *before* introducing systemic change.

This is a consciously chosen conservative position on reform. It does not recommend that change be avoided. Rather, change should be introduced only after cautious and thorough assessment of the probable consequences—consequences that are unintended as well as intended. Our system of presidential selection is remarkably complex and has proved, over time, to be surprisingly responsive to new forces in American society. Adjustments have been made periodically and most have introduced welcome changes. Responsiveness is likely to remain an important characteristic of the system. But continuity is a virtue just as valuable as change—even if it seems less exciting.

Notes

1. Byron E. Shafer, *Quiet Revolution: The Struggle for the Democratic Party and the Shaping of the Post-Reform Politics* (New York: Russell Sage Foundation, 1983).
2. Ibid., 524.
3. James W. Ceaser, "Political Parties—Declining, Stabilizing, or Resurging?" in *The New American Political System*, 2d ed., ed. Anthony King (Washington, D.C.: AEI Press, 1990), 112.
4. Samuel Kernell, *Going Public: New Strategies of Presidential Leadership* (Washington, D.C.: CQ Press, 1986).
5. Ceaser, "Political Parties," 113–114.
6. Robert D. Loevy, *The Flawed Path to the Presidency 1992: Unfairness and Inequality in the Presidential Selection Process* (Albany: State University of New York Press, 1995), 150.
7. *Congressional Quarterly Weekly Report*, February 28, 1987, 380.
8. *Congressional Quarterly Weekly Report*, March 2, 1991, 558–559.
9. Dom Bonafede, "Scoop or Snoop?" *National Journal*, November 5, 1988, 2793.
10. Wilson Carey McWilliams, "The Meaning of the Election," in *The Election of 1988*, ed. Gerald M. Pomper (Chatham, N.J.: Chatham House, 1989), 180.
11. Martin P. Wattenberg, "From a Partisan to a Candidate-Centered Electorate,"

in *The New American Political System,* ed. Anthony King (Washington, D.C.: AEI Press, 1990), 140.

12. Doris A. Graber, "Yes—The Media Do Inform," in *Controversial Issues in Presidential Selection,* 2d ed., ed. Gary L. Rose (Albany: State University of New York Press, 1994), 109–110. Data on media coverage from *Media Monitor* 6(7), no. 2 (August–September 1992); and 6(9), no. 2 (November 1992).

13. Robert D. Loevy, "No—The Media Do Not Inform," in *Controversial Issues in Presidential Selection,* ed. Rose, 124.

14. Ibid., 143.

15. A book dealing with such consequences is Nelson Polsby, *Consequences of Party Reform* (New York: Oxford University Press, 1983).

16. John Aldrich, "Presidential Selection: A Critical Review" (Paper presented at Presidency Research Conference, University of Pittsburgh, November 11–14, 1990). See also Aldrich, "Methods and Actors: The Relationship of Processes to Candidates," in *Presidential Selection,* ed. Alexander Heard and Michael Nelson (Durham, N.C.: Duke University Press, 1987).

17. Richard Rose, "Learning to Govern or Learning to Campaign?" in *Presidential Selection,* ed. Heard and Nelson, 73.

18. One might argue that Bush could claim equal if not more extensive government experience than John Major, selected to succeed Margaret Thatcher as British Prime Minister in November 1990.

19. *The Gallup Report,* March 1988, 9–11.

20. Thomas E. Cronin and Robert D. Loevy, "Yes—It Is Time for a New Presidential Nominating Process," in *Controversial Issues in Presidential Selection,* ed. Rose, 28–36.

21. Robert D. Loevy *The Flawed Path to the Presidency 1992,* chap. 25.

22. Everett Carll Ladd, "No—It Is Not the Time for a New Presidential Nominating Process," in *Controversial Issues in Presidential Selection,* ed. Rose, 37–46.

23. For 1988, a total of $14.1 million in independent expenditures was reported to the FEC, with $10,054,000 favoring the Republican ticket and $568,000 the Democrats. Negative spending was $146,000 against the Republicans and $3,499,000 against the Democrats. *Statistical Abstract of the United States, 1990,* Table 447 (Washington, D.C.: U.S. Government Printing Office, 1990). 1992 figures taken from Herbert E. Alexander and Anthony Corrado, *Financing the 1992 Election* (Armonk, N.Y.: M.E. Sharpe, 1995), Table 5.2.

24. Alexander and Corrado, *Financing the 1992 Election,* chap. 5.

25. James L. Lengle and Dianne C. Lambert, "No—Presidential Debates Should Not Be Required," in *Controversial Issues in Presidential Selection,* ed. Rose, Table 1, 196.

26. David W. Abbott and James P. Levine, *Wrong Winner: The Coming Debacle in the Electoral College* (Westport, N.Y.: Praeger, 1991), 32–37.

27. *Congressional Quarterly Weekly Report,* December 17, 1988, 3526–3527; Carol Matlack, "Backdoor Spending," *National Journal,* October 8, 1988, 2516–2519.

28. Although Wallace actually earned forty-five electoral votes, he received forty-six because one elector in North Carolina (which went for Nixon) cast his vote for the Alabama governor. In 1960, 1972, and 1976, single electors in Oklahoma, Virginia, and Washington also cast their ballot for a candidate other than the one who received the popular-vote plurality in their state.

29. Most of the proportional plans have suggested lowering the winning electoral-vote requirement from a majority to 40 or even 35 percent to avoid the possi-

bility of having the election go to the House. They have also proposed that, if no candidate receives the requisite proportion of electoral votes, the two houses of Congress, meeting jointly and voting as individuals, should choose the president.

30. *Winner-Take-All: Report of the Twentieth Century Task Force on Reform of the Presidential Election Process* (New York: Holmes and Meier, 1978), 4–6.
31. Abbott and Levine, *Wrong Winner*, 153.

Selected Readings

Abbott, David W., and James P. Levine. *Wrong Winner: The Coming Debacle in the Electoral College.* Westport, N.Y.: Praeger, 1991.

Best, Judith. *The Case against the Direct Election of the President: A Defense of the Electoral College.* Ithaca, N.Y.: Cornell University Press, 1975.

Diamond, Martin. *The Electoral College and the American Idea of Democracy.* Washington, D.C.: AEI Press, 1977.

Longley, Lawrence, and Alan Braun. *The Politics of Electoral College Reform.* New Haven, Conn.: Yale University Press, 1975.

Rose, Gary L., ed. *Controversial Issues in Presidential Selection.* 2d ed. Albany, N.Y.: State University of New York Press, 1994.

Guide to the 1996
Presidential Race

Schedule of 1996 Presidential Primaries and Caucuses

BY THE MIDDLE OF 1995, states were still jockeying for position in the 1996 contests. This was particularly true for Iowa and New Hampshire—states that seek to retain a margin of at least eight days and seven days, respectively, before the next states' contest.

Date	State	Procedure	Parties participating
Feb. 6	Louisiana	Caucus	Rep.
Feb. 12	Iowa*	Caucus	Dem./Rep.
Feb. 20	New Hampshire*	Primary	Dem./Rep.
Feb. 24	Delaware*	Primary	Dem./Rep.
Feb. 27	Arizona	Primary	Rep.
	N. Dakota	Primary	Rep.
	S. Dakota	Primary	Dem./Rep.
March 2	S. Carolina	Primary	Rep.
March 5	Alaska	Caucus	Dem.
	Colorado	Primary	Dem./Rep.
	Georgia	Primary	Dem./Rep.
	Idaho	Caucus	Dem.
	Maryland	Primary	Dem./Rep.
	Minnesota	Caucus	Dem.
	Vermont	Primary	Dem./Rep.
	Washington	Caucus	Dem.
March 7	Missouri	Caucus	Dem.
	New York	Primary	Dem./Rep.
March 10	Nevada	Caucus	Dem.
March 12	Florida	Primary	Dem./Rep.

	Hawaii	Caucus	Dem.
	Maine	Primary	Dem.
	Massachusetts*	Primary	Dem./Rep.
	Mississippi	Primary	Dem./Rep.
	Oklahoma	Primary	Dem./Rep.
	Rhode Island	Primary	Dem.Rep.
	Tennessee	Primary	Dem./Rep.
	Texas	Primary/Caucus	Dem./Rep.
March 17	Puerto Rico	Primary	Rep.
March 19	Illinois	Primary	Dem./Rep.
	Michigan	Primary	Dem./Rep.
	Ohio	Primary	Dem./Rep.
	Wisconsin	Primary	Dem./Rep.
March 23	Wyoming	Caucus	Dem.
March 25	Utah	Caucus	Dem.
March 26	California	Primary	Dem./Rep.
	Connecticut*	Primary	Dem./Rep.
March 30	Virgin Islands	Caucus	Dem.
April 2	Kansas	Primary	Dem./Rep.
April 13	Virginia	Caucus	Dem.
April 23	Pennsylvania*	Primary	Dem./Rep.
May 7	Dist. of Columbia	Primary	Dem./Rep.
	Indiana	Primary	Dem./Rep.
	N. Carolina	Primary	Dem./Rep.
May 14	Nebraska	Primary	Dem./Rep.
	West Virginia	Primary	Dem./Rep.
May 21	Arkansas	Primary	Dem./Rep.
	Oregon	Primary	Dem./Rep.
May 28	Kentucky	Primary	Dem./Rep.
June 6	Alabama	Primary	Dem./Rep.
	Montana	Primary	Dem./Rep.
	New Jersey	Primary	Dem./Rep.
	New Mexico	Primary	Dem./Rep.

*Change in the date still possible.

Profiles of Prospective Candidates in the 1996 Presidential Contest

Republican Candidates

Lamar Alexander, lawyer, former governor of Tennessee

Although presenting himself as a conservative "outsider," Lamar Alexander has spent considerable time on the political inside. He served as secretary of education under President George Bush; he served two terms as governor of Tennessee; and before that, he worked as a legislative aide in the Nixon White House and as a congressional staff member. Alexander's early campaign had a populist theme, with the candidate proclaiming the need to dismantle the federal government. At times, he has encouraged a return to a part-time, citizens' legislature, but that appeal has diminished since the Republicans' 1994 sweep in Congress. In general, Alexander supports limited government, advocates a cut in the capital gains tax, opposes preferences for job and educational applicants, and urges no reductions in defense spending. Although less well known among Republican voters than some other contenders, Alexander is viewed by his competitors as a serious opponent, organizing a strong cadre of advisors and fund-raisers. If the American people are looking for yet another "outsider" to fix Washington, then Alexander's message could carry him to the White House.

Patrick J. Buchanan, conservative columnist

This is the second bid by Patrick J. Buchanan for the GOP presidential nomination. He was unsuccessful in 1992, placing a distant second to the Republican incumbent, Bush, but his challenge proved more damaging than most analysts had expected. Buchanan's political views and experience have changed little since. He is an ultraconservative, advocating a foreign policy that many describe as isolationist—including ardent opposition to the North American Free Trade Agreement (NAFTA) and other trade deals. He vehemently denounces illegal immigration and what he perceives as a loss of "traditional values." His prime-time speech to the 1992 Republican national convention delighted the party's right wing by announcing a "holy war" for the hearts and minds of the American people. Despite the intensity of his supporters, Buchanan must be considered a long shot for the nomination, but he will put pressure on other candidates to address the concerns of an important segment of the Republican party. Buchanan has never held elected public office. Most recently, he has been a national commentator, after serving in the Nixon and Reagan White Houses as a speechwriter and communications director.

Bob Dole, U.S. senator from Kansas

Bob Dole is the clear front-runner in the Republican presidential nomination field for 1996. Dole is not new to GOP presidential politics; he was the party's vice-presidential nominee in 1976, and he made runs for the presidential nomination in 1980 and 1988. Plagued by disorganization and occasional infighting in previous campaigns, Dole initially appears more willing to follow advice from his campaign organization. He is portrayed as a candidate with extensive experience and maturity, one who has "earned the right" to be the next president. Citing popular conservative beliefs such as tax cuts, government downsizing, and shifting power back to the states, Dole aims to attract a broad-based conservative constituency. As a long-time fixture in the Senate (thirty-four years in Congress) and as his party's leader since 1984, Dole has always been a pragmatist, constructing bargains and compromises with presidents and Democrats. These included endorsing several tax increases during the 1980s. In 1988 Dole refused to sign a pledge against future tax increases; in this bid for the nomination, he signed such a pledge on the first day of his candidacy. In the same way, Dole has shifted to more conservative positions on gun control and affirmative action, though his long-time record has been as an advocate of balanced budgets and beneficial social programs, including aid to the handicapped and support of civil rights. Dole is a decorated World War II veteran who sustained serious wounds. Should he win the nomination and general election, he would be seventy-three years old on inauguration day.

Robert K. Dornan, U.S. representative from California

A fierce and outspoken conservative, Robert K. Dornan has earned a following for himself among the GOP's right wing. Much like Buchanan, Dornan's presence in the race will force his competitors to place greater emphasis on social issues. He focuses on what he perceives as a "moral breakdown" of American society and preaches the need for a "virtuous" people; solutions to economic problems are secondary to Dornan. Although cultural conservatives represent a growing segment within the Republican party, political strategists suggest that Dornan's campaign will alienate centrist voters. As a nine-term congressional representative, former air force pilot, and talk show host, Dornan is best known for his feisty outbursts in the House, most recently directed at President Clinton. During the campaign season, Dornan could embarrass both Phil Gramm and Lamar Alexander, who claimed draft deferments during the Vietnam War.

Phil Gramm, U.S. senator from Texas

Phil Gramm was the first officially declared candidate in the race, announcing on February 24, 1995. He describes himself as the only "genuine conservative" among the Republican presidential nominees. Gramm is likely to be the best-funded candidate; he set the all-time record for a single fund-raising event: $4.1 million. In early polls, a majority of Republican voters had not formed an opinion of Gramm. He places the elimination of the deficit as priority number one, and emphasizes his earlier budgetary stance displayed in the Gramm-Rudman-Hollings budget balancing act of the 1980s. He has pledged to dismantle the welfare system, steadfastly apply the death penalty, end hiring quotas and preferences, and strengthen the U.S. military. Before being elected to the House as a Texas Democrat in 1978, Gramm was an economics professor at Texas A&M University. He left the Democratic party in 1983, gained reelection to the House as a Republican, and after two years ran successfully for the Senate, winning reelection in 1992. Considered a serious challenger to early front-runner Dole, Gramm could be plagued by his draft deferments during the Vietnam War.

Alan Keyes, conservative commentator

Alan Keyes came closest to holding elected public office when he ran unsuccessfully for U.S. Senate seats in Maryland in 1988 and 1992. A Harvard-educated African American, Keyes held several posts in the U.S. Department of State during the Reagan administration, and later served as interim president of Alabama A&M University for a year. He will be asking the public to move him from a radio studio and the public lecture circuit to the White House. The central focus of his presidential campaign will be family values, including opposition to abortion, teenage pregnancy, and homosexuality. Keyes will find a crowd of competitors on the right wing of the Republican party with Buchanan, Dornan, and Gramm taking similar stands on the same issues and all being better funded. His chances for victory are miniscule, but he could influence the direction of the debate and help change the Republican party's image.

Richard G. Lugar, businessperson, U.S. senator from Indiana

Although Richard G. Lugar has been a senator since 1976 and held a major post as chair of the Senate Foreign Relations Committee, he is little known to the national electorate. He previously served as mayor of Indianapolis and had been considered for vice president on three occasions. Lugar is seen as combining a number of desirable traits: personal steadiness, confidence in crisis situations, and the capacity to reach bipartisan agreements. He is not, however, a captivating speaker or dynamic campaigner. Although his current post as chair of the Agriculture Committee gives him a major role in redesigning farm policy, his long-term emphasis clearly has been on foreign policy, a potential detriment during a campaign expected once again to focus on domestic issues. Unlike his Republican counterparts, Lugar places deficit reduction above tax cuts for the middle and upper classes. He has proposed replacing the income tax system altogether with a national sales tax.

Arlen Specter, lawyer, U.S. senator from Pennsylvania

When he entered the race, Arlen Specter adopted an unorthodox Republican stance. He firmly supports a woman's right to choose an abortion, directly attacks the party's religious right for obscuring distinctions between church and state, and is generally perceived as a social moderate. Specter advocates a switch to a flat tax, an idea gaining popularity throughout the Republican party. Specter described himself as a disciple of the Barry Goldwater philosophy, which preaches the "need to keep the government out of our pocketbooks, off our backs, and out of our bedrooms." Although he has been seen as a social libertarian, few political analysts give him much chance to succeed, lagging far behind his competitors in campaign fund-raising. While Specter seems to have potential to pick up support, it is unlikely his effort will prove fruitful in 1996.

Pete Wilson, lawyer, governor of California

Any major California candidate must be regarded as a serious contender for the nomination, and Pete Wilson adds political skills to the mix, as demonstrated in 1994 when he came from far behind to win reelection as governor of the nation's most populous state. He has demonstrated a mastery of modern campaigning and the knack to identify and run successfully on "hot-button" issues including crime, welfare, immigration, and, increasingly, affirmative action. In exploring his candidacy, Wilson has been developing a message that focuses on clear distinctions between "right" and "wrong," as well as the government's unfairness to those who are doing the "right thing." As governor, Wilson has a major advantage in gaining support from the largest bloc of delegates attending the Republican convention. The state also gives him a wealthy fund-raising base. However, the governor had promised *not* to seek the presidential nomination if his bid for reelection was successful (Clinton violated a similar pledge in 1992), and if elected to the presidency he would be succeeded by the lieutenant governor, who is a Democrat. In addition, Wilson is regarded with suspicion by the party's conservative wing, including the outspoken Dornan. He has raised state taxes and supports a woman's right to choose. Like Alexander, Wilson could seek to run as an "outside" candidate, although he has held public office continuously since 1966, including stints in the state assembly, as mayor of San Diego, and seven years in the U.S. Senate.

Democratic Candidates

Bill Clinton, president of the United States

Resilience has been the hallmark of Bill Clinton's first term in office, as it was during his 1992 campaign. Clinton labeled himself the "Comeback Kid" after the 1992 New Hampshire primary, when he survived campaign incidents that would have forced most candidates out of the contest. Instead, he persevered and won an impressive—although far from resounding—victory, garnering 43 percent of the popular vote. His first year in office was similarly shaky, marked by extended controversy over efforts to revise military policy on homosexuals, the perception of an unsteady foreign policy, clashes with the media, and a long delay in formulating health reform proposals. Health reform and campaign finance reform, two centerpieces of the administration's platform for change, failed to pass a Democratically controlled Congress and face virtually no prospect for passage under the Republican Congress elected in November

1994. There have been some successes, including passage of NAFTA, establishment of AmeriCorps, restoration of democracy in Haiti, the resumption of Middle East peace talks, a growing economy, and a declining budget deficit. Like his record, Clinton's public approval ratings have been mixed, at best—anemic much of the time with little chance to establish a record of accomplishment now that the Republicans control Congress. Nonetheless, Clinton has substantial political skills and an impressive intellect, is a quick learner, and continues to emphasize potentially attractive themes, including change, the future, and moderation. Clinton hopes to do something no Democratic president has done since Franklin D. Roosevelt—gain reelection to a second term. As the crowded field of Republican aspirants scramble to win support with conservative activists, Clinton could become the safe candidate for voters seeking a moderate to lead them into an unsure future. Initial speculation about a political challenge mounted within his own party had largely disappeared by the middle of 1995, but then Clinton angered most of his own party by proposing a compromise on balancing the national budget that accepted large cuts in Medicare and Medicaid, programs the Democrats had been defending against Republican threats. This move made a liberal challenge more likely.

Richard A. Gephardt, lawyer, U.S. representative from Missouri

If for some reason Clinton were to exit the 1996 campaign or the party's liberal wing sought to unseat him, Richard A. Gephardt would emerge as a strong contender. Now serving as minority leader of the House, Gephardt would bring extensive experience and name recognition to a presidential campaign. He entered Congress in 1976, became the House majority leader in 1989, and inherited the top Democratic leadership position in 1995. Gephardt established name recognition when he unsuccessfully sought the Democratic presidential nomination in 1988. No hint of personal or political scandal emerged from the media's close scrutiny. After Super Tuesday in 1992, those who doubted that Clinton could lead the Democrats to victory launched an effort to convince Gephardt to jump into the presidential race, but he demurred. Like Clinton, Gephardt is a political moderate with extensive knowledge about a wide range of public policies. Speculation about his renewed presidential aspirations mounted when the Democratic leader announced a tax proposal in December 1994, just two days prior to Clinton's own version. Gephardt's tax cut ideas, as well as his ideas for reforming welfare, are similar to Clinton's. Although it remains unlikely that any Democrat would challenge a sitting president, Gephardt would bring clear assets to such an effort.

Independent Candidates

Jesse Jackson Jr., U.S. senator from Washington, D.C. (non-voting), chair of the National Rainbow Coalition

A public figure for more than two decades, Jesse Jackson ran unsuccessfully for the Democratic presidential nomination in 1984 and 1988. A charismatic speaker and veteran of the civil rights movement, Jackson could play the role of political spoiler by entering the 1996 presidential race either as a Democrat or as an independent. Jackson was a non-factor in the 1992 election and expressed dissatisfaction with what he perceived as the Clinton-Gore ticket's abandonment of traditional liberal policy positions. In addition, Jackson felt that the promises made by Clinton in 1992 have not been met, calling the president a "dream buster" for African Americans and other minorities. Although many political analysts do not see Jackson as a potential presidential candidate, a Jackson bid for the presidency, like that of Buchanan in 1992, could divide the party of the incumbent president. By challenging Clinton for the Democratic nomination, Jackson could force Clinton to pay more attention to the left. As an independent candidate, Jackson could be even more worrisome to Democrats because he could deprive Clinton of votes in pivotal states such as Ohio, Michigan, and Illinois.

H. Ross Perot, businessperson, independent candidate in 1992

H. Ross Perot became a national figure in the 1992 presidential election through his strong personality, his insistence that issues avoided by the other two candidates be discussed, his service as a vehicle for voter anger with Washington, and his financial independence. Perot first became known for his much publicized efforts during the Vietnam War to free prisoners of war held in North Vietnam. In 1978, he again made headlines when he rescued two of his employees who were imprisoned in Iran. In 1992, Perot ran as an independent candidate with a novel twist. Everything about Perot's candidacy was unconventional, and by June of 1992, Perot was running even with Bush and ahead of Clinton in the polls. With this sudden success came additional pressure and media attention. The campaign fell apart as a result of Perot's limited knowledge of conventional politics and his fiery temper. He withdrew in July only to reenter the race in October 1992 and to become a force during the campaign's final month. He received 19 percent of the popular vote, demonstrating the depths of the public's dissatisfaction with politics-as-usual and its powerful demand for change. He emerged as a frequent critic of the Clinton administration and campaigned aggressively against NAFTA, an effort that included a televised debate with Vice President Gore. Even if he does not run in 1996, Perot, through his organization United We Stand America, will seek to be a political force, potentially assuming the role of "kingmaker" by pressuring candidates to address his issues of concern.

Colin L. Powell, former chair of the Joint Chiefs of Staff, public speaker, and writer

Colin L. Powell has been called the "knight in shining brass." After helping to engineer the American victory in the Persian Gulf War and battling the Clinton administration over a revised policy on gays in the military, Powell retired from active duty to write his memoirs and hit the lecture circuit. In early January 1995, Powell's popularity and prestige was the highest among U.S. public figures. With near-universal support, Powell could be a formidable presidential candidate, but given his lack of political experience and uncertainty about his positions on a broad range of public issues, some political analysts question whether his popularity could be translated into votes. Is Powell a Democrat or a Republican? His answer is "neither." He has stated that he is developing a political philosophy, but he considers it an evolutionary process. One media consultant summarized the uncertainty about Powell by describing him as "a riddle wrapped in a mystery inside a uniform." He has refused to take a stand on several highly charged social issues, including abortion and gun control. He believes that social ills stem from a lack of traditional family "values," and he is a committed centrist. As one might expect, Powell lacks expertise on domestic issues and in the operations of a political campaign. Like Perot, Powell benefits from the public discontent with Washington, but he confronts the daunting historical record of failure by third party candidates.

Lowell P. Weicker Jr., former governor and U.S. senator from Connecticut

Lowell Weicker has been in public life since 1962, serving first in the Connecticut House of Representatives, the U.S. House of Representatives, and from 1971 to 1989, in the U.S. Senate. In 1990, Weicker became governor of Connecticut, running as an independent candidate of A Connecticut Party. Weicker has always been known as a political "maverick." His independence won him respect in many quarters, but it also cost him the support of the dominant, conservative wing of the Republican party. He is considered a liberal on social issues, and has often battled with GOP conservatives. Unlike Perot and the other prominent independents, Weicker has experienced the problems of being an independent executive confronting a legislature dominated by the two major parties. However, with Perot and Jackson considering independent campaigns for 1996, there may be little room for an additional independent candidate.

Results of 1992
Presidential Primaries

1992 Republican Primary Results

	Turnout	Buchanan	Bush	Duke	Others	Uncommitted
New Hampshire (Feb. 18)	174,165	37.4%	53.0%	—	9.7%	—
South Dakota (Feb. 25)	44,671	—	69.3	—		30.7
Colorado (March 3)	195,690	30.0	67.5	—	2.5	—
Georgia (March 3)	453,987	35.7	64.3	—		—
Maryland (March 3)	240,021	29.9	70.1	—		—
South Carolina (March 7)	148,840	25.7	66.9	7.1	0.3	—
Florida (March 10)	893,463	31.9	68.1	—		—
Louisiana (March 10)	135,109	27.0	62.0	8.8	2.1	—
Massachusetts (March 10)	269,701	27.7	65.6	2.1	0.9	3.8
Mississippi (March 10)	154,708	16.7	72.3	10.6	0.4	—
Oklahoma (March 10)	217,721	26.6	69.6	2.6	1.2	—
Rhode Island (March 10)	15,636	31.8	63.0	2.1	0.3	2.8
Tennessee (March 10)	245,653	22.2	72.5	3.1	—	2.0
Texas (March 10)	797,146	23.9	69.8	2.5	0.3	3.5
Illinois (March 17)	831,140	22.5	76.4	—	1.2	—
Michigan (March 17)	449,133	25.0	67.2	2.4	0.1	5.3
Connecticut (March 24)	99,473	21.9	66.7	2.3	—	9.1
Puerto Rico (April 5)	262,426	0.4	99.2	0.3	0.1	—
Kansas (April 7)	213,196	14.8	62.0	1.8	4.8	16.6
Minnesota (April 7)	132,756	24.2	63.9	—	8.8[b]	3.1
Wisconsin (April 7)	482,248	16.3	75.6	2.7[a]	3.7	1.8
Pennsylvania (April 28)	1,008,777	23.2	76.8	—	—	—
District of Columbia (May 5)	5,235	18.5	81.5	—	—	—
Indiana (May 5)	467,615	19.9	80.1	—	—	—

State (Date)	Votes					
North Carolina (May 5)	283,571	19.5	70.7	—	—	9.8
Nebraska (May 12)	192,098	13.5	81.4	1.5	3.7	—
West Virginia (May 12)	124,157	14.6	80.5	—	4.9	—
Oregon (May 19)	304,159	19.0	67.1	2.2	11.8	—
Washington (May 19)	129,655	10.2	67.0	1.2	21.6[b]	—
Arkansas (May 26)	54,876	11.9	83.1	—	—	5.0
Idaho (May 26)	115,502	13.1	63.5	—	—	23.4
Kentucky (May 26)	101,119	—	74.5	—	—	25.5
Alabama (June 2)	165,121	7.6	74.3	—	—	18.1
California (June 2)	2,156,464	26.4	73.6	—	—	—
Montana (June 2)	90,975	11.8	71.6	—	—	16.6
New Jersey (June 2)	310,270	15.0	77.5	—	7.5[b]	—
New Mexico (June 2)	86,967	9.1	63.8	—	—	27.1
Ohio (June 2)	924,572	16.8	83.2	—	—	27.1
North Dakota (June 9)	47,808	—	83.4	—	16.6[b]	—

SOURCE: *Congressional Quarterly Weekly Report*, August 8, 1992, 63.

NOTE: Results are based on official returns except for Ohio, where results are nearly complete but unofficial.

[a] Duke withdrew from the race April 22.
[b] Write-in votes for H. Ross Perot totaled 2.7 percent of the Republican primary vote in Minnesota, 19.6 percent in North Dakota, 7.5 percent in Washington, 7.5 percent in New Jersey, and 8.1 percent in North Dakota.
— indicates that the candidate or the uncommitted line was not listed on the ballot.

1992 Democratic Primary Results

	Turnout	Brown	Clinton	Harkin	Kerrey	Tsongas	Others	Uncommitted
New Hampshire (Feb. 18)	167,819	8.1%	24.7%	10.2%	11.1%	33.2%	12.7%	—
South Dakota (Feb. 25)	59,503	3.9	19.1	25.2	40.2	9.6	2.0	—
Colorado (March 3)	239,643	28.8	26.9	2.4	12.3	25.6	1.6	2.2
Georgia (March 3)	454,631	8.1	57.2	2.1	4.8	24.0	—	3.8
Maryland (March 3)	567,224	8.2	33.5	5.8	4.8[a]	40.6	0.8	6.4
South Carolina (March 7)	116,414	6.0	62.9	6.6[b]	0.5	18.3	2.6	3.1
Florida (March 10)	1,123,857	12.4	50.8	1.2	1.1	34.5	—	—
Louisiana (March 10)	384,417	6.6	69.5	1.0	0.8	11.1	11.0	—
Massachusetts (March 10)	794,093	14.6	10.9	0.5	0.7	66.3	5.5	1.5
Mississippi (March 10)	191,357	9.6	73.1	1.3	0.9	8.1	0.8	6.2
Oklahoma (March 10)	416,129	16.7	70.5	3.4	3.2	—	11.9	—
Rhode Island (March 10)	50,709	18.8	21.2	0.6	0.9	52.9	4.1	1.4
Tennessee (March 10)	318,482	8.0	67.3	0.7	0.5	19.4	0.1	3.9
Texas (March 10)	1,482,975	8.0	65.6	1.3	1.4	19.2	4.5	—
Illinois (March 17)	1,504,130	14.6	51.6	2.0	0.7	25.8	0.7	4.5
Michigan (March 17)	585,972	25.8	50.7	1.1	0.5	16.6[c]	0.5	4.8
Connecticut (March 24)	173,119	37.2	35.6	1.1	0.7	19.5	2.7	3.1
Puerto Rico (April 5)	63,398	1.6	95.6	0.0	1.3	0.1	1.0	0.3
Kansas (April 7)	160,251	13.0	51.3	0.6	1.4	15.2	4.7	13.8
Minnesota (April 7)*	204,170	30.6	31.1	2.0	0.6	21.3	8.8[d]	5.6
New York (April 7)	1,007,726	26.2	40.9	1.1	1.1	28.6	2.0	—
Wisconsin (April 7)	772,596	34.5	37.2	0.7	0.4	21.8	3.4	2.0
Pennsylvania (April 28)	1,265,495	25.7	56.5	1.7	1.6	12.8	1.7	—
District of Columbia (May 5)	61,904	7.2	73.8	—	—	10.4	—	8.5

Indiana (May 5)	476,850	21.5	*63.3*	—	3.0	12.2	—	—
North Carolina (May 5)	691,875	10.4	*64.1*	0.9	0.9	8.3	—	15.4
Nebraska (May 12)	150,587	21.0	*45.5*	2.8	—	7.1	7.1	16.4
West Virginia (May 12)	306,866	11.9	*74.2*	0.9	1.0	6.9	5.0	—
Oregon (May 19)	347,698	31.4	*45.3*	—	—	10.5	12.7	—
Washington (May 19)*	147,981	23.1	*42.0*	1.3	1.0	12.8	19.8[d]	—
Arkansas (May 26)	502,617	11.0	*68.0*	—	—	—	2.9	18.0
Idaho (May 26)*	55,124	16.7	*49.0*	—	—	—	5.2	29.1
Kentucky (May 26)	369,438	8.3	*56.0*	1.9	0.9	4.9	—	28.0
Alabama (June 2)	450,899	6.8	*68.2*	—	—	—	4.8	20.2
California (June 2)	2,752,029	40.2	*47.5*	—	1.2	7.4	3.8	—
Montana (June 2)	116,899	18.5	*46.9*	—	—	10.8	—	23.9
New Jersey (June 2)	399,913	19.5	*59.2*	—	—	11.1	2.9	7.3
New Mexico (June 2)	180,770	16.9	*52.8*	1.9	—	6.3	2.8	19.4
Ohio (June 2)	1,032,851	19.0	*61.2*	2.4	2.2	10.6	4.6	—
North Dakota (June 9)*	31,562	—	*12.6[e]*	—	—	—	87.4[d]	—

SOURCE: *Congressional Quarterly Weekly Report*, July 4, 1992, 69.

NOTE: Results are based on official returns except for California, Montana, New Jersey, New Mexico, North Dakota, Ohio, Oregon and Puerto Rico, where results are nearly complete but unofficial. Percentages may not add to 100 due to rounding. The winner is indicated in italics.

[a] Kerrey withdrew from the race March 5.

[b] Harkin withdrew from the race March 9.

[c] Tsongas suspended his campaign March 19.

[d] Perot write-in votes totaled 2.1 percent of the Democratic primary vote in Minnesota, 19.1 percent in Washington, and 28.4 percent in North Dakota (which was the winning total).

[e] Clinton's vote in North Dakota came on write-ins.

* indicates a non-binding "beauty contest" primary.

— indicates that the candidate or the uncommitted line was not listed on the ballot.

Democratic Primary and First-Round Caucus Winners

Caucus States	Turnout	Brown	Clinton	Harkin	Kerrey	Tsongas	Others	Uncommitted
Iowa (Feb. 10)	30,000 *	1.6	2.8	76.4	2.5	4.1	0.6	12.0
Maine (Feb. 23)	13,500 *	30.3	14.8	5.2	3.0	29.0	1.7	16.1
Idaho (March 3)	3,090	4.5	11.4	29.7	8.0	28.4	0.8	17.2
Minnesota (March 3)	50–60,000 *	8.2	10.3	26.7	7.6	19.2	3.9	24.3
Utah (March 3)	31,638	28.4	18.3	4.0	10.9	33.4	2.7	2.3
Washington (March 3)	60,000 *	18.6	12.6	8.2	3.4	32.3	1.5	23.2
American Samoa (March 3)	n/a	—	4.3	—	8.7	—	—	87.0
North Dakota (March 5–19)	5,000 *	7.5	46.0	6.8	1.2[a]	10.3	2.4	25.9
Arizona (March 7)	36,326	27.5	29.2	7.6	—	34.4	—	1.3[d]
Wyoming (March 7)	1,500 *	23.0	28.5	14.2	—	11.7	0.4	22.3
Democrats Abroad (March 7–9)	4,000 *	12.2	26.6	6.9	—	36.8	17.5	—
Nevada (March 8)	6–7,000 *	34.4	26.6	—[b]	—	19.6	—	19.4[d]
Delaware (March 10)	2,500 *	19.5	20.8	—	—	30.2	—	29.6
Hawaii (March 10)	3,014	13.6	51.5	12.7	0.4	14.3	—	7.5
Missouri (March 10)	20–25,000 *	5.7	45.1	—	—	10.2[c]	—	39.0
Texas (March 10)	———— Not Available ————							
Virgin Islands (March 28)	343	4.1	39.7	—	—	—	—	56.3
Vermont (March 31)	6,000*	46.7	16.8	—	—	9.3	2.2	25.0
Alaska (April 2)	1,100*	33.1	30.9	—	—	1.3	—	34.7
Virginia (April 11, 13)	n/a	11.6	52.1	—	—	—	—	36.3
Guam (May 3)	1,000 *	20.0	49.0	—	—	—	—	31.0

SOURCE: *Congressional Quarterly Weekly Report*, July 4, 1992, 70.

NOTE: By and large, caucus results were compiled by the state parties and reflect either the share won of delegates to the next stage of the caucus process or a tally of the presidential preferences of caucus participants. No results were available from the March 10 precinct caucuses in Texas. In most cases, the turnout figures are estimates. The winner of each caucus event is indicated in italics.

[a] Kerrey withdrew from the race March 5.

[b] Harkin withdrew from the race March 9.

[c] Tsongas suspended his campaign March 19.

[d] Vote for uncommitted and others was combined in tally.

* indicates turnout estimate.

— indicates that the candidate was not listed on the caucus ballot or that his votes were not tabulated separately.

N/a indicates not available.

a p p e n d i x   d

Results of Presidential
Contests, 1932–1992

Year	Republican nominee (in *italics*) and other major candidates	Democratic nominee (in *italics*) and other major candidates	Election winner	Division of popular vote[a] (percent)	Division of electoral vote[b]
1932	*Herbert Hoover* (incumbent president) Joseph France (former senator from Missouri)	*Franklin D. Roosevelt* (governor of New York) Alfred Smith (former governor of New York) John Garner (representative from Texas and Speaker of the House)	Roosevelt (D)	57–40	472–59
1936	*Alfred Landon* (governor of Kansas) William Borah (senator from Idaho)	*Franklin D. Roosevelt* (incumbent president) None	Roosevelt (D)	61–37	523–8
1940	*Wendell Willkie* (Indiana lawyer and public utility executive) Thomas E. Dewey (U.S. district attorney for New York) Robert Taft (senator from Ohio)	*Franklin D. Roosevelt* (incumbent president) None	Roosevelt (D)	55–45	449–82
1944	*Thomas E. Dewey* (governor of New York) Wendell Willkie (previous Republican presidential nominee)	*Franklin D. Roosevelt* (incumbent president) Harry Byrd (senator from Virginia)	Roosevelt (D)	53–46	432–99

Year	Republican contenders	Democratic contenders	Winner	Popular vote	Electoral vote
1948	*Thomas E. Dewey* (governor of New York) Harold Stassen (former governor of Minnesota) Robert Taft (senator from Ohio)	*Harry S. Truman* (incumbent president) Richard Russell (senator from Georgia)	Truman (D)	50-45	303-189
1952	*Dwight D. Eisenhower* (general) Robert Taft (senator from Ohio)	*Adlai Stevenson* (governor of Illinois) Estes Kefauver (senator from Tennessee) Richard Russell (senator from Georgia)	Eisenhower (R)	55-44	442-89
1956	*Dwight D. Eisenhower* (incumbent president) None	*Adlai Stevenson* (previous Democratic presidential nominee) Averell Harriman (governor of New York)	Eisenhower (R)	57-42	457-73
1960	*Richard Nixon* (vice president) None	*John F. Kennedy* (senator from Massachusetts) Hubert Humphrey (senator from Minnesota) Lyndon B. Johnson (senator from Texas)	Kennedy (D)	49.7-49.5	303-219
1964	*Barry Goldwater* (senator from Arizona) Nelson Rockefeller (governor of New York)	*Lyndon B. Johnson* (incumbent president) None	Johnson (D)	61-39	486-52

Year	Republican nominee (in *italics*) and other major candidates	Democratic nominee (in *italics*) and other major candidates	Election winner	Division of popular vote[a] (percent)	Division of electoral vote[b]
1968	*Richard Nixon* (former Republican presidential nominee) Ronald Reagan (governor of California)	*Hubert Humphrey* (incumbent vice president) Robert F. Kennedy (senator from New York) Eugene McCarthy (senator from Minnesota)	Nixon (R)	43.4-42.7	301-191
1972	*Richard Nixon* (incumbent president) None	*George McGovern* (senator from South Dakota) Hubert Humphrey (senator from Minnesota) George Wallace (governor of Alabama)	Nixon (R)	61-38	520-17
1976	*Gerald R. Ford* (incumbent president) Ronald Reagan (former governor of California)	*Jimmy Carter* (former governor of Georgia) Edmund Brown Jr. (governor of California) George Wallace (governor of Alabama)	Carter (D)	50-48	297-240
1980	*Ronald Reagan* (former governor of California)	*Jimmy Carter* (incumbent president)	Reagan (R)	51-41	489-49

Year	Republican nominees	Democratic nominees	Winner	Popular vote[a]	Electoral vote[b]
	George Bush (former director of Central Intelligence Agency)	Edward M. Kennedy (senator from Massachusetts)			
	John Anderson (representative from Illinois)				
1984	Ronald Reagan (incumbent president)	Walter F. Mondale (former vice president)	Reagan (R)	59-41	525-13
	None	Gary Hart (senator from Colorado)			
1988	George Bush (vice president)	Michael S. Dukakis (governor of Massachusetts)	Bush (R)	53-46	426-111
	Bob Dole (senator from Kansas)	Jesse Jackson (civil rights activist)			
1992[c]	George Bush (incumbent president)	Bill Clinton (governor of Arkansas)	Clinton (D)	43.2-37.7	370-168
	Patrick J. Buchanan (presidential speechwriter in Nixon administration, director of communications in Reagan administration, and conservative national spokesman)	Jerry Brown (former governor of California)			

[a] Division of popular vote is between the Republican and Democratic nominees. Percentage may not add to 100 due to rounding.
[b] Division of electoral votes is between the Republican and Democratic nominees.
[c] H. Ross Perot (businessperson) ran as an independent nominee, garnering 19 percent of the popular vote and 0 electoral votes.

Index